Where Beards Wag All

Where Beards Wag All
The Relevance of the Oral Tradition

❦

GEORGE EWART EVANS

Illustrated by David Gentleman

'Come home, lord, singing,
Come home, corn bringing,
'Tis merry in hall,
Where beards wag all.'

THOMAS TUSSER

FABER AND FABER LTD
London

First published in 1970
by Faber and Faber Limited
24 Russell Square London WC1
Printed in Great Britain by
Latimer Trend & Co Ltd Plymouth
All rights reserved

ISBN 0 571 08411 7

© *1970 by George Ewart Evans*

Date of Return

For Katherine, Sarah and Theodore

Y Llafurwr

Hawdd i lafurwr hoywddol
hyder at Dduw Ner yn ol.
O gardod, drwy gywirdeb,
o lety, ni necy neb.
Ni rydd farn eithr ar arnawdd,
ni char yn ei gyfar gawdd.
Ni ddeily rhyfel, ni ddilyn,
ni threisia am ei dda ddyn.
Ni bydd ry gadarn arnam,
ni yrr hawl gymedrawl gam,
ni addas ond ei oddef;
nid bywyd, nid byd heb ef.

Iolo Goch: (14th C.)

The Farm-worker

For the worker in the corn-bright field
It is easy to trust in Providence.
Out of a good heart he'll give
And guest-room he'll not refuse.
Nor will he give out opinion
Except on plough, its beam and breast-shine;
And on his land he'll spurn dissension.
He'll neither make nor go to war,
Nor harry a man to take his substance.
He'll never press us hard,
Nor will he claim false privilege.
Enduring is second nature to him:
There is no living, no world without him.

From the Welsh; by G.E.E.

Pray now, buy some: I love a ballet in print a-life,
for then we are sure they are true.

The Winter's Tale, IV, iii.

Acknowledgements

I wish to thank all those who gave me so much help in the writing of this book. Most of my informants have been mentioned in the text, but I should also like to thank Lionel Reynolds for his valuable suggestions; also Dr. Iorwerth Peate, Dr. Dilwyn John, Victor Bonham-Carter, Nicholas Bagenal, Diana Batchelor, David Thomson, Irene Fleming, Roger Fowler, John Slater and Geoffrey Goddard. The Arts Council of Great Britain gave me a grant which made the writing of this book much easier than it would otherwise have been: I am most grateful. Colin Owen of Burton-on-Trent has allowed me to include his table, setting out some statistics of the migration of East Anglian workers to Burton, and I appreciate his kindness.

I wish to make grateful acknowledgement to Lord Ritchie-Calder, Dr. Anne Ross and Robert Waller for permission to quote from their work, and also to the Cambridge University Press and the editors of *The Dairy Farmer* and *The Village*.

I am greatly indebted to David Gentleman for the drawings he has made for this book, and also for the excellent photographs he took for inclusion in it. I make grateful acknowledgement to the following for the loan of old photographs: Margaret Meek, Frederick Copping, Albert Harry Rumsby, Dick Last, Cecil Runeckles, Rufus and Olive de Pinto; and also Malcolm Freegard for copying some of the photographs.

Finally, I wish to express sincere gratitude to my publishers, especially Peter du Sautoy, for the care and attention they have given to this book.

9

Contents

❦❦❦

Contents

Illustrations

❧❧❧

13

Illustrations

Abbreviations

E.F.P.P. English Farming Past and Present (1961 edition)
A.F.C.H. Ask the Fellows Who Cut the Hay
H.I.F. The Horse in the Furrow
P.U.P. The Pattern Under the Plough
F.A.V. The Farm and the Village
T. Literal transcript of a tape-recording

Introduction

This book has been written out of the conviction that members of the old prior culture in rural Britain are able to give information about a past which is far more extensive than their own life-span. This culture was effectively displaced in most regions by the first quarter of this century; and I call it a *prior culture* because— in spite of its being primitive in many of its forms—to characterize it as a *primitive culture* would be to make a doubtful value judgement and to suggest that in all its aspects it had little that is worth preserving. I believe there is sufficient evidence in the following chapters for the worth of certain modes of this culture, just as there is also evidence to show that it is well that certain of its features have ended even if they have not been forgotten.

But the book's main concern is to illustrate the importance of the oral testimony of those people who grew up under the old culture: how, in spite of the apparently total break during this century, some of the values of this culture still concern us today; and how oral testimony, the oldest form of *recording* known to man, will still have its uses in an age when scientific methods of keeping records are likely to multiply still further. The reader, however, will be able to judge for himself whether or not these claims are valid. What will probably occur to him on his first approach to this subject are the common-sense questions: can the oral tradition be relied upon? can we trust the word of mouth and use it as evidence of any kind? can we give it historical weight? This is not the place to set out a detailed apology for the oral tradition as historical evidence: many writers have long ago proved its value and used it with profit. But this much can be said. Oral testimony has to be used with care and a proper awareness of its limitations. The same principle, however, applies to written and printed sources which are often oral in origin, and do not acquire some sort of mystical value by the simple process of being put on paper. Although this is often overlooked, a written document has to be looked in the face, so to speak, as searchingly as any informant. The fact that a document was written perhaps a few hundred years ago does not of itself frank it with the mark of truth; even if the contents of the document are accurate, its context—who wrote it, what for and under what circumstances—should ideally be known before we can use it without reservation as historical evidence. In seeking oral information one should be fully aware of the informant's background, and should look for information precisely in those sectors where he has first-hand knowledge. It is no use, for instance, expecting a farm-worker to be accurate about the dates of historical events that occurred even during his lifetime. Usually they are beyond his ken because they did not impinge upon him directly. But in any department of his work (and this goes for all the rural craftsmen) he cannot be faulted. In my experience of recording the skills and crafts of the old rural culture I have found that the testimony of the craftsman is more accurate than the average printed source. He is, moreover, able to give a fuller account, with all the local variations, of his craft; and in the very process of describing it he uses a wealth of vocabulary and illustration that does not often find its way into the more concentrated written descriptions that are concerned with techniques alone.

In the province of rural skills and crafts the oral tradition also holds much of the old empirical knowledge that is worth preserving. Scientists today are usually impatient of any claim that the old knowledge has worth. Much of it is, it must be admitted, marginal if not negligible: it was certainly not acquired 'scientifically' and by its nature does not lend itself to proof by replicable experiment. But some of it has stood the test of an extended experiment in the social laboratory of the old culture which has lasted for a few thousand years; and this knowledge, and the attitudes that go with it, still makes sense when it touches on the 'human' sciences like medicine or soil-use where human beings and animals are directly involved in so far as they consume the products taken from the soil. In these fields there are so many variables that the modern scientific method cannot be applied with the same confidence as in the purely physical sciences.

In these fields even the most unlikely and bizarre material sometimes has practical value. For instance, a few years ago I tried to investigate the claims of the old East Anglian horsemen to control their horses by supposedly magical means. I searched for the principle or pattern that lay behind their methods and attempted a rational explanation of the undoubted substance that informed some of their claims. In publishing one of the recipes[1] used by a nineteenth-century Suffolk horseman I was in no way concerned with its practical usefulness but quoted it merely as an example of the principle involved in many of the old horse-whisperers' methods of control. Here is the recipe:

'It is For Catching Wild Colts and Vicious Horses on Aney Feild or Common (For a long distance)

'You must get by the wind and take with you scented cakes made as follows: half lb of oat flower mixed with Treacle and slack baked. Then sweat it under your arms. The cakes to be scented with the oil of origanum, oil of cinnamon, oil of fennel, the oil of rosemary and the oil of vidgin. If you have not time to bake the cakes you must scent a piece of gingerbread and give him that, and it will answer the same purpose.'

On the surface the above appears rather comical and quite impractical, but a few weeks after it was first published I received the following letter from Scotland:

[1] *P.U.P.*, p. 209.

'[You] referred to the horsemen of East Anglia and the near extinction of this class of old time country craftsmen. As a pony-breeder I was particularly interested in the herbal prescription for "taming" horses, and I must say that *I found the concoction to work exactly as claimed.* For some time I have wondered whether it would be possible to obtain a copy of the notebook (written by a Suffolk horseman) from which this prescription was taken. I would be interested to learn whether you could help me in this respect.'

But too large a claim should not be made for oral testimony in respect of its ability to transmit knowledge. What it can do admirably is to supplement existing documentary evidence. But occasionally (an instance is given here) a body of factual knowledge does exist only in the memories of men and women; and it would be lost, or greatly attenuated, were it not taken down before they died. But oral testimony can help the researcher both in town and country most of all by giving flesh to the material he has gathered from other sources. In the process of talking with real people, facts and statistics take on a new significance; and his sympathies being directly engaged he can place the knowledge he has gained elsewhere in a wider and more essentially human setting. Like the anthropologist, through working in the field he becomes inescapably aware of universals which overlap and to a large extent make meaningless the rigid compartments into which studies of the past are divided. Similarly the oral testimony of people of the prior culture can help those studies which are primarily concerned with the present—economic or sociological surveys, for example—by demonstrating how dangerous it is to theorize about any region without a knowledge of those human attitudes that are referable to the area's recent or remoter history. Most of all, oral testimony can help humanize those studies that appear to be suffering from an increasing *mechanization*, tending to give almost exclusive importance to processes, methods and statistics—all things made more freely available by the new competence of the machine. This is undoubtedly a reflex of the highly complicated industrial society in which we now live, where men are becoming statistically little more than predictable things and where the overriding principle is that a business must pay and the over-all problem is the free play and application of an untrammelled intelligence. But intelligence alone will only sterilize the work of the historian and the sociologist; for their disciplines are humani-ties rather than sciences: they are concerned with whole men and not with the abstractions of science; and they are committed to use feeling and a stabilizing intuition to govern the uninhibited drive of the intellect that claims to be pure and objective.

In order to illustrate the worth of the oral testimony of people of the prior culture I have taken most of my examples from East Anglia. I have done this because this is the region I have studied most: I am sure, however, that many other parts of Britain would have served equally well for this purpose. But I believe the oral tradition to be of especial importance in this region because it is mainly the voice of a class of people that have had little op-portunity to speak for themselves. They have left few letters, diaries or written accounts of any kind; and apart from a few outstanding figures like George Edwards, the Norfolk M.P. and spokesman for the farm-workers, there have been few to speak directly on their behalf. Another fact has bearing on this question: in East Anglia the mass-education movement of the last century— unlike those areas of Yorkshire and the Midlands, for instance, which are close to large industrial complexes—made little impact on the rural population. There was no surge towards book-learning: on the contrary, there is strong evidence that there was a resistance towards it. I myself have been told by a number of older people that reading was not encouraged in their homes; and in any case there were few books available for them to read; although the availability of books depended to a large extent on the schoolmaster or parson who happened to be in the village. But many parents actively discouraged reading; and three East Anglians who were born in different districts between 1880 and 1905 have told me that reading was frowned on at home as it would tend to make them dissatisfied and would take them 'out of their station in life'. The older generation, therefore, in spite of compulsory education persevered in the old culture which was almost entirely oral. For that reason they were its chief carriers,

21

unaffected by the newly evolving culture, the so-called *culture of print*; and what to them in the present context was considered a disability has to us proved an advantage, enabling them to provide us with rich material relating to a long historical past.

Mention has been made of the old East Anglian's awareness of his 'station in life'. This is discussed later in the book, and is related to the social hierarchy which seems to have been the inevitable accompaniment of the arable-farming culture of this region. In recent years there has been a tendency to play this down and to make a retrospective fusion of the old, well-defined social strata. It has been unfashionable to discuss *class*; and it has gradually displaced sex as the dominant social taboo. But oral testimony can reveal what were the true attitudes towards this most powerful determinant of social relations, and it can help us to assess how far these attitudes and assumptions about class—many of them barely conscious—are operative today.

In describing the old culture I have included stories and even village gossip; and a reader may well respond to this material with the objection: 'Is it worth taking notice of such trivial facts and stories even if they are sometimes amusing?' Although the material does not aspire to be history the question itself is closely related to a more fundamental one: what does the historian consider his purpose to be? If it is only to 'record' the past, the more momentous the facts he includes and the more trivial facts he leaves out the better it will be for his reputation. But many people will maintain that the historian is under an obligation to interpret as well as to record; and whatever his own views about this he is committed to interpret even before he sets himself to his task. For he has to have at least a provisional framework of selection—an *interpretation* in which he brings into play his judgement of what is valuable and what is not—for the reason that he is aware, however dimly, that it is not possible to put everything in. Often it is the trivial, the remark made on the side, the piece of gossip, that reveal the attitudes (perhaps unconscious or only barely realized) that will be of the greatest value to him in arriving at an assessment of more weighty facts. The anecdote, the tit-bit of gossip may well take him right into the heads of the people

he is writing about, and may well convince him that an appreciation of attitudes is an important and essential complement to a
knowledge of facts. For it is vital to the historian to know, as far
as he can, not only what the people he is writing about actually
did but what they thought about what they were doing. In this
respect the old Roman's aphorism, *Omnia tendunt ad opinionem*, is
very much to the point. What one thinks and makes of the facts is
at least as vital as the facts themselves; and this is as true for the man
who is writing history as it was for the people who were living it.

I have not attempted to cover all aspects of the oral tradition.
It would have been too large a task. Instead I have concentrated
on the tradition that derives directly from the particular nature
of the region's predominant historical work, arable farming, and
the society that grew up around it. I have done this because of my
conviction that the *work* is the biggest single factor in determining
a region's character; and the oral evidence I have recorded here
appears to confirm it.

A short note about the way I collected my material. If I knew
an informant well and he knew and appreciated what I was about,
I did not hesitate to use a notebook. But if I suspected that the
sight of a notebook would dry up information at the source, I
memorized the salient points of a conversation; wrote up the

interview as soon as I could; and if I was in doubt about some aspect of it or wanted fuller information, returned repeatedly until I got it right. Whenever it was practicable I used a tape-recorder for collecting information for this book: with some informants I used both tape-recorder and notebook. In the text I have distinguished between these last two methods by marking transcripts of recorded tape with a letter T at the beginning of each passage. These passages are direct transcripts of the informants' words with only occasional cutting of needless repetitions which would slow up the reading. But I have been careful to keep those repetitions that are part of the dialect speaker's idiom, one of the devices he uses—like the poet—for more effective communication. I have included the full transcripts wherever possible because they are likely—for reasons that are stated later—to acquire a greater value than a perhaps smoother rendering of the content of an informant's conversation.

Part One

Craftsmen

timber jim

1 The Wheelwright

Craftsmen are completely reliable informants when they discuss their own work. Their craft, after a lifetime's application to it, is in their bones and they do not go wrong in describing it; in the same way they seldom, if ever, fall below the standard they set themselves in the actual work. To a man who has spent his life at a certain work or craft it is a point of honour to describe its details fully and without distortion: the work has become a part of him; and to give a wrong description or to make an error of fact would be like an offence against his own person. He would no more give a botched account of the process he is describing than he would scamp his actual work in the field or the workshop. In his work his standard is the highest and this carries over into his recounting of it.

The wheelwright's craft, owing to the prominence given to it by George Sturt and others, has become almost the *classical* craft of the old country community. But like the blacksmith's craft it had in its heyday primacy over most other crafts because transport in both countryside and town were so dependent upon it. For the above reason it may seem superfluous to put down some of the experiences of yet another wheelwright. I do so, however, because local variations in the craft and in the craft-terms are worth recording and local customs linked to the craft are in themselves informative.

27

Percy Wilson (born 1884) of Witnesham, Suffolk is a wheel-wright and carpenter who practised his crafts almost into his eightieth year. He started his apprenticeship at fifteen and completed it at the age of twenty. During this time he got one shilling a week for the first year, two for the second, three for the third, five for the fourth and seven shillings for his fifth and last year. When he became a journeyman he received fifteen shillings a week. Gradually his weekly wage was raised to eighteen shillings, and it remained at this sum until the death of his master. He then took over the shop and carried on the business himself.

'When I was an apprentice we used to go out during the winter to cut down the trees we wanted. We put them on a *timber jim*—a large-wheeled trolley—and carted them home into the yard. If we wanted to make cart shafts we got a tree as near as we could to the shape of the shaft; if we wanted timber for felloes the more bent the tree was the better; if we wanted timber for pommel-trees we cut down a perfectly straight boled tree—if we could find one. Some of these pommel-trees were ten to twelve feet long—the ones they used with the harrows—and they had to be straight. So we chose a straight tree to avoid waste of timber.

'In winter, when the weather was too bad to do outside jobs on the buildings and so on, we used to get a tree on to the sawpit (the bark had already been stripped from it). Then we had to decide what thickness we wanted to cut it. For instance, we'd cut it into inch boards to make coffins; another time we'd cut two-inch boards for various kinds of work; sometimes three inches. If it was for shaft work it would come up to four inches and very often a lot of heavy work was over four inches. But before we started sawing we had first to mark the tree: we *chalked* it. The chalk-line would be prepared. A boy looped the end of a ball of string around his hand while the wheelwright held the ball itself. As the string unwound the wheelwright whitened it with a piece of chalk until he had sufficient length of whitened string. This was then laid lengthways down the centre of the log, fixed in position, and was then pulled away by the wheelwright who let it snap, transferring the chalk-mark to the wood. If he was making coffin-boards, for instance—thirteen boards to a foot—he'd get a compass and mark off the width each side of the centre-line and at each end of the log. Then transferring the cord and snapping it at each mark he'd get a series of parallel lines down the length of the log. Then with the *plumb-bob* or plumb-line which was hung from the centre-line down at the end of the log he was able to find the centre on the under surface of the log. When they'd got this they turned the log over and marked the under surface exactly as they'd done the top.

'When the tree had been marked out the boy—the bottom sawyer—got into the pit: the wheelwright was the top sawyer and was in charge of the work. You had no job to keep warm even in the frostiest weather: you'd have to have your coat off. Each sawyer had to see that he kept to the line while he was sawing; and it was pity help the boy if he didn't keep to the line down in the pit though sometimes he could hardly see it. But occasionally when the saw didn't go straight it couldn't be blamed on the boy. That was when the saw *hollowed*. It would be in the proper cut both at the top and the bottom of the tree but it would bend slightly in the middle. You could always tell when a saw was *hollowing* by the noise it made. When it was running smoothly it made a sweet swishing sound like music; but when it was hollowing it was as if it was groaning; a labouring sort of sound. And, of course, it would make sawing terribly hard work. Hollowing was due to a faulty sharpening of the saw. If one of the teeth was a little longer than the others, or if they were set a bit differently it would cause the saw to hollow. And it did considerable damage then: it bent over so that it cut a slice out of the next board; and with a bad hollow I've known it cut right through the next board and spoil the one beyond—that's if it was a terrible bad hollow.

'We fixed the tree over the sawpit by resting it on rollers or *rolls*. The rolls we used were about five inches in diameter, absolutely round with holes at each end for you to insert an iron rod. For light work we used a three-inch square length of wood placed across the pit: we called this a *transom*. As the sawing of the log or tree advanced we'd move the rolls forward or backward as the case may be. To do this we pushed iron rods into the holes and levered the rolls into position. The log was held firm over the pit by iron hooks or *holdfasts*.'

William Hewitt (born 1887) who was in charge of the timber yard of the Campsey Ash Estate at Tunstall, Suffolk used hexagonal rolls which were less likely to shift, while sawing was in progress, than the round ones. The method of using rolls in a sawpit is referred to by Thomas Tusser who wrote in the sixteenth century in his *Husbandly Furniture*:

> *A frower of iron for cleaving of lath,*
> *With roll for a sawpit good husbandry hath.*

Some Suffolk craftsmen maintain that the first sawpit was an ordinary draining ditch on a farm; and that the bricked pit in the wright's yard was only an improved and well-sited ditch. This seems very feasible, but though it was probably the first device used in the sawing of timber it was not the only one in East Anglia. It is certain that a sawing frame was used in both Norfolk and Suffolk when it was necessary to cut a log away from the site where it was to be used. I first heard of it from an old craftsman, Albert Heffer, of Farnham in Suffolk. He had seen one when he was a boy at the beginning of the century. From his description it appears to have been like the arrangement sometimes pictured in medieval manuscripts:[1] a log upended and resting obliquely on two trestles. The saw used was the frame type, and one man stood on a trestle over the log, the other below it and operated the saw more or less as in a sawpit. This type of frame and saw was commonly used in shipbuilding, and this may account for its adaptation to other uses along the East Anglian coast.

Percy Wilson told me: 'Travelling sawyers used to come round asking for work, though my master rarely employed any of these men; neither did I. But one of them once sharpened a saw for us; and he made a right good job of it and charged two shillings. You could employ travelling sawyers on piece-work: they charged 5s 6d a hundred feet for sawing. The hundred feet were calculated like this: Supposing you had a tree ten foot long and a foot in diameter. Well, in estimating the sawing of the tree they measured

---

[1] *A History of Technology*, Oxford, pp. 387 and 392–3.

from the deepest cut, the one in the centre of the tree. Although the cuts further from the centre were, naturally, not a foot deep (and the outside ones were very shallow) they all *counted* as a foot deep. So if a sawyer made ten cuts in a foot-diameter log ten feet long it would count as a hundred feet and he'd get 5s 6d. It was thirsty work, of course; and the travelling sawyers were always heavy drinkers. They lost a lot of sweat and they had to replace it with something; and beer was safer than the water.[1] The men who did this sort of work usually operated from the town. They'd walk the six or seven miles from Ipswich, and they'd usually be at our shop by 7 a.m.

'Here are some of the vehicles we made before the First World War: a tumbril for a cost of £10; a Scotch cart £14; a harvest carriage or wagon for £40 and a road wagon for £30. A Scotch cart[2] was popular round here. I made a lot of them. They'd carry about a ton. We had to buy some of the wood to make this sort of cart as some of the work—the sides and the front of the cart— was in pitch pine, nine-inch by one-and-a-half-inch planks. We had none of that kind of wood growing round here at that time so we got it from Brown of Ipswich. A good Scotch cart would last for a tremendous long time. Some people used to say to me: "Will you come out to my farm and have a look at my new Scotch cart? Something's wrong with it." *New* used to make me laugh! Because when I'd seen the cart I'd recognize it and I knew it was one I'd made seven, eight or perhaps nine years before. But that didn't signify. It was still new.

'In making the Scotch cart we cut the sills out then the rest of the framework, the front bar and the back ledge, and we bought the one-and-a-half-inch pitch-pine planks I told you about and they were put in on top of the others and bolted through. The rest of the timber we cut in the pit; and it had to be at least a year old, nicely dry so there'd be no shrinkage. Then we'd put in the floor; and then we'd have the wheels to make.'

---

[1] The home-brewing of beer was important in this respect when the water-supply was a well (usually contaminated) or even a ditch or pond. It was noticeable that in Suffolk in the 1950's these were still the only sources in some districts, and water as a drink was therefore taboo.

[2] See *F.A.V.*, pp. 102–3.

The wheels are the wright's distinguishing mark of his trade. It is the wheels that separate him off from the craft of carpenter: a wheelwright is equal to any job in the carpenter's craft but a carpenter cannot make a wheel. Percy Wilson confessed that making the body of a Scotch cart—or of any vehicle for that matter—was a much simpler job than making the wheels:[1] 'The first thing with the wheel was the nave [hub or stock]. In the winter we had already cut up pieces of ellum ready for naves. They were about seventeen to eighteen inches long. We selected two pieces for naves of the cart we were making and we put them in turn on a crude sort of lathe. This lathe was driven by hand with a huge wheel about six feet high. It drove on to a pulley about four or five inches in diameter—so you can see the gearing was tremendous. The boss used to hold the chisel, the gouge, and he'd *round* the piece of ellum. Then he'd take a broad chisel and clean it up. Then he'd cut the hoops on—the places where the iron bands that went round the nave would fit—all ready. The iron bands were usually one-and-a-half-inch by three-eighths-inch, but the Scotch cart had a wider one at the front of the nave—about two inches. Then he marked out and put some lines on with a chisel, so they wouldn't rub out. These were the places where he'd fix the spokes into the nave. Then came *morticing the nave*, cutting the holes out into which the spokes would fit; then cutting the spokes themselves, driving the spokes into the nave, pulling the shoulders of the spokes ready for the felloes. After this came *rounding it* [the wheel], seeing that the spokes were the same length from the nave to tip to get the wheel perfectly round. For morticing the nave and fixing the spokes in the right position we used a *guide* (or gauge) a slender bar of wood with a sliver of whale-bone at the end. The next job was cutting out the felloes. Then came putting on the felloes and what we called *riving*[2] the

---

[1] For detailed description see George Sturt, *The Wheelwright's Shop*, Cambridge (1963), chapters 18–27.

[2] Sturt (ibid. chapter 21) called it *ringing* the wheel. Riving (pronounced to rhyme with giving) meant hammering the felloes on to the spokes. This East Anglian word is undoubtedly related to the Orkney word *rive*: to work energetically (H. Marwick, *The Orkney Norn*, Oxford, 1929). It is Norwegian in origin and probably an earlier form than *ringing*.

1. Foundry Yard, Bungay, with a Cameron plough

2. Silver Jubilee George V, Bungay Foundry (Rumsby's), May 1935

3. Coronation Display, George V, June 1911

4. Queen Victoria's Diamond Jubilee Display, June 1897

wheel: this was hammering on the felloes. This was nothing to do with putting an iron tyre on the wheel: we sent it to the blacksmith for that but only after we'd put on the felloes to our satisfaction. He would put on a three-quarter-inch by three-inch iron tyre.

'The road wagons were built to carry three tons. They had two pairs of shafts and often they were pulled by four horses, two in the shafts and two in traces. The harvest wagon was very strongly made but lighter than the road wagon. It had one pair of shafts. A wheelbarrow (which cost a pound, iron-work and all) wasn't

Peasenhall: furnace for heating iron tyres

such an easy job as it might appear. A wheelbarrow wheel was the most difficult of wheels to make: it had a spoke to each felloe— four spokes, four felloes. The spokes were made from oak riven down with the grain; and for ordinary wheels were about two foot six inches in length. They were laid up to get properly dry. When you morticed the spoke into the nave you numbered each one so that it would fit perfectly into the mortice you'd cut for it. In making the wheel for a Scotch cart the spokes were not tapered very much. They had shoulders. Here's how the vehicles went as regards spokes and felloes:

Road wagons: 6 felloes; 12 spokes
Harvest wagons: 6 felloes; 12 spokes
Tumbrils: 6 felloes; 12 spokes
Scotch carts: 7 felloes; 14 spokes.'

The extra spokes and felloes in a Scotch cart were probably needed on its home ground where a strong wheel was essential on a rougher terrain than is to be found in East Anglia. This strong wheel was responsible for the extra cost of a Scotch cart.

'We also made all the smaller things needed on the farm. I've mentioned pommel-trees: we also made whipple-trees, and also a lot of *seals* for horse-collars. I've got a lot of patterns for seals in my workshop still. I believe we called them seals for heavy horses and *hames* for ponies. An axe handle—we made scores of them— cost a shilling.

'When the vehicle was finished we painted it up. Then one of the travelling craftsmen came out from the town and *lined* the cart, trap or wagon we happened to be making: that means he painted the finishing touches, the lines on the wheels and the panels. The liner did nothing else except lining and sign-writing. To line the cart he used long, narrow brushes he called *pencils*. He dipped these in the paint and lined the spokes, felloes, and sides of the vehicles as a final decoration. I well recollect one liner who used to come out here. He would walk from Ipswich and get to Witnesham soon after 6 a.m.—a five or six miles' journey. And then he'd be in a rare way because our employer was not out of bed. Like a good many other liners he enjoyed a glass of beer. In fact this one used to drink like a herren [herring]. He'd soon be shouting at the window to call the boss up to go and get him some drink—usually home-brewed beer. One of the first things he said on reaching here in the early morning was: "Is the boss up? Are his blinds up?" As soon as the boss was stirring he'd get his mug of beer; and then he'd start his lining, and not before.

'I recollect him once doing a job for us, on a Scotch cart I believe it was—but he didn't finish it. The customer wanted it urgently, so my boss sent me to Ipswich on the bike to try and get him to come out and finish his job. When I got to his house I found he was in a bad way: "I can't do it," he say. "Look at my hand!" His hands were shaking so much he couldn't have held a brush much less use it. "You finish it for me," he say. "You can do it!" So I had to go back and finish the lining on that particular cart. It's true I did a bit of lining at other times, but it wasn't my job.

'But he was a splendid craftsman—they all were, both in lining and in sign-writing. The main secret of the craft was to get the paint exactly the right consistency. We used to mix the paint for them before they came but the liner himself used to add the *turps* to make the paint run exactly right so that he could make the brush run from the top to the bottom of the spoke without dipping it in the paint—one movement. He'd dip once and he'd go a tremendous way round the rim of the wheel even without dipping again. On the rim of the wheel he'd put one broad line and two thin ones. He had two widths of brushes—a broad and a thin. He put his paint on a palette-plate and dip in his pencil as he called it, and he added the *turps* until it was exactly right, not too thick; do, it wouldn't have gone far enough without dipping again. If it was too thin it would run and make a worse mess than the other. One movement on the spoke would be enough; one stroke like an artist's, from underneath the felloe right down to the top of the nave. But he wouldn't start until he saw the boss's mug of beer: once he had that inside him he would go'.

2 *Foundry Craftsmen*

This chapter is included to illustrate how the value of industrial archives is enhanced by having a living member of a firm to fill in the bare, written accounts and to answer the questions that arise from them.

In the Suffolk town of Bungay a small iron foundry business started at the beginning of the nineteenth century and lasted until 1968. It grew up to serve the domestic needs of the town (stoves, firebacks, smoothing irons, and all the general ironwork linked with the house) and also the farming needs of the countryside around it. In fact the account books show that the bulk of the work was agricultural. It was undoubtedly one of those small family businesses—at first hardly distinguishable from a blacksmith's shop—that grew up at the beginning of the last century in East Anglia in response to the needs of the new farming improvers. Townshend, Coke and Arthur Young had led the way and stimulated farmers to use new methods and new machines; and lesser known men like the Biddells in Suffolk[1] had enthusiastically followed the lead and had begun to experiment. They quickly showed the need for efficient ploughs and other implements specifically designed to suit local conditions; and the ingenuity of local smiths was extended to carry out the design required and often set out by the farmer himself. Out of these

[1] *H.I.F*, Part Two.

small businesses grew firms like Smyth, Murton Turner, Garrett, Ransome, Sims and Jefferies, some of which became world famous. The Bungay firm of Cameron (later Rumsby), although its *Cameron* or *East Anglian* ploughs attained some fame and were exported to the colonies, did not grow beyond a maximum size of thirteen employees.

It would be interesting to speculate why one particular small firm went ahead and expanded while another remained comparatively static. But to compare Ransome, Sims and Jefferies of Ipswich with Cameron-Rumsby of Bungay in an attempt to adduce general reasons would probably be unprofitable. For, apart from the obvious advantage the Ipswich firm had of a site in a much larger town with a correspondingly quicker rate in the exchange of fertile ideas, the difference in drive and temperament of the founders would be a critical factor in a firm's expansion. We do not know enough about the Cameron family to make a comparison but it is likely that the first Cameron was not the equal of Robert Ransome who first set up a similar, small family business in Ipswich in 1789. But one thing is certain, the Ransomes' accidental discovery of a method of *chilling* plough-shares enabled the firm to get ahead of their competitors and to remain ahead right throughout the country. At least the Cameron-Rumsby, Ransome, Sims and Jefferies comparison is instructive in this particular because the Bungay firm was induced to make an agreement with the Ipswich iron-founders granting them a licence to fit Ransome's patent-chill shares to their plough, as they themselves did not possess the secret and expertise of the chilling process. The Ransome sign over the shop door [see Plate 3] was a long-standing evidence of this agreement.

The earliest entries in the Cameron account books are for the years 1820–5, though the first twenty-eight pages of the earliest surviving ledger are missing; and it is likely that the firm was in operation at least a few years before 1820. The first known Cameron was succeeded by Daniel Albert Cameron (1841–1900). He employed Nathan Rumsby (1829–1920) whose son, Harry Nathan Rumsby (1872–1945), took over the business after Daniel Cameron's death. Harry Nathan Rumsby's two sons, Albert

Harry Rumsby (born 1899) and Cecil Cameron Rumsby (1905–66) took over the business from their father and ran it in partnership. Two years after his brother's death, in the autumn of 1968, Albert H. Rumsby sold up the business. Shortly afterwards he generously made his account books, photographs and some of his remaining stock available for the purposes of making this record.

'As I've said my brother and me took over from my father. He took over from Daniel Cameron (he's the old gentleman with a beard on the left of the photograph [Plate 1]; and my father is next to him holding a bike). But Daniel Cameron was very fond of tipping his elbow, and for two years before he died my grandfather, Nathan Rumsby (he's the very old man at the bench in the workshop photograph [Plate 6]), had to run the business for him. If you look at the arch photograph for the Silver Jubilee, 1935 [Plate 2], you'll see my father in the centre, me on his right, another brother who's a schoolmaster, and my brother Cecil who was in partnership with me. There you have the family!

'Even before I left school I used to work at night with my grandfather at the bench. I started regular work in the shop in 1915, the second year of the War. The hours were 6 a.m. to 6 p.m. during the week, 6 a.m. to 2 p.m. on Saturday. My grandfather taught me most of the processes in the shop: pattern-making, moulding, casting and fitting (that is, putting together things like Dutch ovens we'd made in the shop). My grandfather had a very high standard of craftsmanship. Work was much slower than it eventually became after the War; but it was very thorough and whatever job you did had to be of the highest standard and finish. Besides, it often happened that if you had a certain job to do you'd have to make the tools you needed before you started on it. But as you see from the account books the range of the jobs we had to do was tremendous. You pointed out one item in the account book for April 10th, 1896:

Mending doll's perambulator 4d   1s 2d
Rivets and 1 screw to *do*.

Well, I repaired a doll's pram a year or so ago. We had all sorts of little, fiddling jobs to do outside our proper work, and I suppose we should have refused them. But as we were living in a small town we had to accept them. For instance, when my father was Town Reeve (in the early twenties) we made the name-plates for all the streets in Bungay. And about that time we also made the Black Dog at the top of the standard on the traffic island near the market-place. Have you seen it? It has a red tongue hanging out of its mouth. It's supposed to be *Black Shuck*[1] the ghost dog they say used to run about Bungay and the marshes. We also made the iron bridge at Ditchingham a mile or so away: the one that goes over the river to Rider Haggard's old place.

'My grandfather, Nathan Rumsby, was a wonderful workman at the forge and at the bench. He had only one eye, but with that one eye he was more accurate than many who had two. Do you know, he could do a job at the forge to almost the exact measurement, so when it came to the bench-work—the filing and the grinding—there'd be the minimum of finishing to be done on it, hardly anything at all. He went to the exhibition of tools in London once, and while he was there he saw a little hand-drill which took his fancy. So he stood and looked at it for some while. He looked at it long enough to memorize every detail. Then he came home and made a copy of it. It's still to be seen in Bungay Museum. He also made a machine for grinding lawn-mower blades. But horse-engines—like the one in the photograph [Plate 5]—was one of his specialties. I've still got the wooden pattern he made for a horse-engine wheel and it's a beautifully-made thing.

'My father was very strict in the shop and there weren't any customs like *First Nail*[2] or *Paying your Footing* or anything like that. The boys who were taken on at the shop had to arrive with boots clean, and they daren't put their hands in their pockets while they

---

[1] The structure was built in 1933 to commemorate the site of the old town pump. On its plinth is a plaque with the following inscription:
'Above: The Black Dog of Bungay which according to the legend appeared in the parish church of St Mary during a severe thunderstorm on Sunday, 4th day of August, 1577:

All down the church in midst of fire
The Hellish monster flew;
And passing onwards to the quire
He many people slew.'

[2] H.I.F., pp. 203–4.

39

were at work. My father was very strict about hands in pockets. If a youngster came into the shop, as they sometimes did, looking for a job, and slouched up with his hands in his pockets, asking:

' "Could you give me a job, Mr. Rumsby?" he'd say: "It's not a job you want!"

'But there was always fooling about with the new boys who got taken on. Someone would grease the handle of a stock-and-die just before they went to use it. Then they'd send the new boy out to the shop for a tin of *gumption* or a tin of *compression*. We were up to all tricks. I recollect we had a short-tempered old woman who lived right near the shop. She was always complaining about something or other. So on the old woman's washing-day—to get our own back—we got a long pole and laid a sack on top of her back'us chimney. Of course, as soon as she got her copper-fire going she couldn't go in the back'us for smoke. Another time, we connected the coil from an old Model T Ford to the water-pump in the yard outside the shop. The pump was shared by many people round about, and we used to watch out for anyone coming to draw water and delight in their expression as they touched the pump-handle.

'I remember, too, the farm-workers sent to the shop from the farms about harvest-time when it was the custom for them to go round the tradesmen a farmer had dealt with to ask for *largesse* money. I recollect one coming in on a certain occasion and saying bluntly: "I've come for the largesse." He was a bit taken aback when my father said: "Oh, the largesse! Well, it hasn't come in yet." But he always paid largesse money to a good customer's men: he couldn't afford not to do so.

'As I've said I worked in my father's shop long before I left school. As soon as I'd finished school of an afternoon I'd go down to father's. I remember Thursday afternoons especially. This was market-day at Bungay; and my father was accustomed to take up some of his stock—smaller items like plough-shares, coulters, and so on—and lay it out in front of the *King's Head*. Then, as soon as I was free, I'd go to him up there and he'd give me the orders he'd taken from the farmers—perhaps half a dozen plough-shares of different sorts, and perhaps as many coulters.

I'd then go down to the shop and load these items into the old hand-cart. It's in one of the photographs [Plate 1]. Many is the time I pushed that round the town with my father's stock. Because the farmers would put up their horse-and-trap at the various pubs in Bungay; and I had to take an order down to, say, Farmer Smith who was at the *Fleece*, the *Angel*, the *Swan* or the *King's Head*. Often too, I'd take a load on the hand-cart down to Gardner the carrier's. This carrier, Gardner, used to go to Norwich every day; and he'd leave different items we were sending out to customers at various places along the route: the *King's Head* at Brooke, the *Railway* at Poringland, and so on.'

The advantages of having a commentator to bring to life various facets of the business do not need stressing. But they are nowhere more apparent than in Albert Rumsby's explanation of some of the more recondite items in the early account books. Here are some examples:

June 28th, 1825 Cock spur and eye for casment   9d

This ancient fastening, whose name so evokes the shape, can still be seen on old windows.

1821 Coulter laid   1s 0d

Laying a plough-coulter meant in effect remaking it. After its edge had become worn through long use the smith welded on to the worn edge a piece of two-and-a-half-inch feather-edged steel; and then the coulter was as good as new.

1829, April 27: 4 Buckles altered   8d
    June 13: Drilling eyes for sales   2d
    July 4:   10 links and 4 swivels for Breechens   1s 8d
           6 new Bits for dutfins   1s 3d

These items are all concerned with horse-harness; and the dates show when the horse and the harness on the farms were under most strain: ploughing and spring-seeding, haysel or hay-harvest, and the preparation for the corn-harvest. *Sales* are the seals or hames on the horse's collar, and the eye took the hook of the plough-traces or the thill-bells of the hames-gear when the horse was between the shafts of the tumbril. *Breechens* is the dialect for breechings, and *dutfin* the dialect (in fact a Middle English word) for bridle.

1829: To 6 Bills pointed & 4 Drawing up the Midl.   2s 6d

These were mill-bills or picks which the miller or mill-wright used for dressing his mill stones.[1]

1824: Grinding and hanging knives   1s 0d

These, according to Albert Rumsby, were the knives of a chaff-cutter. *Hanging* a tool indicates the way in which one part of it is connected to another (cf. the hanging of a scythe). In this instance the knives of a chaff-cutter were 'set off' to the right cutting-angle by means of small wooden wedges.

1827 To Mr James Worts, Bungay
Aug. 7 21 Iron Straks   76 lb.
       5 Do. Do.   17 lb.   £3. 2. 0

Iron strakes were the separate plates fitted to a cart wheel before the use of the iron ring or tyre.

1828 To Mr Aldrich, All Saints
   3 Shars (not case hardn).   3s 6
   1 Tw. Brist   5s 6
   1 A. Brist   5s 0

A *brist* is the breast or plough mould-board.

[1] *F.A.V.*, pp. 146–51.

1827 5 Bills and 3 Pritchells triming   1s 0

Pritchells are mill-bills with chisel ends.

1825 8 Aug. New Sickle   1s 10

One would expect to find a corn-sickle in demand at this date.

Daniel Cameron's price list shows that they sold iron ploughs of three varieties: a swing- (a plough without a wheel) a one-wheeled- and a two-wheeled-plough for prices varying from £3 to £3 5s. An iron horse-hoe cost £2 17s 6d. Cameron's wooden ploughs were also made in three varieties: *skimmer and land wheel*, *skimmer and foot-* and *swing-plough*. They ranged in price from £2 10s to £3 10s. At this time (late nineteenth century) the firm also specialized in making horse-engines for farmers. One of these engines is illustrated in Plate 5. They could be driven by one or two horses, and were used on the farm for chaff-cutting. Cameron's list gives the following description: 'No. 1 horse-gear fitted for one horse with driving wheel, cast iron foundation, frame and cast feet for fixing, intermediate motion, the same fitted with double boss, pole and whippletree.'

It is clear from the account books that the domestic business was as important as the farming trade even if it was on a small scale. The firm specialized in the making of stoves and grates from the beginning; and there are numerous early entries referring to the fitting of a *false-* or *fixed-bottom* grate which could be fitted underneath an ordinary grate as a separate structure. There are also numerous entries relating to *anchors*, the fittings at the end of the iron tie-rods. Long iron-rods were often inserted in old timber-framed houses during the nineteenth century to prevent further damage from *thrust*—the outward pressure of a heavy, steep-pitched (thatched or tiled) roof upon the relatively weak outside walls. *Anchors* or *anchor-heads* were fixed on the ends of the rods and are visible on the outside walls of the building: as their name implies their purpose was to prevent movement. They were of various designs: S-shaped pieces of wrought iron; double-S; a round boss; or a cross.[1]

[1] *P.U.P.*, pp. 66–7; also *A.F.C.H.*, p. 219.

anchor·head

1824	I Anchor laid	2d
1826	Wrd. (?) plate and making anchor	1s 4
1827	Altering anchor	2

One entry about anchors links it with the iron fitting often seen in sixteenth- and seventeenth-century timber-framed houses in East Anglia.

1827	Making anchor and square staple	6d

This is the iron attachment fitted to strengthen the wooden joint between two principal timbers, for example a vertical and horizontal member. It comprises a flat piece of metal with a flange, and a square staple was driven over the metal bar to prevent movement.

Box-irons and box-iron heaters formed a great part of the domestic trade:

1822	Heater to Box iron	2d

In Cameron's price list box-iron heaters are quoted at 2d a lb. The heater of a box-iron is a triangular piece of cast iron that was placed into a fire, taken out when red hot and inserted into the box-iron that was used for smoothing linen, etc. Many country wives in East Anglia used the box-iron until a few years ago: the old traditional type was the most popular; but other, more sophisticated, types survive: a box-iron heated by charcoal; one heated by a methylated spirit arrangement; and a housewife in

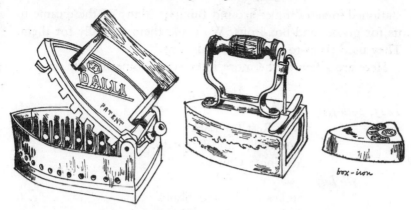

box-iron

Helmingham, Suffolk, used a more elaborately-designed American one. It was heated by charcoal embers which could be livened up by inserting a bicycle pump into a hole in the 'door' of the iron and pumping vigorously.

Another early entry shows that the firm made *heater-stoves* quite early in the nineteenth century. This was a kind of oven, square in shape; and it was specially made for making the triangular pieces of metal red hot before placing them in the box-iron. It was priced at 3s 4d. The following is also related to the box-iron:

1825 New goose iron   1s 8

This is a tailor's smoothing iron, the handle resembling a goose's neck. *Goosing* was the process of ironing with a tailor's goose. The age of the implement can be gauged from the reference to it in the Porter scene in *Macbeth* (Act 2; iii).

> *Come in, tailor; here you may roast your goose.*

There is also a related entry a few years later:

> *Mr Farrow (Hatter), Halesworth*

1827 2 New Hot Irons (33 lb)   12s 0
        New Straw Bonnet Press   £1 8s 7

Albert Rumsby added a note about goose-irons and box-irons: 'During the last war there were many squadrons of Americans stationed in aerodromes around Bungay. Many of these came to us for goose- and box-irons. We made them specially for them. They used them to press their uniforms.'

Here are a few of the more interesting domestic entries:

Mrs Gurneys

1825, 29th June

	New Rest for Lath	16s 0
	Iron Collar and Brass do.	6
	Making 3 Chucks	1 0
5th July		
	Spikes to Crickett Shoes	1. 6
	Spikes to Crickett Shoes	1. 5
	Larth for Rock Bow (?) md.	1. 0

1827, 27 Oct.

	8 Sash Weights	72 lbs	10 0
	1 Chimney bar	8 lbs	2 0

1828, 27th March   *Richard Fulcher (A'tirney)*

	To Shaping Coffee Mill	1 6
	Repairing Kittell	1 2
	To Pulleys, & hook & eye	1 6
	Coffee dore md.	6

1829

16 April	To Repairing Kittell	1 0
22 June	To frying Pan; part new and lining do.	2 0
27 ,,	New bottom to water Pot	1 3
6 Oct.	New Scuppit spade or shovel	3 0
	New fire pan Spone	1 2
	To laying small Poker	8
	To Repearing Cup	9

Albert Rumsby was also able to give notes on the photographs. Plate 1 shows a Cameron *E.H.* plough in the process of assembly. When it was complete it was listed as a two-horse iron plough with round coulter, skim coulter (also called a skimmer or skim-breast), land and furrow wheel. A complete plough is visible over the shop fascia in Plates 3 and 4. The weight of the plough was 273 lb.; and in 1900 it cost £5 5s. The coulter or knife (visible just in front of the share) was fixed to the beam of the plough by a round 'eye' and tail nut. The cast-iron plough-foot (not yet fitted in the photograph, Plate 1) was fitted to a stalk of seven-eighths wrought iron which was held by a square 'eye' fitted to the plough-beam. William Bramsby, Mrs. Albert Rumsby's father (he is standing near the forge in Plate 6) specialized in making these square 'eyes'. Mrs. Rumsby said: 'I often used to hear about square eyes, but it was years before I knew exactly what they were!'

In addition to the robust *E.H.* plough, Cameron made the *E.S.*, a little market-garden plough, the *E.N.*, a lightish plough for a smallholder, and the *E.M.*, a plough that was a little heavier than the *E.N.*

As already stated, the cart in the photograph is the one which Albert Rumsby pushed around the town when he was a lad. 'Behind the cart is the workman named Mays who looked after the furnace. He's holding a heavy sledge-hammer which he used to break up the scrap-iron (it's there in a heap behind him) for melting down in the furnace. Next to him is Albert Nursey, and the tall man next to him is Tom Evans. Old Tom was a very good moulder when he was sober. But if anything went wrong he'd go out and get filled up with beer. The short man next to Tom is holding a ladle, and the end one is holding a forge hand-hammer.'

Plates 2, 3 and 4 show the retail shop at the front of the foundry in ceremonial dress for various state occasions: Plate 2, the Silver Jubilee, George V and Queen Mary, May 1935; Plate 3, their coronation, June 1911; Plate 4, Queen Victoria's Diamond Jubilee, June 1897. The steel structure of the arch is the same one in each photograph. Chinese lanterns figure in the three schemes of decoration; and the small glass, coloured jars, which also held candles, in the earlier two. Part of the legend in the 1911 arch did not photograph because the words were painted in a colour that did not register on the photographic plate. But the most valuable feature of this set of three photographs is the opportunity it gives to study the changes in dress—especially men's headgear —over a period of forty years. The photographs show bowlers, billycocks, a boater, trilbys, a square bowler, and a fine selection of caps.

Albert Rumsby commented: 'In the 1935 photograph [Plate 2] the plough is a Cameron *E.N.* You can see the knife coulter and skim-breast quite clearly. Behind the arch you can see the galvanized corrugated water-cisterns we used to make. Every house almost in the country had one of these to collect rain-water, soft water for washing clothes. The Ransomes' plate in front of the shop was also there in 1911 as you can see. My father, Harry Nathan Rumsby, painted the *Old English* on the arch, but the arch itself had been made donkey's years before this. Of course, I wasn't born when they took the 1897 Victoria Jubilee photograph; but I know that half of the people in it had nothing to do with the firm. They were just passers-by, "visitors" who slipped into the picture to get their likeness drawn! You'll recognize the articles behind the 1911 arch: pigs' troughs. We used to sell a lot of those. The iron rods you see in the 1897 photograph [Plate 4] are fencing stakes. The horse-engine photograph is an interesting one. As you know, the horse walked round and round to drive a fan to blow the foundry furnace. R. Hunt of Earls Colne in Essex made these horse-works; and we used to make gears for them; we fitted up a number of them on farms for driving chaff-cutters. The "intermediate motion" which was inside the barn stepped up the speed. You can see the usual tools in this photograph, too: hammers, ladles and so on. The two men wearing billycocks and standing in the doorway are holding a *double ladle.* The object on the right of the horse circle is the frame of one of the Cameron ploughs. Cameron himself is sitting on the left of the engine-frame, in the centre; beside him is his friend, a pork-butcher from Bungay. I reckon the date of this photograph would be about 1895. We used the horse for taking out gear into the town and the countryside about: so turning the engine wasn't his only job.

'The workshop photograph [Plate 6] is not perhaps as old as the horse-engine one. You can see the type of stove we used to make. My father is standing in front of one with a plough-wheel behind him. That's my grandfather—number one at the bench!'

5. Foundry Yard with Horse-engine

6. Foundry Workshop

3 Saddler or Leather Craftsman

The working horse disappeared from most of the farms in East Anglia in the decade 1950–60. The Second World War had slowed up the horse's displacement by the motor-tractor and the breeding of the farm-horse was given a new stimulus; but as soon as industry was realigned to a peace-time rhythm and tractors came more quickly off the assembly-lines, easing out tanks and armoured cars, the East Anglian farms became almost fully mechanized. By the late 'fifties the working farm-horse had disappeared from most districts of Norfolk and Suffolk. He remained on a few farms singly or in pairs for use in jobs such as seed-drilling and harrowing. An occasional farmer kept a horse or two for unashamedly sentimental reasons, but when they died off sentiment failed in most instances to survive inevitable pressures. Moreover, as the older generation of horsemen retired from the farms younger men became less and less reconciled to being tied to the farms at week-ends simply to bait a pair of horses. Except for a farmer here and there, standing out resolutely against change, and for those farmers in the Fens of Cambridgeshire where there were still jobs for the horse, and economically justifiable ones too, mechanization was complete by the early 'sixties. Already there was growing up a generation of young farmers who had never seen a pair of horses harnessed to the plough.

The country craftsmen who depended on the farm-horse for most of their living faced a bleak future. Many blacksmiths and harness-makers—in the two crafts most closely affected—anticipated the farm-horse's disappearance by closing their shops. A minority, younger, more adaptable and more hopeful, held on and —as far as they could—adjusted their business to the new landscape. The experience of a Suffolk harness-maker, Leonard Aldous (born 1900) of Debenham, illustrates the health of some

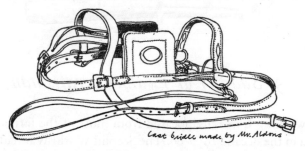

Last bridle made by Mr. Aldous

of the old crafts and the resourcefulness of the craftsmen in riding the changes. He was apprenticed to the saddler's business in 1913. It was an old-established firm some of whose order books date from 1832; and it served a rich arable area which assured plenty of work as long as the horse remained the chief source of power on the farms. After the First World War, however, the tractor began slowly to erode the almost complete dominance of the horse; and although this process was slowed up considerably during the inter-war years by the depressed state of farming, Leonard Aldous found that after taking over the business from his employer he had to adapt continually:

'Our main difficulties, of course, were due to the changes in farming and especially the recession of the horse. But at first it was very gradual and we had time to look around and absorb some of the changes. For instance, after the First World War the self-binder or reaper-binder had come to the front—most of them drawn by horses at first. As you know, the old self-binder had a canvas conveyor-belt which delivered the sheaf of corn after it had been tied. These conveyors often wanted repairing, and that was a regular job for us; and it was directly in our line although many people wouldn't think so. They assume that a harness-maker dealt and worked in nothing else but leather. This is not strictly true. We made headstalls, halters, horse-covers, and the plough-reins or *cords* which, as the name implies, were made from hemp. I've mentioned to you before[1] that there was a rope-walk at the back of this shop during the last century; and the harness-maker worked in fibre as well as leather. They grew hemp in this area and prepared it as well, so work in canvas was well within the harness-maker's traditional craft. As well as repairing the canvas-conveyor we did a lot of work for agricultural engineers, making and fitting belts for the new self-binders they turned out.

'But increasingly, after the last war, the self-binder had to give way to the combine-harvester. So again we had to think because a great deal of our work seemed to be under another threat: we came to the conclusion that we would lose a great deal of our business. The first combine-harvester that came to this district was a *Massey 21*; and it was equipped with a wide web and leather belt. There was, therefore, a fair amount of work for us with that. But then the combine-harvester developed further, and the more advanced machines were fitted with an auger-drive to collect the corn, instead of a conveyor-belt. Again, we thought the business was in danger.

'Yet along came the pea-harvesting machine. It's becoming very popular in this area and is likely to last because farmers are beginning to find out that it's profitable to grow peas on a large scale for some of the big firms like *Birds Eye*. These pea-harvesting machines are fitted with a heavy form of rubberized canvas conveyor-belt; and we've had the idea of making up these belts as well as repairing them. But things are on the move all the time: a new machine has been evolved for picking french beans as well as peas, though we've been able to come in on this because they are using another heavy canvas for it. As far as we can see ahead we will still be in the market.

[1] *F.A.V.*, chapter 11.

'In the early days of the self-binder it was only used for cutting wheat, rarely for other corn; and there were not many repair jobs on it. But these new pea and bean machines are in use for a great deal of the summer—a kind of extended harvest job; and we can then have these machines in the winter to overhaul and repair at our leisure.

'The other day (August 1967) I saw three large combine-harvesters being moved from one part of a big nearby farm to another; and the contrast with the time when I was a boy sixty years ago struck me very hard. At that time, before 1914, I used to see a thrashing tackle being moved along the road by horse-power. Consider the number of horses they used:

> Four horses pulled the old portable steam-engine.
> Three or four pulled the threshing drum.
> Two horses pulled the straw-elevator.
> One horse followed behind with a chaff-cutter:
> One horse with the water-tank.

There were at least ten horses on this job, and it does remind you that our business depended not only on the horse that worked in the actual field but the road or transport horse in a dozen or more different trades. Then there's the difference in speed that one's bound to notice. That old outfit I used to see when I was a boy took a good half-day to move from one farm to another: today a combine usually gets to its job in half an hour at the most.

'But the horse has not completely gone although I don't know of a working farm-horse within miles. Light horses and ponies for riding are increasing in number. There used to be light horses in the district, of course, when I started in this trade; but it was the farm-horse that made the real work for us. You imagine a sight like I've just described: horses doing heavy transport jobs like this, and working hard at the plough and so on and the self-binder. The harness was bound to come under strain, and it needed frequent repair. Though we can grumble at the passing of the heavy horse, the light horse and the pony are coming well to the front, and we are getting a lot of work, harness repair and so on. In fact, the future of the craft looks brighter than it's been for years. There are a dozen jobs we wouldn't have thought of twenty years ago, let alone doing; but we are doing them today and finding they help the business. Take, for instance, the new interest in antiques. On several occasions we've repaired the leather on a pair of old-fashioned bellows. We've done quite a few jobs matching up leather with polished wood on an antique. We've repaired an old landau for a museum, and we've done a careful restoration job on an old writing-case just recently. So, you see, we're still very much in the business.'

4 Whitening-Roll Maker

Most of the rural crafts have been well-documented, especially in recent years; but occasionally a small, marginal craft—now obsolete—has remained in the memories of the older generation. Such a craft is the whitening-roll makers of Stonham Aspal in Suffolk; and the details were told me by W. H. Thurlow (born 1890) and his wife.

The business of making whitening for decorating rooms, shops, dairies and so on, was carried on by one family in Stonham Aspal —the Berry family. As so often happened, the skill came down from one generation to another. The Berrys had a well-established business by the beginning of the last century; and later it went to one of the daughters who married a Stonham man called George Race (Plate 7 shows George and Harriet Race, Mrs. Thurlow's parents, at the time of their diamond wedding). George soon acquired the distinctive name of *Whitening-Maker Race*; and he and his wife carried on the trade for about fifty years until just before the outbreak of the First World War when ill-health and a lessening demand for the product forced them to give up the business.

The chalk for making the whitening was carted from the quarries at Claydon a few miles away. It came in tumbrils, and cost ten shillings a load, delivered to the Races' yard. There it was dumped and taken in pails to the circular crushing-pit. This contained a heavy iron wheel which operated in a way similar to an old cider-mill. The wheel was fixed to a central post or upright spindle by a long wooden axle which projected like a capstan shaft beyond the pit itself. A donkey or a pony harnessed to this shaft walked round, causing the wheel to revolve in the pit, crushing the lumps as it did so. But before the donkey started on its roundabout trek, buckets of water from a nearby pond had been poured on to the chalk, so that when he had been pulling the wheel round for some time a thick, cream-like liquid would have formed in the pit.

One of Mr. Thurlow's sisters recalled that sometimes neither a dickey [donkey] nor a pony were to be had. Then the children had to pull the wheel round. They worked in pairs, one of them being harnessed to the shaft. The old lady remembers being fixed to the shaft with a rope passed over her shoulders and underneath her armpits. There was room for one only to pull on the shaft at a time; but it was possible for her younger sister to *push*. This she did by getting a short forked stick, something like the top of a linen-prop and fixing it against the end of the shaft to give her better leverage.

When the liquid in the crushing-pit had reached the consistency of thick cream they ladled it out and strained it through a very fine wire-mesh sieve into another (rectangular) pit alongside. This was the first of the two straining-pits. These two pits were identical in design and were lined with porous bricks, five 'courses' deep. The bricks were porous so that excess water soon percolated away. While this was happening a scum formed on top of the liquid. They took this off with a trowel and the liquid was then left until it reached the consistency of cream cheese. Harriet Race, who usually managed the making of the whitening with two or three of her twelve children, now took the raw material out of this pit with a trowel and placed it in the second straining-pit. In spite of the sieving there was always an amount of grit at the bottom of the first pit, and she took great care to prevent any of the grit getting into the second.

After it had been left there for a while, the raw material would have reached a 'workable state'. They took it out with trowels and doled it out in equal quantities on to plain tiles, a pile of which was kept handy for the purpose. They then placed these flat tiles, each with its load of whitening, on top of a low wall that ran alongside the pits, 'the whole length of the property'. The wall had been specially built for drying whitening: it was about three feet high—'just high enough for you to work', as one of George Race's daughters described it. The length of time the whitening was left on the wall depended entirely on the weather. If it was hot and sunny, Harriet Race and her children had to be careful not to let it get too dry. If this happened the material would crack and crumble as they tried to handle it. When they judged that it was ready, they took the material and worked each amount into a ball, 'just like dough'. These, in fact, were known as *balls* or *rolls* of whitening. The Race family referred to them as rolls and sold them at 1½d each. They became so skilful in estimating how much of the raw material to scoop out on to each plain tile that the weight of the rolls did not vary appreciably, and four always made up a stone at which rate the whitening was sometimes sold. After being processed in this way the rolls were very brittle; and as they had no form of wrapping great care had to be taken in handling them. The older members of the family collected the rolls in bushel skeps; and after a sack had been placed in the bottom of the donkey cart they loaded them tenderly for delivery around the countryside.

About the year 1860 when George Race was courting Harriet Berry he went with his future mother-in-law to the seaside town of Aldeburgh to sell a load of whitening. It was too long a journey to do in one day with a donkey and a loaded cart, so they slept one night by the roadside. They sold the whitening to a shopkeeper in Aldeburgh. 'His customers used it for whitening dairies, ceilings, bedrooms and living-rooms and even parlours. There was not much wallpaper at that time o' day. People couldn't afford it. And the whitening business used to flourish.' George Race lived until the 'twenties; and although he spent all his life at Stonham Aspal, not much more than twenty miles from the East Coast, his Aldeburgh trip was the only occasion when he saw the sea.

The lavish use of whitewash for interior decoration during the nineteenth century must have been noticed by many people who have in recent years bought timber-frame cottages in East Anglia. In many of the cottages the beams have been thickly whitewashed, and one of the new residents' most arduous jobs has been to strip the beams of their covering. While doing this they have most probably inveighed against the people who were tasteless enough to cover up the beams in the first place. Yet their strictures are not altogether just because fashion is a great dictator; and where fashion says, 'Cover up!' either with whitewash, plaster (or skirt), only the strong-minded can resist; and it would be interesting to speculate how many people today uncover timbers rather to be in the fashion than for the reason that they like looking at studs and beams.

But fashion apart, there was another reason for the frequent use of whitewash—a functional one. It was recommended and, indeed, insisted upon in the interests of cleanliness and public health. A few years ago we lived in a sixteenth-century house in Needham Market. One of the rooms downstairs is beautifully panelled but a former owner told me that, sometime before, they had laboriously to scrape off the whitewash with which the panels had been thickly covered. The full story came out when we discussed the former name of this particular room—the *Boulting Room*. During the late nineteenth and the beginning of this century, the owner of the house had been a baker; and the back premises were the *bake-office*:[1] one room contained the huge brick-oven where the bread was baked and the table where the dough was first made and weighed; in the Boulting Room were the flour boulters, the wooden hutches where the flour was sieved or boulted before it went into the next room for making into dough. The sanitary authorities insisted that bake-offices, like dairies, should be covered with whitewash, and should be kept white with frequent renewals of the wash.

Even at a very early period, however, the wooden walls of bakehouses were so treated:[2] 'After the great fire of London in

---

[1] A once common word in Suffolk; cf. tan-office or domestic offices. Office from Lat. *opificium* contracted to *officium* (*opifex*, an artisan or mechanic).

[2] S. O. Addy, *The Evolution of the English House*, London, 1905, p. 126.

the year 1212 the civic authorities ordered that the cookshops on the Thames, as well as all the bakeries and breweries, were to be whitewashed and plastered inside and out as a precaution against fire. Whitewash and fresco-painting were universally applied to the stone walls of ancient churches, though modern "restorers" always strip them off as a late innovation.' Whitewashing was even older than this. The Romans daubed their buildings and private houses and we can be certain from the word they used to describe the process—*dealbo*—that the colour was white. Therefore it is likely that the making of whitening was a very ancient craft indeed.

5 *The Gardener*

In writings about the countryside gardening as a craft has not been much celebrated because, one supposes, it appeared as a subsidiary skill that most countrymen practised, and had to practise, when wages were very low. But it was also a skill that most countrymen delighted in. It was their form of self-expression, their art; and they thought about it continually even when they were away from their gardens, in the same way as a writer or an artist is continually thinking about his work even when he is not at his desk or his easel. Much of the skill they used in their garden developed out of their traditional knowledge, and they rarely read books or writings on gardening, taking the stand: 'The books won't tell you what to do in your own particular garden. You've got to find out that for yourself.' Although for many this is a counsel of unapproachable perfection, many country gardeners did in fact experiment in their own gardens and develop their own methods.

Such a gardener is Anthony Willet Lankester (born 1893) who until recently had one of the best-kept half-acres in the Suffolk village of Helmingham: although in his later years he did not 'farm' all the land as he once did when he was a younger man. Much of it was latterly put down to grass and fruit trees. But even up to last summer the grass was well kept, the land extremely clean, the crops healthy, and the hedges beautifully kept and trimmed. On one of my visits he told me of his experiment, the growing of winter potatoes. He had noticed that *self-set* potatoes (tubers that had escaped harvesting and had lain in the ground throughout the winter) when they sprouted during the following spring were always healthy and free from frost damage. He therefore decided to try an experiment: to plant some potatoes in the early winter or late autumn, but potatoes that had been specially prepared:

'When I was harvesting potatoes in the early autumn I took out a few and let them lay on the ground, in the sun until they were right green and their skins thick and tough. I let the first frosts get at them and although it *snew* [snowed] they took no harm, as I found out later. This laying on 'em out a-climatized 'em; that's why I done it. And I proved to be right! Then I planted them in late November to early December; and I had a crop from these potatoes at about the same time and of the same amount as I got from the ones I planted in the ordinary way. The advantage with these winter-set potatoes is that they are not harmed by the spring frosts and they are completely free from disease.'

Anthony Lankester has been setting a row or two of winter potatoes for years; and last year (1968) he gave me four or five pounds of main-crop (*Majestic*) that had been sown in the winter. I watched him dig them out. The yield was not less than that from the spring-sown tubers. The winter potatoes had good, firm flesh and clean, healthy-looking skins and they were completely free from blight or blemish. And they passed the ultimate test: they had a very good flavour when—as the gardening writers say—they were brought to the table. Anthony Lankester had developed this method through long observation and experiment. As he told me: 'You notice, you pay regard, you say nawthen, and you try it!'

Frederick Woods (born 1876) of Framsden, an adjoining village, was a gardener of an older generation and a professional. He went to Helmingham school; and he showed me the certificates he won during his last three years at school (1883–5):

'These are Her Majesty's Inspectors' certificates, as you see. When you passed in all subjects and had a regular attendance you had a prize. About six boys and six girls had prizes every year. We were measured for a pair of good strong boots which were fitted before the prize-giving. The boots were made by the village shoemakers round about: Stockings, the shoemaker at Framsden, would make the boots one year, Denny from Otley the next, and the Pettaugh shoemaker the year after that. They shared them out among all the shoemakers in those villages which sent children to Helmingham school. The Tollemaches also used to give shirts and underclothes for regular attenders.

'When I left school I had a wish to become a gardener and to study horticulture. But I had to wait for some time as it was not easy to get in. But at last I got my first start at High House, Campsey Ash, the Honourable William Lowther's place. He was the Speaker in the House of Commons. Then I went from there to Glevering Hall, a few miles away; and from there I went as a second gardener to the Duke of Hamilton's place at Easton Park. At Easton Park I lived in a bothy[1] with two other gardeners. We did our own cooking and we had milk and vegetables free. A woman came in twice a week to clean up, and our sheets and towels were washed in the estate laundry. But we had to see to our own personal washing ourselves. I enjoyed the time I lived in the bothy very much. We used to go out one night a week bell-ringing—*chimes-ringing* not the *science-ringing*—and we used to ring at the services on a Sunday.[2]

'When I started there was a rigid apprentice system in gardening. During my first year I spent my time stoking furnaces and doing other odd jobs like mixing soil and *crocking*; getting the earthenware pots ready for plants. You put a piece of earthenware over the draining-hole at the bottom, and then some soil, and a few pieces of earthenware here and there in it, also a piece of rough turf for drainage, and you then filled it with more soil.

'In my second year I went on to fruit. I remember one of our

[1] In Scotland farm-workers lived on the farm, usually sleeping in a loft above the stables—the bothy. The practice of *living in* died out in East Anglia early last century, so it seems, and this is the first time I have heard the term bothy in this area.

[2] *A.F.C.H.*, chapter 18.

crinkle-crankle wall, Easton Park

main jobs was to *force* the strawberries. But *force* didn't mean just bringing them on quickly with heat as many people seem to think it does. We tried as far as possible to reproduce the same conditions as the plant met when left to itself in the normal growing-season. First the strawberries were planted in '48' pots and then clamped. (I should explain that there were pots of different sizes—still are, of course: '36', '48' and '60' were the ones I was most familiar with. The same amount of clay went into making all the pots—that's how I understood it. '36' pots were the largest because the larger the pots the fewer there'd be in number from a given quantity of clay. You could make forty-eight similar pots of a smaller size from the same amount—and so on.) After clamping the strawberries in the '48' pots we put a hundred or so into a cold frame. Then we put a little gentle heat on them until they were ready. We also grew a lot of *pines* [pineapples] in the stove-houses.

'I spent part of my third year as apprentice in the vegetable gardens. My fourth year I spent in the orchid-houses or stove-houses. Each house had two large saddle-boilers which burned anthracite. We used one stove at a time. The gardener who used it cleaned it out ready for the next one when he took over. A great deal of my time here was spent pruning the vines. We had Muscatel, Lady Downs, Black Admiral and Alexandria Muscats. To grow these last grapes and to get them to develop to their proper colour demanded a tremendous amount of heat: it was a costly business. But it was pleasant to get away from the stove-houses on fine sunny days and to work in the gardens. At this time of year when the pollen of the fruit trees was dry when we were going about our jobs in the garden we never passed a tree without giving it a shake to scatter the pollen and help fertilization.

'But apart from our work in the gardens and in the stove-houses we had a definite daily routine connected with the house. We had to change the flowers in the various rooms, in the hall, in the drawing room, in her Ladyship's boudoir and so on; and, most important of all, we had to decorate the dining table. For breakfast and lunch there were three little pot plants on the table. Dinner was at 8 p.m.; and at 7 o'clock you had to decorate the tablecloth. But first you had to find out from the butler what silver he was going to use. We made a pattern of leaves and flowers on the tablecloth and we had to know where the silver was going to lie before you did this. I recollect a herring-bone pattern I used to fancy; and I carried out this design very often. One of the most important things we had to watch out for was that the flowers didn't obstruct the view of the guests. It wouldn't have done to have that. Next morning the flowers had to be taken off the table well before breakfast-time.

'When I was at Easton Park there were twenty-seven servants. In fact there were so many servants *they* [the residents] hardly knew your name. They were just about aware that you were around the place. When the Duke was in London, every day we had to post off a little *buttonhole*—often carnations—so he'd get it first thing next morning. At that time of day, the ladies used to have a *spray*, the gentlemen a *buttonhole*.'

6 The Ploughman

One of the skills that had the highest acclaim in the East Anglian countryside under the old farm economy was the ability to *draw* or plough a straight furrow and lay a level stetch (a section of ploughed land) so that it looked like a well-made length of corduroy. The skill, too, that could drill a field so that no mark was visible on the seed-bed except the marks of the drill-coulters themselves, won equal esteem. So great was the interest in ploughing a well-finished stetch with mathematically straight furrows, or in the faultless drilling of a seed-bed and so keen was the rivalry between various horsemen that, even after they had spent most of an autumn day ploughing an acre or so in the field, they would spend the rest of it ploughing the land over once again in the cosiness of the inn bar. And on a Sunday morning they walked round the parish inspecting their neighbours' week of ploughing to see if it measured up to the high claims that had been made for it during the detailed preliminary examination at the four-ale bar. Strange as it must seem now, the skill of the old horse ploughman was not recognized outside his own immediate circle. All farm-workers were *labourers* with that term's implication of unskilled and unintelligent toil; and that label stuck to them until recent years. And it must be admitted that the low

8. Ploughman Jack Page and a pair of Suffolks

9. Horse rake

10. Taking corn to the millers, Halesworth, Suffolk

11. Pair of oxen with old Norfolk *gallus* (gallows) plough, North Elham, Norfolk, *c.* 1907

level of wages the farm-worker received appeared to the un-
informed justification enough for not changing their image of
him. But the farm-worker was practised in numerous skills as
well as ploughing and drilling, and no apology is offered here
for including him among the craftsmen as a craftsman of the
highest order. James Seely (born 1894), a Norfolk farmer who
started his career as a horseman, told me:

'The old teamsmen would walk miles round the countryside to
look at other people's work—well outside their own parish sometimes. At the time I'm speaking of, before 1914 when I was called
up, the pubs were open all day during the week but on Sunday
they were closed except during mid-day for a couple of hours;
and then they'd open again in the evening. But if you'd travelled
three miles you could have a drink in a pub at any time on a
Sunday. So the teamsmen [or horsemen] used to walk their three
miles out of the village to get a drink, looking at the ploughing
as they went. Then when they'd had their drink they'd walk
round to another pub till they made their way back home. Some
of them made a real outing of it, looking at the land and saying,
perhaps: "They've got a real good 'un here. Look at his work!"'

'You take the ten-furrow work we had to do on the heavy land
round Kirby Cane. That was tradesman's work. You'd take
years to learn it. You had a nine-inch share to your plough and a
stetch coming out at seven feet ten inches. You used an eight-foot
Smyth drill and your work had to be right to the inch. But that
weren't the only skill: there were half a dozen more: stacking—
it's a rare skill today—thatching, which we had to do on the farm,
hedging, ditching, looking after half a dozen horses, and keeping
them in good condition with little aid from the vet.'

James Knights, a Suffolk horseman who was born at Debach
near Woodbridge in 1880, also emphasized the long training and
the skill needed: 'I started when I was very young—with a good
bloke, too. He put me into the way of a lot of things. He showed
me how to work a horse and how to treat a horse and he also
showed me how to govern a horse. I was thirteen when I started—
that was seventy-five years ago. And I went to plough and I got
on with it all right. Then I went to Yorkshire.'

He worked on the farm and latterly led a stallion, then after a few years he returned:

[T][1] 'At the age of eighteen I was ploughman at Thistleton Hall, Burgh in Suffolk. But after a while I became restless and I had a mind to go to Burton-on-Trent malting because I knew I could earn good money. The farmer say to me, "You've got a pair of good horses and I give you a shilling a week more than I give anyone else (I was getting 12s a week), and I don't see why you want to leave for." But I went and did a few seasons malting before settling back on the Suffolk farm; and the time I'm talking about is a good bit later. I used to lead a drill, an *eight-counter* [coulter] drill, and I used to do a field and you couldn't tell the *wheeling* [after drilling he skilfully covered up the wheel-mark of the drill by drilling right over it so that it appeared as a mark of the coulter]. You couldn't tell which was the wheeling and which had been proved. A man was talking to me not long ago about it: a field that I led by the side of the road at Boulge. I led that field and you couldn't tell the wheeling; and there were seven or eight horsemen from Bredfield come and looked at that one Sunday, and you couldn't tell the wheeling. The oats were about three inches high. You couldn't tell the wheeling on it. That's how straight I'd done it. You got to drive your first horse and lead the one in the shafts. That was a hard job, and you'd got to know how to do it! That's right: two horses at length. That was the time when we were a-drilling on the flat: a big stetch, when they'd begun to put these stetches into one. It would be sixteen yards from furrow to furrow. Then we used to drill it *overwart* [athwart the furrows]. That's how it used to be done.'

The care taken over drilling, and the emulation it aroused among horsemen is illustrated by an Essex farmer:[2] 'I knew of a horseman who'd get up early and make a dummy run over the field he was going to drill later in the day—go over it first with an empty drill so that he could use the coulter marks to get perfect accuracy when he did the actual sowing.'

[1] Throughout the book, this symbol indicates a literal transcript of a tape recording.
[2] Malcolm Carter, Layer de la Haye.

Charles Last, born at Forward Green, Earl Soham, Suffolk in 1878, was one of the champion ploughmen of his district; and his life-story is typical of the farm-worker of that period. Like most skilled head-horsemen he had, too, no misgivings about sounding his own praises. They knew they were good and no false modesty restrained them from asserting it. Ploughing and drilling and managing their horses had been their whole way of life, and why should they not assess it as they saw it? But in every instance where a horseman claimed pre-eminence I always found a farmer, or a contemporary or two, to confirm his claims:

'I went to school at Earl Soham and I paid tuppence a week for going there. I left when I was eleven one Friday afternoon; and by eleven o'clock on the Monday morning I was away. I took my lunch and I was away with a farmer down by Stonham Charch, rooting out docks with a little two-tine fork. The schoolmaster—well he'd got my tuppences and I reckon he didn't much care what happened to me afterwards.

'Shortly after that I went as *back'us boy*[1] to Mr. Fiske's of Whitegate Farm, Creeting. I stayed there till I was twenty-seven years of age. I was a tidy-good man by the time I was seventeen. One of my jobs at Fiske's was with the newspaper. He had a weekly newspaper come by post; and when I started as a back'us boy I had to take the newspaper, as soon as he'd finished with it, to Johnny Field who farmed at Crowfield Hall, a fair step away. When Johnny Field had read it his back'us boy took it to George Stedman's at High Elm, Gosbeck. From there Stedman's boy took it to Kitson at Choppins Hill Farm, Coddenham.

'The next week Kitson of Choppins Hill would have it first, and he'd pay for it; and it would come back along the line so they'd all have it first in turn. It was a weekly newspaper: it used to come on a Friday and I'd take it round usually on the Monday. As soon as the farmer read it he'd tie it round with a piece of string and seal it up with wax for fear anybody else would read it—anybody who didn't pay! But that didn't signify, because there were few boys strong enough at thet time o' day to read what was in the newspapers.

[1] *A.F.C.H.*, pp. 23–7.

'I spent nine harvests at Whitegate Farm, Creeting, using the scythe in all of 'em. I never saw an engine [reaper or reaper-binder] the whole time I was there. At that time you got 9s a week if you were single, and however good a workman you were you wouldn't get 10s until you got married. You could get a woman for 7s 6d in those days [the cost of the marriage-licence]. I went to the farmer and I told him:

"I should be getting ten shillings now."

"Not if you're single," he say.

"Well, I got myself a woman last week."

"You have? Then you'd better bring the certificate on Saturday morning so I can see it."

'At that time we worked from 6 a.m. until 6 p.m., Saturdays included.

'For most of my time I worked for a Needham Market farmer called William Hunt. He was a good farmer with well over 2,000 acres and he'd been farming some while. He'd go over a field with an owd stick with a dock-spud at the end of it: he'd dig his spud into the land and bring up a bit o' the soil and put it in the palm of his hand, and then he'd take it in his fingers and rub it a time or two atween them. If he say, "Thet will do!" you may depend it would do. That farm would go like a rick a-fire. It would *do*:[1] it would go forward and prosper and make him his money.

'One day we were at work with two ploughs; and the man who had the other plough say to me: "There's a woman a-coming along the *headlings* [headlands], Charlie. Who is it?"

"Thet's Mrs. Fiske from Willisham Hall, Mrs. Hunt's mother. Thet that is!"

'We were ploughing-in beans, and he was covering up; and she come along to me and she say:

"You're the head man by the look on it. You got the drill.[2] Now tell me: what do you think on this farm?"

"I don't know nawthen about the farm, Ma'am," I say. "This

---

[1] A very rich and powerful word in the dialect, although small. Here it means prosper. If an animal is 'a-doing well' it is getting fat. O.E. *dugan*. M.E. *dowan* to be strong (cf. doughty).

[2] *F.A.V.*, pp. 38–9.

is the first field I ploughed. But if they all turn over like this 'un, Ma'am, it'll do right well."

"Good," she say. "If Mr. Hunt [her son-in-law] will supply the judgement, I'll supply the money."

'After I'd been there some years I was out a-ploughing one morning and Mr. Hunt, the farmer himself, was there. After a while another farmer came by and come into the field; and as he see me a-going round he say: "You got one good ploughman at least," and when I turned round at the headlings he say to me: "You been at this game some while, Mister."

"More'n three weeks!"

"I dessay."

"I'll tell you what: I've been at this game long enough to git twelve copper kittles."

'And this farmer then turn to Mr. Hunt; and Mr. Hunt, he say: "He's whoolly right: he's got twelve copper kittles. I've seen 'em myself." '

Before mechanization and the coming of the tractor to the farms, furrow-drawing matches for horse ploughmen were very frequent. Charles Last and his father attended every match they could; and they often carried off the first prize, a copper kettle usually, for ploughing the straightest furrow or the best stetch— the neatest with level top and straight furrows as well, a good finish.

Copper kettles were also given as prizes in skittle matches at public houses. Sam Friend (born 1888) of Framsden recalled some of these matches: 'They used to have them regular at Kittleburgh *Chequers*. They'd allus bowl for a copper kittle. Nine-pin bowling but when there was a competition there were usually ten. In the latter part of the time they used to have only three pins. You got two balls for sixpence. I won a kittle at Ashfield *Swan* in 1913. You could have the copper kittle or 12s 6d which was a little bit more than my week's wages at that time. I took the kittle.'

A number of these kettles that were won as prizes were often not used but kept as ornaments, and repositories for bills, receipts and trinkets. Since the last war, antique dealers have done a brisk trade in them in answer to the demand for ornaments for period houses and cottages. Here, also, is a footnote to the mention by Charles Last of newspapers in the country. In more recent years when the old pattern of a weekly newspaper gave way to the daily, farm-workers took the local newspaper on one or two days a week, those days when farm-sales and cottage-sales were advertised—usually on a Wednesday or Saturday. Newspapers and the reading habits of country people are also mentioned in the following account recorded on tape and transcribed without any editing. I include it in full as it is relevant to the training of a ploughman or horseman who had almost invariably to serve his time as a back'us boy before graduating to the plough. Charles Rookyard (1889–1965), a Suffolk ploughman and horse-leader, recorded it just before his death. A description of William Charles Rookyard may assist the reader in investing the account with the overtones that are inescapably present to anyone who knew him.

He was a tall, well-built man over six feet in height. He had a dark, gypsy-looking eye and black hair that had not lost its colour. He had the reputation of being the best horseman in the Helmingham district. But he knew it, and this also got him another reputation: of being a *boosting man*; but most people conceded that there was substance in his boasts and that he could do anything with even the most vicious of horses. He was an old soldier (1914–18) and served chiefly in the Mesopotamian campaign. As a young man he had taught himself to play the accordion and he had taken it with him on service 'to entertain'—as he told me—'my pals in the desert'. He continued to play the accordion and sing in the pubs around Helmingham right up to the time of his death. It was instructive to see him on an occasion like this: his features were lean and he had the look, manner and the individuality of an old campaigner, a veteran repertory actor who was perfectly used to *realizing* his personality. His sense of the dramatic comes over, albeit thinly, in the following transcription, the latter part of which I have included to show some of the hazards of being a back'us boy:

[T] 'One day I said to my mother: "I don't know, Mother; I fare to be fed up with being about here. There's nobody to give me a [regular] job." And as luck happened for me the shop-man then come on a Friday morning from Mr. Cutting's of Mendlesham which we people had dealt with for sixty years. Well, I looked in the paper [he'd brought] and I saw Mr. Hinery Avis, a pork dealer and a good farmer wanted a boy to live in the farmhouse. (No, we never did have a newspaper. This is what my mother's shop-things were wrapped in. That's the only paper you had to read which come with your shop things. Only the farmers had a newspaper.) Well, I see from there that Mr. Hinery Avis of Eye wanted a young chap to live in the house. So off I go!

'I got there and I said: "Good afternoon, Ma'am. Is Mr. Hinery Avis at hoom?"

"Yes, young lad, and what do you want?"

"I see you advertize for a young boy to live in the house, to look after two ponies, exercise four greyhounds, sweep and clean the yards up, chop sticks, get coal in, and keep the harness clean. Thet will suit me lovely!"

"Well," she said, "the boss is not at home. But if you like to go . . ."

"Well, I'm urgent," I said. "I want the job."

'She said: "All right, if you go to Diss *Sun*. That's about five mile from here."

'I'd then come nine miles: hopped, walked, and rid this old *cushion* bicycle which I gave five bob for. And where thet was stony in the road I *had* to walk—fresh stoons from off the field. Then I used to git on and ride the smooth parts. Away I went until I got to Eye. Later I called at Diss *Sun* which I'd niver seen before. I said:

"Please is Mr. Hinery Avis here?"

'He said, "Yes", and he went and told Mr. Hinery Avis; and all the farmers were in there having some lovely drinks; and I don't blame them. He said: "Tell him to come in here." I went into the *Smoke Room* and he said:

"Hullo, young lad, and what do you want?"

"I see you want a boy to live in the house, sir."

"Yes, I want a good lad."

"I won't praise myself up," I said, "but I'll do my best."

"You're the lad.—Well, where do you come from?"

"Mendlesham Old Farm, Mr. Scott's of Mendlesham."

'He said: "Right! I know him. I'll be over there tomorrow morning and get your character and see what sort of a chap you are."

'Well, he come over there and he got my character, and he come right up to my door. He said:

"Good morning, Mrs. Rookyard."

"Good morning. What do you want?"

"I want your son."

"Well, sure alive, you're not going to take my boy from me!"

"Yes, he's crazy to come with me."

"I'm a-going, Mother, say what you like. Bundle my owd things togither and tie a piece o' string round 'em and throw my best shoes into the cart, and I'll soon be off."

'So we got into the cart and I said: "Fare thee well, Mother. I'll come and see you afore long."

'Well, I went over there and got the job; and Mr. Hinery Avis was pleased with my character and my people's character, and I set to work right straightaway, cleaning, going ahead and doing what I could; and I got on wonderfully well; and in less than three months thet gentleman [and his wife] said to me: "We both come to speak to you in your little kitchen, Charlie."

"That's all right, lady," I said, and the boss said:

"I want you to do this job for me: I want you to come and fetch me at Diss of a night with the pony, and I want you first to take a load of pigs to Dickleburgh; go back with another load of bigger pigs, and then take them to the farm, unload 'em, put the other pony in the cart and come and fetch me at night at Diss. And you'll ast in there what time I'm a-going to get home."

"Right, sir."

'I got to Diss about 11.30 p.m. and asked for him. They said:

"It's no good you a-troubling after him yet, Charlie. He won't come yet.

"All right. I'd better go and speak to him."

"Right. I'll tell him you're here."

'He [the farmer] said: "Tell the boy to come in here and he can hev a drink."

'I went in and he said:
"What do you want, Charlie?"
"I'd like half a pint of old, sir."
"Give the boy a pint!"

'He'd got plenty of drink by this time; but it didn't worry me.
Well, do you know, it got to twelve o'clock and I dussn't ask
whether he was ready or not, because there was a lot in there like
that—all sportsmen. Do you know, it went until half-past twelve
before he came out; and I had to get him hoom—which I did
and we got him to bed as best we could.

'Thet time o' day my boss, Mr. Hinery Avis, used to have
casks, two or three, standing in his cellar: you could keep a
hundred gallons of beer in them. And the beer was fed with
horseflesh and raisens and different sage-stuff out of the garden.
And a cask like them at that time o' day was never cleaned out.
Time they got three-quarters empty they used to brew again.
They made three lots o' beer: there's what they called best beer,
the seconds, and the third was for the farm chaps in the summer-
time when it was hot and dry. Right! And you didn't want only a
couple of pints of his best beer—which was as black as vinegar—
and that would make you fall about. Which we weren't allowed
to touch.

'But to come to this: I done a very bad thing once. Now my boss was out—and he'd told me when I first went there and he drew the beer: he got some of this lovely beer out of this here hundred-gallon cask and he said:

"There," he said, "boy! You can have the beer out of any of these other casks but don't touch mine, the best beer."

"All right, sir."

'But he gave me a taste of thet, and do you know, I thought to myself: I should like to know where he put the key for this; in which I done wrong.

'When he went out that day I found this key on top of the big cask which was a foot higher than I was, and I turned the tap on; and to my surprise I got let down; and it learned me a lesson. I turned this tap on and I got a pint of this lovely beer out—and what happened was I couldn't turn the tap off!

"There," I said to the servant. "I don't know what I'm a-going to do now. You'd better bring a pail."

'She brought a pail that would hold about a gallon. So I filled this pail and I said:

"Go and find me up a nice little cork. I don't know! This is going to fling me, I reckon. I'll be sent home else I'll git a hiding."

'Anyhow she got this cork and I put this cork up the spout of the tap—which was a brass tap—and stopped the beer. I took the pail of beer into the hoss-stable and covered it up with a bag. And the horsemen came in next morning and I said:

"I don't know if there be any of you here like a drop of beer."

"Thet we do!"

"There you are then. I'm a-going to git into trouble. I turned his brass tap on and I cannot get it back."

'And I couldn't either; it was the last time it had turned.

'Now, my master after he'd been up an hour or two allus liked a drop of his lovely beer. He went down there and he found this cork up in the spout. He wanted to know where I was, immediately. I told him:

"I'm very sorry, sir. I went to the wrong cask."

"There! You knew which one to go to for the best lot, didn't you? You young rascal you! That found you out. That's one mark against your character."

"Yes, I'm very sorry."

"Never mind. I'll look over that, Charlie," he said. "But here! Will you promise me you'll niver touch it no more?"

"Yes,"

"Well, I'm going to have a different turn-out. I'm going to have a tap put in here which goo with a little lock."

"A very good idea, sir."

"And then I shall know it'll be safe."

"All right," I said, "I'll niver do wrong no more." '

7 Steam Ploughing

The steam-engine, although specially developed for use in agriculture, made comparatively little impact on the economy of farming in East Anglia and none on the social structure if we compare it with the changes that followed the introduction of the internal-combustion engine. There appear to be two main reasons for this: the equipment was too expensive for an individual farmer to run;[1] and this, along with the amount of capital tied up in the whole steam tackle, prevented it from being used except by those farmers who were farming on a large, capitalist scale. Secondly, the physical layout of large areas of the East Anglian countryside was against the use of the steam-ploughing tackle. The fields were often too small and of an irregular shape, whereas steam ploughing to be satisfactory and economic needed a square or rectangular-shaped field of a considerable acreage. The difference in the layout of the fields in Suffolk and Cambridgeshire noted in the following account illustrates this.

The first disadvantage—the cost of the equipment to the individual farmer—was to a large extent surmounted during the first half of this century by the contract system. Contractors, who were perhaps millers or large farmers, owned small cohorts of steam-engines and their tackle and hired them out complete with teams of men; and ploughing and cultivating was done on contract—at so much an acre.

[1] *A.F.C.H.*, p. 105.

Joe Thompson, born 1901 at Clopton, Suffolk, was in charge of a steam tackle for many years; and he gave me an account of his career after leaving school. He is an example of the versatile and ingenious countryman who has the adaptability to turn his hand to most jobs he meets: farm-engine man, bee-keeper, gardener, hedger, bricklayer and house-repairer. His story shows how the uncertainty of the times he has lived through compelled him to master not one skill but several. He is short in height but built as strongly as an oak door. The liveliness of his eye and the quickness of his movements dispel any impression of heaviness that at first glance might be deduced from his build:

'I started on the farm after leaving school at thirteen and a half. I worked on the farm until 1915 when I transferred to the Helmingham estate. Many of the men from the estate had been called up and there was plenty of work there for a young lad. I worked on the estate as a bricklayer's labourer until 1919. In this year the men who'd been called up returned home. They had their jobs back and I was made redundant. I had no dole and I was obliged to do odd jobs like going round the Helmingham half-acre allotments dibbling corn and so on in the old-fashioned way with a pair of dibbles.

'About that time I followed the thrashing-engine from farm to farm for miles round, walking or cycling. I recollect going to Gosbeck Hall on one occasion. I'd heard the night before that the thrashing-engine was going there the next day. I went there in the morning early. There were nine others there all looking for jobs —to be taken on while they were thrashing the corn. The farmer was leaning over his gate as we all came up to ask for work. He looked at us and pointed to three men: "You are married, you are married and you are married. I'll take you three. I really don't want anybody but since you're married I'll take you." The rest of us had to go home. This was in 1920. I went dibbling a lot in that year, chiefly on the allotments belonging to the Helmingham estate. Lord Tollemache was very strict about these allotments when he was in his reign. He came round and looked at them and he'd stop at any allotment and inspect it.

'Later that year I got a job as cook-boy with Mr. Dawson's

steam-engines of Rushmere, near Ipswich. He'd got three or four sets of ploughs and five road-rollers—all steam. I worked there for a season with a ploughing-set. As you know, there are two steam-engines in a ploughing set. One engine was fixed at each side of the field and they pulled the plough backwards and forwards between them by means of a steel-ropes or cable. At the end of each *bout* one engine moved a few yards forwards along the side of the field while the second was pulling the plough across the field: it was then ready to pull the plough back as soon as the other engine had finished its bout.

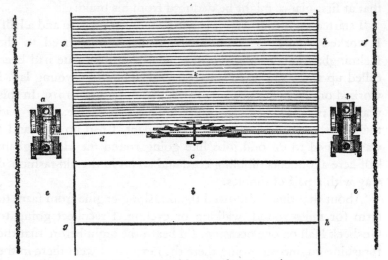

Traction of steam-plough by means of two steam-engines.

a b Two steam-engines, with drum and windlass.	*d* Wire rope between engines.	*g h* Open furrows of ridges.
c Balance plough.	*e e* Headridges.	*i* Unploughed land.
	f f Fences of the field.	*k* Ploughed land.

'The plough itself had two sets of furrows: one at each end. One set ran free on one bout and was engaged on the next. A man sat on the plough structure to guide or steer it. He was called the steersman. A steam plough-set was made up of two steam-engines and the implements—plough, mole-drainer and cultivator—the water-cart and the living-van. A gang of five men worked it: the foreman, two drivers, a steersman and a cook-boy. When they were working they all lived in a van where there were two double-bunks and a single, or three single and a double.

The foreman always had a single bunk: that was his privilege. During the day the bunks folded up against the side of the van. We had a little portable range for cooking but when I was cook-boy I rarely used the oven much except for baking a few potatoes. Most of the food was boiled—salt pork, salt beef, meat-puddings, and currant duff. We fried bacon for breakfast. In the summer we did our cooking out of doors. We had an old *devil* like a grid, and we set it up in the open.

'My job as cook-boy started well before it was light. The foreman used to wake up early and call the two drivers and the cook-boy. The drivers went out immediately into the field and took the dampers off their engines—the plates on top of the funnels to prevent the fires from drawing. They then raked out and made up their fires to get the steam up. Perhaps they'd left their engine with a pressure of 100 the night before. By the morning it would be down to 40, and they had to get it up again quickly. In the meantime, as cook-boy, I used to make the tea; as soon as this was done I gave the foreman his tea, also the steersman or cultivator man, as he was sometimes known. I had a mug of tea myself and then took tea out to the two drivers in the field. If they were using the cultivator and not the plough the steersman went out and they started work and the cultivator went up and down the field between the two engines exactly as the plough did. But a plough always needed four men to operate it; the other implement three.

'I then went back to the van after giving the drivers their tea and I made breakfast, and ate mine with the foreman. Then us two went out into the field and relieved two of the men there. The foreman went as driver for one of the engines and I did the steersman's job. When the first two came back from their breakfast and the steersman took over from me I went back to the van with the second driver and got him his breakfast. My job then was to do the beds, wash up and generally clean up the van. I'd perhaps then go to the nearest shop for food and tobacco. Then came the same procedure for dinner. Then I made tea again at 4 o'clock. I would be free after this until they left off work, usually at dusk.

'My job then was to get a couple of buckets of hot water from the engine for the men to wash in; and then it was time to get supper. It was eat, work, and sleep mostly. But when I became a driver I would welcome a chat in the evening because you were on your own all day with no one to talk to; and even if there was any conversation you couldn't hear it like as not because of the noise of the engine. We used to have some tales in the van, I can tell you, mostly after work or on wet days. The hours were long, from dawn to dusk; and meant finishing at 10 p.m. in the summer. We had the standard agricultural wage—in the early 'twenties it was about 25s—plus acre-money. Each man had 6d an acre for every acre that was worked (ploughed, cultivated or mole-drained). The cook-boy got 3d an acre. The foreman was in charge and got more than us men. We worked a six-day week, finishing at dinner-time on a Saturday. The foreman had instructions from the owners about which farms he had to go to, and if he had requests to do more work on the farms in a certain district he could use his own discretion.

'Before going on to a farm the foreman went on before to find the best way to get to the fields and so on; and then he would lead the engines to where we had to work. When we moved the tackle the foreman drove the first engine and the second driver steered; the first driver drove the second engine and the steersman steered. Like a puzzle, ain't it? The first engine took the implements; plough, cultivator and drainer; the second engine dragged the living-van and the water-cart. The cook-boy rode on the van, and when we were going downhill he used to jump out to put the brake on. The season lasted from the end of March until the end of November. The foreman and the two drivers went into the owner's yard with the two engines to help with repairs and overhaul; and the steersman and the cook-boy became redundant.

'After one season in Rushmere, I went to a firm called Pamplin, Brothers of Cherry Hinton, Cambridge. I did four seasons with them and went up from cook-boy to driver. The Cambridgeshire fields were much better suited for the steam plough: they were big and usually regular in shape. The land was firm when we went on to it but if the weather turned wet you'd got to get off it

12. Steam plough engine with driver

13. Steam plough engine with driver and steersman

14. An overgrown field
in the 'twenties.
The original hedge
is on the right

15. Washing day on a Suffolk farm, *c.* 1930

16. Helmingham 'double-dweller'

pretty quickly. The Fens were the most tricky for working in. It was right treacherous near the dykes. If you got near a *sand-gall* the engine would drop into it and then you'd be in trouble. The light land, though, made the worst wear on the implements. The sandy, gritty land would wear out the shares and the cultivators. I once remember a farmer coming out while we were cultivating (this was on light land). He cast his glance at the work and said: "You ha'n't got much of a point in there!" He wanted the cultivator to go in as deep as we could get it.

'As I said, it was a pretty lonely job, and as a driver you didn't do much talking. But you could do a bit with the engine-whistle. There were a number of recognized signals:

> One sharp blast meant *stop*.
> Two pips meant *start*.
> Three pips brought the foreman.
> Four pips brought the cook-boy.

A long blast followed by a short one brought either coal or water. A man from the farm fetched these; and since he'd been carting all the time you were there, as soon as he heard the signal he knew which one you wanted.

'It was hard work but we had some jolly times. The gangs I worked in got on well together and we rarely had any trouble. You got about a lot and met a lot of different people; and now and then folk used to come out into the fields to see you and have a chat.

'I got taken back on to the Helmingham estate in 1925, and I then had a job as a bricklayer until 1940. Then I went to work for Mr. Styles of Bocking Hall, Helmingham. He bought two plough engines; and I drove them for him during most of the last war. I never did find anything—remains or anything like that—in the fields. About the only thing I found was wasps' nests, and when that happened the chap on the cultivator used to catch it then. But I remember once a plough-set I was working on pulled the water-main to pieces at Stonham. We were actually using a mole-drainer and it caught the pipe: something had to go! Mr. Styles sold his engines in 1946. The trouble was that the steam-engine

F   81 couldn't compete with the big caterpillar tractors. One man with a diesel *crawler* would do the same sort of job as a steam-tackle with four men and a cook-boy. That's what killed the steam-traction engine. But I didn't tell you how I did one season (May to November, 1924) with *Bert Stocks' Fair*. I was the engine driver and drove a Burrell traction engine. The big Burrell drove the dynamo for lights and so on while the Fair was working; and it was also used as a tractor when the Fair moved from place to place. Working with the Fair was a relief to me: I liked it very much. When we were on the move my engine pulled the centre engine (a portable) and the gantry on which the portable engine rested while it was driving the big roundabout. It also pulled a living-wagon and the *water-dandy* (two tubs balanced on a frame). When we were going to a new site, Bert Stocks used to stand on the field and guide us to the exact spot where he wanted the engine to stand. We went all over East Anglia, to flower-shows, galas—like Needham Market and Stowmarket, the Trinity Fair at Southwold, Aldeburgh Regatta, Walton-on-the-Naze Regatta—and so on. I got five shillings a week more than a farm-worker and one free meal—a cooked dinner at the middle of the day. When the Fair was set up I was often an odd-job man as my engine was stationary. I used to take money at the coconut stalls and mealtimes I'd relieve the drivers from the centre engine that drove the horses and the crocodiles. I also did turn and turn about on the big Burrell engine. The Fair people were good company, genuine people; side-show men and all—all decent people.'

The visit of the steam plough to a farm demanded the farmer's co-operation. George Sadler (1905–66), a Cambridgeshire farmer's son, recalled the occasions when the engine came to his father's farm at Whittlesford during the First World War:

[T] 'When you got harvest over we'd be getting on this old steam-plough job. That's another *nice* job we used to be on, carting water for these steam-plough engines. I know, these old engine men would blow their whistles at 3 o'clock in the morning. Do you know, we had to cart water for them! They'd take three loads one day and two loads another—for each engine. There'd be two of us, with a trace hoss and one in the shafts of these big old carts. At 3 o'clock in the morning they'd pip three times: that was water. When they pipped twice that was coal. Then we used to have to be out there with these here horses and water-carts. We had to pump! We didn't pull under a thing where we turned a tap and filled it. All pump! If you pumped it out of a damn ditch or pond you had to dig a hole so you get the nose of your old pipe in, to fill that with water so you could pump into the cart.

'Carting water for *ship* [sheep], that's another job we had to be full at in the summer-time. All day long we'd be doing that. I think one summer—in the 1921 summer—that was one of my jobs: carting water, water, water, water!—all day long. Pumping it. The old water-cart I had took 700 pumps to fill it up; and I had this damned old mare that wouldn't take the foal.[1] I used to back her up against the pump, just get the trough in, start pumping, when she'd step up about a foot so the trough fell out of the cart. Well, if that wouldn't make anybody swear I don't know what would. Perhaps the blasted flies would be biting her: up she'd go again. You'd get down and you'd think: How many pumps have I had now? 100 to 150? You'd got to pump 700 to fill the trough up. And by the time you'd done that they wanted another lot.

'But on this carting water for the steam-engine. I know I got a four-year-old hoss one morning—blast! he was a good hoss, too—carting water. The old whistles went about 3 o'clock; and of course we had to get into the stables earlier then to get the horses baited because they all had an hour and a half bait. (And you always had to do the tails up summer-fashion and winter-fashion. There was never a hoss went out unless that's tail was done up. It had to be left long with just a little braid on the top, with a little bit of straw, for the summer [to enable the horse to keep away the flies]. The whole lot would be done up from the bottom as a winter *do-up* to stop the mud and that from getting on it.) Well, I got three parts across this field with this load of water and this hoss wouldn't budge another inch. He wouldn't face that

[1] *F.A.V.*, p. 119.

83

engine at no price. So the old man on the steam engine he said: "Wait till I get this cultivator acrost, I'll have him up here!" So when he got it across he unhooked his rope (it was a wire rope he used to pull the old steam ploughs backwards and forwards) and after I'd taken off the trace-hoss he hooked the rope on to the shafts and he pulled him right up to the engine; pulled this hoss and water-cart right up to the engine, right to the side of the engine and held him there with a rope. The old hoss was doing all sorts of things but laying down. And the engine driver sucked his water out and let him go. But I tell you, the third load I went acrost there about 7 o'clock that night he didn't want no rope pulling him acrost there. He was too damned tired: he went across next time all right!'

Part Two

Agriculture

❧✿❀✿❧

Hales Barn, near London

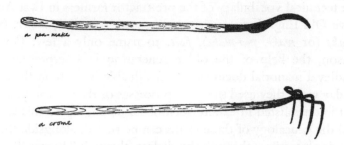

a pea-make

a crome

8 Farming and the Depth of Oral Testimony

The importance of the testimony of the older generation that took part in East Anglian farming prior to the introduction of the self-propelled machine needs no emphasis. Arable farming has here been the main line of farming since the beginning of the historical period; and farming itself has been both the mother and the nurse of the East Anglian culture. It has given this culture its individual stamp and is responsible for its remarkable continuity up to the beginning of this century. The older generation that reached manhood before the First World War are in a true sense historical 'documents' in that they can teach us some of the techniques of the age-old farming that mechanization displaced and communicate to us something of the cultural atmosphere and attitudes within the society which was the old farming's context.

To take first of all the technical content of the old generation's testimony about farming: there is hardly a period in farming history to which this generation could not supply an oral footnote. The essentially Roman and Romano-British methods of harvesting corn with the sickle were known to them as also were the threshing of corn with the flail and the Roman method of *thorough draining* called bush-draining. They used, in East Anglia up to the 'twenties, a primitive wooden plough that was the same in its bare essentials as the Saxon *carruca*. Many, too, of the names of what Tusser called *Husbandly Furniture* and much of

87

the technical vocabulary of the pre-tractor farmers in East Anglia have Old English roots: words like *seals* (or *seles*), *thiller, beetle, meake* (or *make, pea-make*), *fleet*, to name only a few. For this reason, the help of the older generation in interpreting early medieval manorial documents is invaluable because in their day-to-day work they used the same processes or the same implements as the ones listed in extant documents belonging to this region; and the genealogy of these terms can be traced, alongside the old farming practices, through the dialect, through Thomas Tusser's *Five Hundred Good Points of Husbandry* back to the medieval *compoti* [manorial inventories] and by deduction back to a much earlier period. A compotus from Easton Bavents in Suffolk (dated Michaelmas, 1344) would be familiar to an old East Anglian horseman, or teamsman as he was called in Norfolk, once he had been given help with some of the words. He could point out that he had used most of the tools and that he was familiar with most of the items that are under the heading *videlicet in granario*. The measures are exactly the same as the ones he used: *1 bussellus frumenti; 3 busselli et 2 peks siligonis* (winter wheat or rye?); *1 quarterium 6 busselli avene grosse* (oats). He would recognize *4 wedhokes* by their name, also *4 Kelers*[1] and *4 Tynes* (Chaucer's *teine* and the East Anglian dialect *tine* a fork-prong); and although he would not be familiar with *4 furce pro garbis* (pitching forks) and *3 furce pro fimis* (dung forks or *muck-cromes*) by these names he could point out their surviving counterparts and demonstrate their use. He could show, too, exactly how to use a *seminale de virga* (a seed-hod or *sidlip*) as soon as the Latin phrase had been made plain to him. The phrase *1 bussellus ligni cum ferro ligatus* (a wooden bushel[2] strengthened with an iron band) would make his eye light up as soon as it had been interpreted.

Another manorial document from Suffolk, *An Extent of the Manor of Horham, 1356*, has an amount of farming data listed under *Various Memoranda*. Like the previous one it was transcribed by J. M. Ridgard, a local historian, and illustrates the help that farmers, who once practised the old type of farming in Suffolk, can give in illuminating medieval farming documents.

[1] *A.F.C.H.*, p. 223.   [2] *F.A.V.*, pp. 90–1.

Here are four examples from the *Extent* with comments by Charles William Rogers (born 1903) who farms at Boundary Farm, Ilketshall St. Margaret, not many miles from Horham:

j. *The jurors say that a manorial plough-team can plough, at wheat-sowing time and throughout the winter, three roods of land per day; and a day's work is worth 6d.*

'Three roods, or three-quarters of an acre used to be a day's ploughing under the old system of farming on the heavy lands in Suffolk. If a man and a pair of horses ploughed three-quarters of an acre on a heavy-land farm it was considered a good day's work.'

ij. *And the team can plough one acre a day during Lent, during the times for sowing peas and oats, and at the time of the third ploughing. And a ploughwork is worth 8d.*

'This was the peak period of the spring ploughing. The days were getting longer and they would be able to do a longer *journey*,[1] and they wouldn't be ploughing as deep then as earlier in the farming year; therefore they would be able to plough more.'

iij. *And the team can plough half-an-acre a day, worth 5d, in summer at the time of ploughing the fallow-land*

'Ploughing a long fallow or summer-tilth was a very hard and slow job for the man and his horses, and it would have been the same when they had oxen. If the land hadn't been broken up it lay in big clods; and a man could not do more than half-an-acre: he couldn't stand it. Even then he'd have to do the ploughing early in the morning before the heat of the day.'

This is confirmed by another farmer's, James Seely's, account of ploughing a summer-tilth (see page 101, below).

iv *And one acre of land can be sown with two bushels of wheat.*

'Today, using modern varieties of wheat, we sow rather more than two bushels per acre. The old varieties of wheat would tiller out more. There was more growth to each plant, though of course the overall yield of the modern varieties is greater.'

[1] *H.I.F.*, p. 40.

89

This correlation of the older generation's memories of the pre-tractor farming with the existing records has also another facet. To some historians, at least, the claim that much of the farming in late nineteenth-century East Anglia had not changed to any great extent—in the use of hand-tools and the processes connected with them, for example—since the Romans may seem a gross overstatement. What about the big improvements, they will object, the introduction of the machines for which East Anglia has always been famous? It was the East Anglian firms already mentioned that pioneered these machines. This is perfectly true but we must beware of mistaking the part for the whole. The larger farmers with a fair amount of capital, the landowners with plenty (especially those landowners like the Tollemaches who were able, as brewers, to inject strong stimulants into any failing enterprise) and the industrial capitalists like J. J. Mechie and Lord Iveagh whose capital was virtually unlimited, could adopt the new machinery and experiment with new methods immediately. But the smaller farmers who were in the majority were forced by their very position to carry on with the older methods. Although the scythe used with cradle or bale, to give one example, had displaced the sickle for the harvesting of corn on most Suffolk farms by the middle of the last century, and the scythe itself had to a large extent given way to the reaper and reaper-binder by 1914, the old method of reaping by hand still persisted into the 'twenties; and on some Suffolk farms it was used in the 'fifties, though admittedly for special jobs like clearing the headlands for a machine or the saving of wind- or rain-laid crops.

The farming depressions of the last hundred years (an acute one is discussed in a later chapter) gave the small farmer little opportunity to bring his farming methods up to date, especially as the depression that began in the late 1870's lasted without real intermission until 1914, the period of industrial expansion when the new machines were coming on to the market. Lack of ready money and an inbred conservatism which is a characteristic of the small farmer everywhere induced him to carry on with the old tools and the old methods long after they had been superseded on the bigger farms. An example is the thorough- or under-draining just mentioned. East Anglia, particularly north Essex and Suffolk, was the pioneer region of under-draining; and with Perthshire in Scotland was well in advance of other parts of Britain. Some of the first clay-tiles, and later the earthenware-pipes, were laid in East Anglia because the principle of under-draining had been understood and practised from early times. Yet most of the smaller Suffolk farmers were still using the ancient method of bush-draining for the simple reason that they could not afford the outlay for earthenware-pipes. In East Anglia at the lowest down-curves of the farming depression—1890 and 1930— the polarity of great wealth and intense poverty was sharply reflected in the farming itself as well as in the social scene. At one pole there was a small minority of improving farmers with at least a fair amount of capital; at the other was a majority of smaller or medium-sized farmers with little capital at all, who were still forced to use some of the primitive methods that their forebears were using many centuries before.

The farming records of this period also reflect this polarity with some accuracy. In local archives there is an abundance of records deposited by the more progressive, enterprising, and well-equipped farmers and landowners or trustees of large estates. But, there is—or there appears to be so far—an almost complete hiatus in the records of the smaller farmers. The reasons for this are understandable. The small, or even the middle-sized, East Anglian farmer was seldom well-read and could not appreciate the historical importance of written documents; and, even when he did, native caution, independence or simple guile persuaded him that there was no point in letting other people pry into his affairs: an attitude that in later years has been hardened by the relentless activities of the tax-inspector and his ally the tax-collector. Moreover, the large farmers were proud to make public the record of their successful farming: the small farmer who had for years walked the tight-rope between a bare subsistence and bankruptcy had no such incentive to expose the bitterness of his long struggle. I have known more than one farmer—and at least one who was public spirited enough to give freely of his time to the community—destroy their records rather than risk their exposure to other people. The records of the occasional small farmer I have been allowed to see lead me to believe that their absence from the overall account of farming during the last hundred years is a serious one; and to rely solely on the records of the more prosperous farmers to give a true picture of the farming of the period is akin to reading the glossy papers without the corrective of the more stolid and perhaps dull columns of print. The oral testimony of the smaller farmers and the farm-workers who remember this period can at least help to correct the picture, even if they can give only a few of the actual details that are lacking.

But this oral testimony of the smaller farmer and the farm-worker is valuable not only for the facts they can supply to help in constructing a full account of the period but also what they *think* of the facts. The farm-worker, especially, was rarely articulate on his own behalf during the period we are discussing—from about 1880 onwards. It is true that he sometimes gave evidence at a Government enquiry, and this evidence was included in a Government report.[1] But here he was a man making an appearance in a public place on a matter that was not of his own choosing. At most, the farm-worker would reveal only a little of his attitude towards the position in society in which he found himself; and even if he attempted to do this it would probably have been considered irrelevant. But an innate cautiousness usually prevented him from expressing anything that was remotely like an opinion on this. He would give nothing away: he would not reveal what he really felt. His cultural environment, the precariousness of his position—of 'being under the thumb'—had conditioned him not to speak his innermost thoughts in public. He recognized that his daily work took him into a peacetime battlefield where any false move he made would find him without a job and probably without a house. The farm-vacancies advertisements in the local papers with their frequent coda: *Union men need not apply* were enough to warn him of the true position if warning were needed. The contest between the farm-workers and the wealthier East Anglian farmers was particularly bitter

[1] *The Agricultural Labourer*, A. Wilson Fox, 1893.

under the old system of farming. All evidence shows that the farm-worker was at the base of a very steep social pyramid. He was the footings, the man out of sight, who was rarely called upon to give evidence. He had to take what was given him, and he had no status at all, being little different from the medieval serf. It is questionable whether or not it was always so: it was certainly so after the 1873 movement to form an agricultural workers' union, the *lock-out* by the farmers and the consequent falling away of the men's unions. The East Anglian farmers actually started the lock-out of the farm-workers in their attempt to prevent the formation of their trade union; and when Dr. Fraser, Bishop of Manchester, made a protest at the farmers' action in a letter to *The Times*, it was the farmers of East Anglia who answered him most vehemently. G. E. Fussell wrote:[1] 'For some reason, I am not quite certain what reason unless it was that here the great 18th century improvements had taken place and the tenant farmers were wealthy men and occupiers of large farms, the contest between them and the unions seems to have been peculiarly bitter in East Anglia.' Whatever the reason it is clear that after the lock-out the wealthier East Anglian farmers remained frightened men and acted cruelly accordingly. No other explanation can account for the embittered and unequal struggle. That things were not right was clear to a Government Commissioner[2] and induced him to make the mild comment:

'The relations between employer and employed are of a more cordial character in the Northern Counties than in the Eastern, though many farmers in the North say the men are more independent than they were twenty years ago.'

Now this may strike the reader as a very partial viewpoint, and very much like revealing a personal bias in a very inappropriate place. But it is a considered viewpoint arrived at after talking to and questioning dozens of farm-workers who lived through the period; and I quote a Suffolk farmer's—an exceptional farmer's—account which I think goes some way to confirming it. John Goddard[3] was by no means a small farmer as

[1] *From Tolpuddle to T.U.C.*, p. 77.   [2] A. Wilson Fox, op. cit. p. 23.
[3] *A.F.C.H.*, pp. 103–7.

his testimony shows. He has given here an outline of his farming practice and, what is more to our present purpose, an unequivocal statement about the social environment in which he grew up and farmed. His account carries all the more weight in that it was not given out of bitterness or failure but in the fullness of life after a long career as a successful farmer with a solid reputation among his peers in the county:[1]

'I was born in 1855. I am an old man now. At the present time I am farming only 300 acres. I left school when I was twelve. Since then I have worked on the land, and it has been a rough road, and uphill all the way. Don't talk to me about the good old times. They were *wicked* old times. Men in the fields used to work from dawn to dark, six days a week. As a small boy I remember working with them. My mind very often was on sport: fishing, catapults, cricket. But nothing would induce *them* to leave a minute before time. One of them would pull out a big old watch and announce the verdict: "Time to go another bout." At the end of the week they drew a wage of nine or ten shillings, barely enough to keep body and soul together. It was little better than serfdom. The poorer they were, the bigger their families. They had to bow and scrape and cringe to the parson and his wife. They had no status and no independence, and how often they had to rely on charity.

'Farmers themselves were not much better off. The year 1879 was long talked of as *Black '79*. I saw barley sold then at less than five shillings a sack, and wheat at less than ten shillings. The land could not be let. Landlords had to farm their estates themselves or let them go. Even with labour so ridiculously cheap, many farmers could not carry on.

'As the eldest of six sons I started farming on my own account in 1876. Everything was dear then and it was not a good time to start. Then three years later came the slump. To give one example of its effect: my father's farm valued at £5,500 in 1876 dropped in value to under £2,000. Good times, indeed! The squire and the parson ruled the villages. The worker was a slave. Farmers

[1] Told to a reporter of the *Dairy Farmer* and printed in Vol. 15, No. 2 at Ipswich, February 1942.

were often at the mercy of absent landlords whose stingy lease agreements and their dirtiest work was done by their agents.

'I began in a small way, at the bottom of the ladder on less than a hundred acres of heavy land. My parents could do little to help me. I had to meet a high rent of £2 per acre and pay the tithe myself. I soon realized it was impossible for a small farmer to live. A brother, farming on a similar scale, was of the same opinion. So we formed a partnership, and were fortunate to get the offer of a 300-acre farm. That was the turning point, in 1888. This step, like everything else in farming, was a gamble but it came off. I am no believer in small farms or in wheelbarrow farmers. Bigger farms means bigger fields, lower overheads, and a full day's work for every man.

'Nor am I a believer in half-measures. To "go the whole hog" has always been my motto. Whether with crops or stock I have always tried for big returns and *quick* returns. This means spending money, feeding well, ample manuring, high farming. For fattening stock, for example, my plan was always to feed "to the danger point". My baby beef, from Red Polls, came to maturity at under two years, and weighed 10 cwt. It could only be done by giving calves a good start in life and suckling them on the cow. The same with crops. We made a lot of farmyard manure— the straw must always go back to the land, you know. We kept a flock of 500 ewes, and as many as 80 breeding sows, fattening up to 800 hogs each year. On top of this, we spent plenty of money on artificial manures. Anything to aid and abet the crops and get the heaviest possible yields. There is as much expense in handling a poor crop as in handling a good one.

'Horses, too, when doing heavy work must be fed well. Mine were rationed at six stone of corn each per week. But you can't farm with horses alone in these days. You must use a tractor if you would keep abreast of your work. Tractors can be most useful on stubbles after harvest and for autumn ploughing.

'I have never been a big dairyman. I have kept Red Polls, because they are hornless, and the Suffolk breed for a Suffolk man. They never sleep in, neither summer or winter. I have never had any trouble with their bags, nor any other serious health trouble, with the exception of an occasional case of milk-fever. Principally, they have always lived off the farm, getting very little concentrated food. When grass is past its best I have found nothing better than marrow-stem kale, fed in the open; and I have a particular liking for kohl-rabi for dairy cows. During the last war (1914–18) we sold milk, but afterwards we found we could do better by rearing calves on cows and producing baby beef.

'Well, we had bad times and good times. The last war came within the latter category. But there were difficulties then. Labour was scarce, the farms were stripped of the younger skilled men. We had to make do with boys and old men; and I had fourteen women land-workers, local women who did everything: hoeing, spreading manure, carting corn—and did it well. Twenty years ago, in partnership with my son, I farmed 1,500 acres, much of it light land. Farming, as I have said, is a gamble. I recognized this and took the plunge, hiring big farms when nobody else would look at them. If you never bid you'll never buy much!

'At present we farm three farms, of heavy and mixed soils, about 800 acres altogether. But my farming activities, now that I have reached the age of eighty-seven, are confined to the 300-acre farm where I now live, and have lived for fifty-four years of my life. In this war [1939–45] we've got to grow everything possible whether it pays or not. There isn't a penny profit in growing corn, unless it's malting barley. This last harvest was a terrible time. I employ 15 men on 300 acres; but it took us seven weeks to get it in.

'One thing I think important, that applies to every farm, and that is unity between masters and men. My mother used to tell her six boys the story of the miller who showed his sons how difficult it was to break a bundle of sticks, how easy it was to break them one by one (Hitler must have learned that lesson). We learned it: the lesson that unity is strength. We were taught to stand together and help one another; and that is what we've done, not only among ourselves but with the men on the farm. I think I can say that on my farm we all think well of each other. We are

17. Helmingham smithy with *trav'us*

17a.
Detail of smoke-hole
in smithy roof

18.
Joe Thompson
and his corn-drill

18a. Detail of drill mechanism

all interested in the farm, and ready to help each other in misfortune. I have always been on the side of the working man, for I've been through the mill myself.'

I myself can vouch for this last statement. When I spoke to John Goddard at Tunstall a few months before his death in 1953 I lived in the adjoining village; and I had long heard of his reputation as a good employer. The workmen who had been with him for most of their lives demonstrated the truth of this reputation better than words. An incident, too, happened a few years before to show that John Goddard meant what he said. A man who had been in his employ for many years in a weak moment stole some corn to take home for his fowls. He was caught and expected instant dismissal. Instead John Goddard pardoned him and the man stayed with him until he retired.

9 Farm-Worker to Farmer

The account of his life given me by James William Seely, born at Lound near Lowestoft in 1894, throws light on the question, what was it like to be a farm-worker in East Anglia before and immediately after the First World War. He was a farm horseman or teamsman for the first part of his life, and he rented a seventy-acre farm in Norfolk in 1937.

'My father was a fisherman, and he used to go to sea from Lowestoft. We lived at Lound for the first five years of my life and I can just recollect my mother, Elizabeth Seely, selling beer at three farthings a pint in a little off-licence place in the village. But I was really too young to know much about it; though later on I heard some of the old 'uns say that this beer—which they called *traffail*—was much better than the beer they used to serve at five times the price in pubs after the War.

'When I was five we moved from Lound to Hales, near Loddon in Norfolk. My father was still going out from Lowestoft, fishing; but when he was at sea he got nawthen sent home. The men who went out from Yarmouth used to get ten shillings a week sent for their families but the Lowestoft men got nawthen. While my father was away my mother used to go to the shop and get food for the family *on the mace*[1]—*on tick*—against the time my father come back from fishing. But sometimes if they were out

[1] Probably *mease*, a measure or barrel of herrings. The fisherman had credit on the strength of the catch he hoped to make.

98

of luck they had no fish to turn into money and they finished up in debt. After we'd been at Hales for a few years Father went to Penzance fishing for mackerel. They returned in debt and shortly afterwards he died. My mother had four boys and a girl: I was the eldest but still quite young—eight or nine—and she had to go to the Board of Guardians. They allowed her three-and-sixpence a week. They said she was young and able-bodied and could work. So she took in washing and did all manner of little jobs. I had to pump water for her most mornings afore I went to school, and my younger brothers did too. I remember the rows in the morning afore we went about who was to get the water up: "I got one more pail than him," was how it used to go on. Then we had a mile-and-a-half to walk to Loddon school. Then every Saturday morning us three children who were old enough to go to school had to take attendance cards they'd given us to the Relieving Officer to show him we'd been attending school all the week. If we'd been absent it would be marked on the card, he wanted to know exactly what we'd been doing on that day. I suppose it was to see that us children didn't earn any more money working out of school. That was the time when we saw more dinner-times than dinners. A lot more! We took bread-and-jam to school with us. We allus took a mess of bread'n jam for dinner. Of course, as we went along on the roads there'd be turnips then, and we'd get over the field and have a turnip or two, pull a turnip and eat it. That's how half the kids lived that time o' day—turnips and swedes raw. Where they kept sheep and had locust beans we thought that were a good feast, locust beans. Everybody had a job to live where there was a large family.

'I left school when I was twelve and went to work at Hales Green on a farm on the big estate, Kirby Cane Hall: it was about two mile for me to walk. The hours were 6.30 in the morning till 6 o'clock in the evening during the summer, 7 to 5.30 in the winter. I recollect my first haysel, I was working with a few men cocking the hay, and the steward came along towards the end of the day and he say: "Are you going to finish this tonight?" The men agreed to do this as it would mean threepence overtime, threepence an hour, enough for an ounce of 'bacca. Of course

I stayed and worked with them. But when we came to be paid on the Saturday night the steward gave me my week's wage, three shilling—I was getting a tanner a day—and nawthen more. So I say to him: "What about my overtime?" and he say: "You're only a *quarter man*.[1] You'll have to work another extra hour next week, and then I'll give you three ha'pence." That's how they carried on that time o' day. The good owd days!'

Percy Wilson told me a similar story of an earlier period. It happened near his home at Witnesham, Suffolk and he recalled it to illustrate the hardness of the farmers in bargaining about wages. 'This was in my grandmother's time at Witnesham and it happened just below here. There was a gap in the hedge of the field that led on to the main Ipswich road; it was just at the top of the hill below here. A woman was weeding here—she used to get eightpence a day from the farmer—cutting thistles out of corn most likely. Well, one day as she was weeding, a swarm of bees hung on a branch near this gap. Now her husband was a bee-keeper, and she slipped home, got a skep and hived these bees. At the end of the week she went to get her money from the farmer and he said:

"How many days did you do, woman?"

"Six," she say.

"That you didn't!"

"I did."

"Well, what about those bees you hived?" (Somebody had told him, else he'd seen her himself.)

"Oh, that didn't take more'n ten minutes."

"Never mind. I shall have to cut you half a quarter [a penny] all the same."

"Half a quarter! Who ever heard of half a quarter! Here, you better take a quarter, and I hope you get rich!" '

James Seely continued: 'But the farmers are much more civilized today than they were then. Near us was a farmer who was known throughout this district as *Slap-arse* Wharton. If a boy had done something wrong on his farm he'd take down his trousers and tan him with suthen. No farmer would lay a hand on any-

[1] *A.F.C.H.*, p. 89.

body today. They don't swear as much either. In the owd days they were allus swearing, calling the men lazy buggers who didn't earn their day's pay. I recall the time when there was an owd bor on the farm; he was called Billy Killington. The farmer had put him out *holling* [ditching]; and at the end of the day Owd Billy had cut himself a stick he fancied out of the hedge. He walked home with this stick, and the farmer happened to meet him on the road. On the Saturday night while the men were being paid Owd Billy stood counting his money over and over in his hand:

"What's up, Killington?"

"You've given me eleven shilling instead of twelve," Owd Billy say.

"That's all you're worth. You can't call yourself a full man, doing a full day's work, if you got to have a stick to walk home with!"

'At that time o' day you dussn't get wrong with your master. If you did you got the sack and you were finished. You were in a right muddle because if you went for another job the first thing the farmer would ask you would be: "Why did you leave your last place?" If you told him you got wrong with the farmer he'd say straight away:

"Well, you'd better get right with him then. Go back and apologize."

'You were right under and you couldn't move; and there was no one to protect you. If a farmer knew you had joined the union you'd get the sack.

[T] 'I stayed there at Kirby Hall for about four year. I got so I went to plough after a year or so. I went to plough when I was fifteen, ploughing a long summer-tilth, jumping from one clod to another. They used to summer-till the land then, plough all summer long on the owd heavy land. They used to plough it about four times all summer long,[1] and git the seed in a week or so early for the next harvest. That was the land they couldn't get on during the spring time: it was ploughed late and had no frosts and that, so they couldn't get the crop in. That's why they made

[1] *H.I.F.*, pp. 128-30.

a summer-tilth; they were forced to make 'em because they couldn't git the crop in on this old heavy land.[1] But they could get the seed in for next year's harvest very early. I've seen 'em up there drilling the wheat in one field when the next field was still *on the shock*, the harvest hadn't been carted. That was Kirby Hall way. They used to have several acres long summer-tilths. It wasn't easy walking while you were a-doing one of these. It was hard work, June and July, for men and horses. It was all clods, big owd hard clods. We used to have a Bungay plough (Cameron) for that job, an all-iron swing plough. No wheel; we couldn't use a wheel on a long summer-tilth; it were a swing plough.'

Almost as soon as war broke out in 1914 James Seely joined the army. He served throughout the war with the Eighth Norfolks, gaining the rank of sergeant and also the Military Medal:

[T.] 'We'd just finished harvest that year, and two or three of us were walking out on the Sunday night just after war had been declared, and one of us say: "What about joining the army?" So off we went to Norwich the next morning. As we went in we see the posters along Bracondale there, the recruiting posters: *Kitchener's Army. Sign for Three Years or the Duration of the War.* One of the lads say: "I'm not a-goin' to sign on for the duration. The war will be over by Christmas and then we'll be setting on our ass at home again!" That's how we were. Of course, we didn't go straight to the recruiting office. We'd been paid off for the harvest and we all had a pound or two. So we went into the pubs. By the time we came to join we were a bit merry.

'As you know, when you join the army you have to take the oath on the Bible. But they were a-joining up in droves at that time, mostly young chaps—many of 'em under age; many who were only seventeen years old said they were twenty just to get in! We were a very big crowd in the room at the same time, so what the officer did was to line us up in a semicircle in front of his table; and the chap at the end put his hand on the Bible and the rest of us had to touch the man in front on him, so we all kinda joined to the man who had his hand on the Bible. But

[1] Similar conditions existed last year (1969) on some of the heavy land of East Anglia, and farmers were forced to make long, bare fallows.

suthen went wrong with our crowd. There was a chap there with his *whole-falls*—the flap in front of his trousers, his fly, it were like a sailor's; they used to wear them then—it was hanging wide open; and o' course, us others couldn't stop a-laughing. But the officer got angry and he sent us all outside shouting out: "This is a serious business! A Serious Business!" Of course, it *were* too.

'I first went to Shorncliffe in Kent; then Colchester, Salisbury Plain; and then France. I got to France on the 15th May 1915 and I stayed there until the 21st February 1919. We had a proper training at the beginning of the war, but I remember later drafts coming out to us—young lads from the Lancashire cotton mills, for instance. They joined the army, had *leaf*, were sent to France and were killed—all in eight weeks. Young kids! Passchendaele was the worst because of the mud and the water. You couldn't make trenches because if you dug down more than a foot or so it would fill up straight away with water. We had to make a hollow in the mud, and we lay there like swallows: we used to long for the dark so we could stand up and straighten our legs.

'But do you know, I think the happiest time I ever had was in the army; though there were some funny times, real bad times. But I think I can say I had some of my happiest times in the army. When we'd be overtopped with mud and water in the trench there'd allus be someone say something to make you laugh. You allus had a laugh, even if you'd been a-cryin' two minutes afore that. Somebody were sure to say or do suthen so you could have a good laugh. We were once in a dug-out, I recollect: there were only owd bits o' wood on the top of it. And it were a-raining and a-raining! You were up to and over your knees in water in the trench: it was supposed to be *our* dug-out and it was coming through these bits o' wood and we were a-sodden wet through and cold. And there was a chap there—he was a sort of chapel preacher—and he says: "Oh," he say, "I've had enough on it!", he say, "I've a good mind to shoot myself," he say, "with this lot. I can't stick it much longer."

"Out!" said one of the blokes. "Out! Don't you shoot your-self in our 'front room'. Get out and do it!"

'And another one say; and went to give him a push: "Go on," he say, "Go on! No! shoot yourself out there. Don't do it in our parlour!"

'Of course he were a *rum* sort of bloke: you couldn't make much out of him. We used to have rum come up in the trenches. He allus used to take his rum ration and go throw it out. He wouldn't drink it. He was seen a-doing that two or three times, and I told the sergeant: "You don't want to give him no rum. He'll chuck it out." So they niver give him no rum for two or three days; but then he come up after it. He say he was going to take it as a medicine. He wasn't going to throw it out: he'd take it as a medicine! He was in my platoon. A *rum* bloke!

'We were all Norfolk chaps in my platoon. There were one or two educated chaps but most on us were all sort of uneducated. We all clicked in in one lot: we all kept together. We could get on with Norfolk chaps better than a Norfolk chap could get on with a Londoner. But I met some good Londoners, some good Norwichers, too—good soldiers. But with our own sort o' slang we all kept together and got on better. I had a bloke along o' me his name was Bond; he come from Attleborough, and he was my batman. That was 1918 time and we were a-pushing the Germans back. And all our rations were sent up, and we had to take these with us the next morning to follow up the Germans. I said to Bond: "You want to look out when the rations come up to git us a can o' water," because our water allus come in petrol-cans. "If you can git a can o' water I'll git a bag o' rations." Well, he got a bet! He got a petrol-can o' rum, the rum for the Company—two gallons for the whole Company! I said: "You want to keep care o' that. Keep your head on it so nobody don't pinch thet during the night."

'Well, he kept his head on it, but he kept a-supping on it as well. When we went out next morning before we *fell in* they [the Germans] blew a bridge up down the road. I found that this here chap Bond was so drunk—and it was the first time we'd fallen in with civilians after driving the Germans back; these had been taken prisoners, French women. And of course they were a-welcoming us there; they'd got their doors open and so on—and he was so drunk he slipped in one of these doors and just laid on the couch—drunk.

'But he never came back to us; he never did join the Regiment no more. And when the war was over and I got back home I went over to Attleborough and I ask a chap if he knew him. He looked in the charch where they'd got all the people who'd joined the army in the 1914 war. Bond! He wasn't a resident of Attleborough; but he'd come there to work for Gaymer; and he was put down *Missing*. What happened to him I don't know; whether the owd women ate him, I don't know. But I never did see no more of him after that.'

James Seely's experiences while he was in the army may appear out of place in the context of this book. I include them because his statement that his days on the Western Front—in spite of the horror and the squalor—were the happiest of his life seems to be some sort of commentary on the greater part of a lifetime spent in what is often regarded as the idyllic English countryside. It may have been idyllic to some but evidently not to the people who lived as close to the land as James Seely did.

[T] 'I came back to the farm in 1919. The wages were better then, but in a couple of years they had dropped back again, worse than what they were before we went out. They dropped to twenty-four shillings in 1921, but the cost of living had gone up; and this was hardly as much as twelve shillings before the war started. But the war had changed the men who had been in the army. They were better educated. Before they went out some on 'em had niver been in a train, or slept a night from hoom. They had a different feeling when they come back: they were not going to do the same things or put up with as much as they'd done afore they went out.

'But I worked on, and in 1937 I rented a small, seventy-acre farm from Lord Canterbury's estate. It's called Washingford. The place had been terribly neglected: it was full of blackthorn and whitethorn bushes—like trees some on 'em—all over the place. But the farms were going cheap then. A farm across the way there, Poplar Farm, Sisland, was sold about the same time for £1,110—210 acres at about £5 an acre. It was in bad state, of course; the dykes were all full and the hedges had all grown up and were spreading across the fields. But today that same farm would probably fetch over £300 an acre. Yes, between the wars nobody had any money in farming. Yes, there were farmers round here, in different farms I can mention, they had no money. I know one man had thirty cows. He bought a motor car but before the year was out—during the last quarter—he couldn't tax it. He didn't have no money. It was bad for everybody; good farmhands that could thatch, plough, do anything on the farms were walking the road. I recollect when I had the thrashing tackle after I got this farm so many men turned up asking for a day's work I could have manned two tackles and had some men over. There were stone-pits over there just behind the house: they belonged to the county council. They put some of the unemployed to work there: three days a week for a married man, two for a single.

'Lots of farmers had milk at that time. The farm I worked on during the 'twenties, they kept cows. They could only sell their milk summer-time when the visitors were at Yarmouth, eightpence a gallon they got for it. I carted milk to Loddon to take to Yarmouth. It cost three ha'pence a gallon for the lorry, so that was sixpence ha'penny a gallon. Some of them were sending it to Stowmarket and they got less. The land was all bushes. You could get on to any field and nobody would never see you. There was nine acres up the road there you could ha' hid up there—anywhere, it was all bushes. When the *War Ag.* [Agricultural Committee] took over I asked 'em would they send the gyro-tiller—an owd engine that come round and twizzle everything round—I asked 'em would they use it and do that field for me. They say: "No, we'll never force you to plough that. You'll never get forced to plough that up." But I ploughed it on my own. I got a steam-engine with a rope and we pulled out all the owd bushes and then I ploughed it with horses. It was better, too; the gyro-tiller did a lot o' harm on some fields.

'I worked horses all the time. I had a young chap drive a tractor for me for a short time, but I didn't have him long, as I say, and I don't drive a tractor myself so I kept to horses till I retired after that bad winter in 1962. I recollect it was that year I was out ploughing with a team of horses, and a traveller come to see me. He'd travelled well over a hundred miles that day he told me and I was the only man he'd seen working the land. It was too wet for the tractors to go on it but I could work without doing the land any harm.

'When I was a young man I never felt the cold, and I never felt tired. Now I know all about the east wind, and I can't move my left leg without having the *screws*.'

Market bell, Norwich

10 The Auctioneer

The auctioneer in the countryside is in a unique position to judge the state of farming in the area in which he operates. His profession demands that he has a fair knowledge of the land and its livestock, and he knows from experience what methods and what qualities enable one man to 'go ahead' and what lead another to disaster. An auctioneer sees much more than he can, or will, talk about; and if he has been in the region for a long time—invariably the case with the East Anglian auctioneering firms—there is hardly a man in the area who can give a better estimate of the general farming and the skill or otherwise of each individual farmer.

Aston Gaze, until he retired, was a member of a well-known East Anglian firm which has operated for many years from Diss on the Norfolk-Suffolk border. He entered the business at the beginning of the inter-war farming depression; and his memories of that period of twenty years are invaluable in supplementing the bare statistics of farming in the region during that disastrous period:

'I left school in 1920 and went into my father's business of auctioneering. My early life as an auctioneer coincided with the big farming depression after the First World War. Farmers who were farming land that was a bit ugly went under by the scores. Even on the good land where the farmer hadn't enough capital to look after it and have it properly drained he couldn't hold on. He'd be getting a yield of eight combs of wheat and ten combs of barley per acre. But that wasn't good enough: it gave him no leeway. This is understandable when you recollect the price of wheat at that time. Yes, I remember selling some of father's wheat during that period—in Diss market at nine shillings a comb (and even then one farmer boasted he could afford to grow wheat at that price! but he was unusual). That was in 1923. It was only the farmers who worked the best land, land that would yield about fourteen combs an acre, who survived. The farmers round North Walsham in Norfolk, for instance; and those around Eye, Stradbroke, and Framlingham in Suffolk. On the ugly, poorly-yielding land such as that between Halesworth and the Suffolk coast the farmers couldn't keep going. A great deal of the land went back. Little of it was cultivated at all; the hedges grew out and what there was of farm land was nothing but rough pasture.

'Those Suffolk farmers who managed to keep going on the better land only did so by not sparing themselves or their men. They supervised every detail in the men's work. On the whole the Suffolk farmers adapted themselves better to the depression than did the Norfolk farmers. In west Norfolk thousands of acres of land—which at that time were all on the big estates—were given up and the landlords could not let it at any price. The late Mr. Leonard Mason took over huge stretches of west Norfolk, and it was like a big ranch. This was in the 1920's.

'The farm-workers were in a terrible plight, and the farmers were sorry for them but could do little about it. During the 1914–18 war their wages had reached 46s a week, which was reasonable as prices were then. But after the War the wages were eroded down to 19s a week.[1] Many of the men were out of work: they were not eligible for the dole and were put on "relief". They worked in the stone pits and at breaking stones for the road at 4s 6d a day; four days a week for the married men and two for the single men.

[1] G. E. Fussell, *From Tolpuddle to T.U.C.*, chapter 6.

'The prices of the farms at that time will give you some idea of the state of agriculture during the depression. Land was almost given away. I know of a village grocer who bought a 100-acre farm (with farmhouse) for £400, the sort of land that's fetching £300 an acre today. I hired a small farm myself when I was still working as a young auctioneer; but it was only by injecting the farm with half my salary that I could keep it going. I drew enough to live on each week; and the rest of my salary, which was not much, I drew each month. All that money went into the farm. At that time I could have bought a farm of 240 acres for £1,200, only one of the conditions of sale was that the buyer had to pay £200 in cash for the transaction, the rest to remain at 4 per cent. I couldn't raise the money. The man who did so recouped his money by cutting down some timber on a piece of low land on his farm. That farm, too, has changed hands several times since at good prices.

'Most of the farmers who were in difficulties would manage to hold on until they were unable to pay their workmen. That was the final crisis. But before they got to this stage all their livestock would most likely have been sold for cash. They'd go from one tradesman—blacksmith, harness-maker, miller, threshing-contractor and so on—to another because they'd outlasted their credit with the original one; keeping on, holding on, hoping all the time that things would change. But when they failed to get ready money to pay their workmen they knew then it was the end of the road: "A Deed of Assignment for the Benefit of Creditors".

'When it came to that it was not unusual to find workmen who hadn't been paid for as long as five weeks. As preferential creditors, of course, they were paid first and in full. And do you know, I never once came across an instance of a workman at this time leaving a farmer because he couldn't pay him.

'The 1926 Strike saw the lowest point in the bad times in East Anglia. After this things began to pick up a little. The State intervened. The Government started the sugar-beet industry, and that was the beginning of a big improvement. Although the contract price for growing sugar-beet was not a very big one, it was a definite contract and it helped farmers tremendously. Again, sugar-beet got the farm back on to a healthy and realistic rotation. Before this farmers had been growing cattle-beet (mangolds) and swedes and turnips as a root-crop. But it had become a kind of dead crop because raising cattle was not paying. Now they had a good break-crop which in addition helped them out of their difficulties.

'The improvement from 1936 onwards was real; but of course the results of the worst times showed right up to the time of the outbreak of war in 1939. It is, in retrospect, a very significant fact that whereas those who went under in the early 'thirties paid four or five shillings in the pound, those who had the real bad luck to "nearly make it" and succumbed to circumstances just before the War paid out in full or nearly so—even sometimes with a little over.

'These were the casualties: we all were—or nearly all—insolvent; "too poor to break". Those who managed to carry through those bad days can appreciate that we are now, in spite of all we can with justice complain of, in a very different case. But we who have seen them and have heard from our fathers of a similar state of things in the 1890's are uneasily aware that it can happen again. The younger generation—to whom this depression is only an old man's gloomy tale—press on with every confidence in these days of inflation; and they believe they will never have to face times such as their fathers and grandfathers saw. I wonder.

'Among those who survived the depression best I would put those who managed to hold on to their flocks of sheep. The yearly cheque for the lambs was perhaps the largest single item in the farmer's income; but twelve months of unrelenting hard work, constant attention and scheming went into it. Then there was the wool, sold by auction at Diss, in the maltings near the station. That cheque and the cast-off ewes was supposed to *mend the flock*; that is, buy in shearling ewes to keep the numbers up and also a ram.

'I was brought up in Diss, and some of my most vivid memories are of Diss Lamb Sale. The sale was held each year on the last Thursday in June. Before the Second World War every East Anglian farm had a folded flock of about 200–500 sheep and a shepherd and his *page*. Most of the lambs we handled were from Suffolk ewes crossed with a Cotswold ram. (The Cotswold, a biggish white-faced sheep, is the nearest representation of the old English sheep on which England's wool-prosperity of the Middle Ages was based. As with the Australian sheep, the merino is supposed to come into its remote ancestry. In the 1920's and 1930's about 1,000 to 1,500 of these rams were bred by a few specialists in their native Cotswold Hills, and in two or three places in Norfolk and Suffolk, solely for siring the big lambs which the trade of this time required. The breed was not of general utility and is now almost, if not quite, extinct.) These lambs—what we described as "Half-breds"—came from this first cross, both dam and sire: they had speckled markings on the face.

'Diss wasn't the only lamb sale, of course. There were sales at Attleborough, Harling, Swaffham, Hempton Green, Watton and other places in Norfolk; and there were the Suffolk lamb sales as well: Bury St. Edmunds, Stowmarket, Melton—and so on. But Diss was the largest in East Anglia. Some of the lambs came from mid-Norfolk, some from local flocks, but most from Suffolk; Oakley, Gipping, Needham Market and Framsden sending entries of 500 to 1,500.

'Before the day of the sale the pens for the sheep were set out with wooden hurdles on the cricket meadow. It was a work of art to arrange twenty-five or more rows to hold all the sheep. We always managed to do this and to spare the actual cricket pitch. On the night before the sale the shepherds and their helpers who were bringing lambs from a distance would turn them into one of the meadows of a friendly farmer within striking distance of the town. When I went to the cricket ground at 5 o'clock on the sale morning the streets would be so full of sheep you could hardly move. We set to work and counted in 10,000 or 12,000 before we had breakfast. In handling the sheep we had the help of a family called Garland who were extremely accurate sheep-counters, as were Sam Last and later *Muskey* Scoulding who also set the hurdles. We started selling at 10 a.m. and usually finished round about 5 p.m. By that time we'd have sold anything up to 25,000 sheep.

19. Taking sheep to Haddiscoe marshes, Norfolk, *c.* 1915

20. *Quanting* hay on the Norfolk Broads in 1886 (a quant is the pole used to propel the boat). The Pettingill family towed their boat by rope when they gathered hay off the rands: they used a quant to keep the boat off the bank

21. Stradbroke (Suffolk) church, *c.* 1864. The three Stradbroke photographs were taken by J. C. Ryle's daughter

22. Stradbroke street, *c.* 1864. J. C. Ryle is standing in the centre of the road

'On that day the whole town of Diss used to be given over to the sheep. One of the first things to be done was to go round the town with wooden boards to cover up all the drain-gratings to prevent the sheep from breaking their legs. Very few of the roads were tarred then; and during the Sale there was plenty of dust about. The air was also thick with the complaints of old ladies grumbling about the sheep that had invaded their front gardens. All the small boys of the town stayed home from school to help the drovers; and they had a whale of a time.

'As they were sold the sheep were sent off by rail and driven off by road. Diss railway station was a poor place for people on that day: passengers had to manage as best they could. The sheep were loaded over the passenger platform: 250 to 300 wagons loaded with sheep used to leave Diss station on a Sale day. Drovers also used to take out the sheep by road and deliver them to farmers who'd bought them. A drover would go out with, perhaps, a 1,000 sheep. He'd have an old pony and trap, two or three dogs, and maybe a boy. He'd drop the sheep at the various farms after he'd planned out his journey. *Drover* Green was one of these. He'd take out the sheep from Diss and deliver them to farms ten miles the other side of Dereham. We trusted these drovers entirely; and when they next came in to Diss they would give us an account of their itinerary, telling us that Farmer So-and-so was a couple of sheep short, or that someone else had one or two too many.

'Bob Williamson of Holt, a large farmer and sheep dealer, used to walk his purchases of over a 1,000 sheep home himself. Mrs. Williamson used to meet him at various points with the car. Several times I remember taking them in to tea with my grandmother who lived opposite the sale yard; and—at nearly ninety— thoroughly enjoyed the day and was visited by many of her old friends.

'The sheep sales held their importance up to the last War, but tended to diminish. The War hastened their decline: too much of the entry consisted of 'Entire Flocks' (all the ewes on the farm sold as well as the lambs). It was not exactly that sheep did not pay: other things paid better, and the folded sheep, once the

H   113

mainstay of many a farm, does not fit in with modern farming. The smaller sales shut down one by one. Diss succumbed last in 1966, after nearly a hundred years. By this time it had gone down to a very small affair. Sheep-selling in East Anglia is now concentrated on Fornham, near Bury St. Edmunds, where thirty or forty thousand sheep and lambs are sold in the course of the season. My sons and myself have a little flock of a hundred ewes. Most of the lambs go off to the butcher, only the smaller ones to Bury. And that is the only flock within miles of Diss.'

Helmingham Hall

11 *Open and Closed Villages*

One advantage of oral testimony about conditions in East Anglian villages before 1914 is that it serves to emphasize the dangers of generalization even about villages in the same district. Indeed there was often a great contrast between villages situated in contiguous parishes. The contrast usually depended on one village being *open*, the other *closed*, or *close*.

In the closed or estate village there was at least the appearance of a well-ordered existence which was symbolized by the neat cottages, the well-kept gardens and allotments, the excellent repair of the farmhouses and farm buildings, the well-kept hedges and the overall appearance of thoughtful planning of the village landscape. And if the landowner or squire was benevolent and active on behalf of the people of his village this outwardly convincing appearance of things would even bear closer examination. For the benevolent landowner, in the tradition of a just aristocracy, treated tenant-farmers and farm-workers alike and would sometimes intercede on behalf of the worker if he suspected the farmer was using him wrongly.

In the open village where there was no dominating landowner or squire, where were a number of tenant-farmers perhaps paying rent to absentee landlords, where some of the cottages were tied to the farms and others owned by rural 'capitalists' like small tradesmen or speculators, where families came in and moved out of these 'free' cottages consequent on their paying or not paying the rent, conditions were often squalid in the extreme. The appearance of these villages told most of the story, especially during the worst troughs of the farming depressions, and the under-surface reality was not very different from the external squalor. The conflict between farmer and farm-worker was softened by no mediator; malnutrition among the children was usually worse than in the closed villages; and there was that deep-seated resentment at unashamed exploitation by employers against whom there was no appeal, a resentment that became inbuilt, continuing for generations long outlasting the worst social conditions and the intense class conflict which were its cause.

Arthur Wilson Fox, who prepared the 1893 Report,[1] mentioned the contrast between the two types of village at that date, and his comment reflects the polarity—the existence in the region of the two extremes—referred to above:

'When comparing the cottages in the two Eastern counties with those in the three Northern ones [Northumberland, Cumberland and Lancashire], I should say that the worst and the best are to be found in Suffolk and Norfolk, the worst being chiefly in open villages, where impecunious owners or small and greedy speculators are frequently the landlords, or where "lifeholds" are numerous. The best are nearly always situated on farms or in "close" villages, belonging to landed proprietors, who build them without expecting a direct return for their money, perhaps with the object of attracting a good class of farmers and labourers, or of improving the appearance of their property, or it may be to serve a philanthropic end. In addition it is frequently the practice for owners of estates to keep the management of the cottages in their own hands, and thus the internal and external repairs are properly attended to.'

There is a story from Suffolk which sums up the conditions in the open type of village at the end of the last century and for a

[1] P. 16. See also A. Wilson Fox, *Agricultural Wages in England and Wales During the Last Half Century*, London, 1903; reprinted in *Essays in Agrarian History*, Vol. 2 (1968), pp. 133–6 for lowness of wages in arable counties, especially Suffolk; also p. 153 for poor state of cottages in Suffolk villages.

long time afterwards. A horseman applied for a job with a farmer who had a few years before built himself a *model* farm with the most up-to-date farm buildings and all the latest equipment. After the usual preliminaries and a tour of the farm, the farmer offered the horseman the job. He accepted and the farmer said: 'Right. I'll now show you your cottage.'

After seeing the cottage and looking contemplative for a moment or two the horseman asked:

'D'you mind if I sleep with the hosses?'

It would be misleading, however, to contrast open and closed villages simply on the level of material conditions, or even while bearing in mind the advantages of having a well-disposed and powerful father-figure who was at hand to temper the worst effects of injustice. The differences and similarities between the two types of village are much more subtle. Men and women are not necessarily happiest where physical conditions leave little more to be wished for. If they feel that these conditions have been won at the expense of their freedom or by the surrender of their human dignity their content is soon corroded; and eventually they find their lot as oppressive as they would have done under overt poverty. For in the long run it is a man's spirit and not his body which is the arbitrator of his own condition, and once his spirit has given judgement no amount of blandishment will completely win its consent.

But it would be as well to examine a closed village in some detail, to pick out some of its characteristics, and to attempt to capture some of its social feel. The Suffolk village of Helmingham has been owned by the Tollemache family since the sixteenth century, but it was given its present form in mid-nineteenth century by John Tollemache (1805–90).[1] He sold some of his estate at Bentley in Suffolk and used the money to construct a model village which was to become an embodiment of his views on solving the agrarian problem of his day. He also attempted at Peckforton and Dorford in Cheshire to give physical shape to

[1] Formerly *Halliday* of Peckforton Castle, Chester. High Sheriff of Cheshire, 1840; M.P. for South Cheshire, 1841–68 and for West Cheshire, 1868–72. Created Baron Tollemache of Helmingham, 1876.

his ideal of a progressive landlord sincerely concerned for the welfare of the people who lived on his estate. The Government *Report on the Agricultural Labourer* (1893)[1] shows that he had gone some way towards attaining his ideal:[2] 'Mention has been made of the late Lord Tollemache as a model landlord but it must not be forgotten that other landlords have done their share in the matter of small holdings.' 'On the estates of Lord Crewe, Lord Tollemache, Sir Henry Broughton and others, a number of men are continuously employed and these work much shorter hours and average higher wages than those paid on the farms; but they are a class apart. . . . By far the greater portion of the cottages are held by the estate owners and let directly to the labourers.' 'In addition to the farms as given in the returns of the Peckforton estate of Lord Tollemache there are on this estate 255 labourers' tenements, "three acres and a cow", of which about 170 are in the Nantwich Union. The term "three acres and a cow" was, I am informed, invented by either the late Lord Tollemache or Mr Cawley, father of the present agent.'

Whether or not Lord Tollemache or his agent or someone else invented the phrase it was used as a rallying cry by Jesse Collings, one of the Liberal M.P.s who was active in the late nineteenth century in the formation of a farm-workers' union. Yet the proposal was an old one:[3] 'Thomas Becon in 1540 had suggested that landlords should attract to every cottage enough "land to keep a cow or two"; and Arthur Young had advocated at the time of the later enclosures the letting of a small area of land to help the farm-worker keep his self-respect and to compensate for the loss of his grazing rights with the enclosure of the commons." [4]'What Young deplored was the loss of a golden opportunity of attaching land to the home of the cottager.'

Intelligent and far-seeing landlords like John Tollemache realized that there would be no health in the economy of the countryside until some reparation was made to the farm-worker

[1] Poor Law Union of Nantwich (Cheshire), Roger C. Richards, Asst. Commissioner.
[2] Ibid., pp. 97–8.
[3] *E.F.P.P.*, p. 123.
[4] Ibid., p. 215.

for the loss of his grazing land, either on the commons or road-side verges; and—more important still—the loss of his self-respect that were consequences of the enclosures of the eighteenth and nineteenth centuries. But shortage of pasture in an arable area like Helmingham probably induced John Tollemache not to attempt to apply the classical formula there. In Helmingham he laid out his farm-workers' tenements on the plan of a pair of cottages to an acre of ground; half an acre for each tenant and room for a couple of pigs in the corner of his holding. The cottages were laid out, here and in the surrounding villages, on a conventional plan adjoining the roads through the villages. They are semi-detached or *double-dwellers*, as the local term is; there is a pleasing interval between each pair and they are built at a distance of ten or fifteen yards from the road itself. The plan (page 130) shows how each cottage lies on a half-acre plot divided from his neighbour's half-acre by a central fence or hedge. The scale of the rent for cottage and land can be gathered from these sources. The 1893 Report (page 20): 'The price of allotments in Norfolk and Suffolk generally varies from £1 to £2 per acre, which does not seem unreasonable'; and a Helmingham woman referring to the beginning of the century: 'My mother used to pay £4 5s a year for the rent of the cottage, the garden and the allotment. It was raised to £4 15s later on.'

On entry to the cottage the farm-worker or estate employee signed an agreement with John Tollemache, not with the farmer who directly employed him. A note in the 1893 Report[1] relates to Nantwich, Cheshire, and to his practice on his estate there; he appears to have done the same at Helmingham: 'By far the greater portion of the cottages are held by the estate owner and let directly to the labourers. The number of farm-servants, i.e. those who live in the farmhouse, in Cheshire is very considerable so that the farmers are not so anxious as they are in Warwickshire and elsewhere to have a number of cottages in the farm take. There is, however, a custom on Lord Tollemache's estate and elsewhere, I was told, to permit the farmer to exercise one option with regard to certain cottages. If one happens to be empty the farmer

[1] Roger C. Richards, Asst. Commissioner, p. 97.

may nominate a tenant and in the absence of a very strong reason to the contrary the nomination is accepted, but after that the farmer has no further voice in the matter.' That meant that in nearly all cases John Tollemache had strict and direct control both of the tenant farmers and their workers. From the worker's standpoint it meant that he was not liable to be evicted from his cottage at the whim of the farmer: the Lord stood between them. The same practice obtained in other parts of East Anglia:[1] 'In Norfolk Lord Walsingham lets 192 cottages out of 196 direct to labourers. Lord Leicester lets all of his (over 1,000) direct to the labourers. In Suffolk on the Duke of Grafton's property there are 235 cottages, fifty-five of which are let with the farms, and 180 direct to labourers.' This had two great advantages for the landlord: he could keep a direct check on the condition of his property, ensuring that the cottage was kept in good state and repair; and, again, he could keep a check on the persons who came into the estate and—as will be shown—he could hasten the removal of those he wanted out of it.

Here is a copy of the cottage agreement at Helmingham:

Cottage and Allotment

An Agreement made this 15th day of March 1884 Between John, Baron Tollemache of Helmingham in the County of Suffolk, of the one part and George Stockings of Helmingham in the County of Suffolk of the other part. Whereby the said John, Baron Tollemache, agrees to Let and the said George Stockings to Hire all that Messuage, Tenement of Cottage with Yard, Gardens and Allotment Land thereto belonging situate in the Parish of Helmingham, from the 11th day of October 1883 for one quarter of a year and so on from quarter to quarter until tenancy hereby treated shall be determined by three months' notice by either party herein named

Yielding and paying unto the said John, Baron Tollemache, his Heirs or Assigns, the yearly rent of Four pounds twelve shillings, by four quarterly payments in advance if demanded by,

---

[1] A. Wilson Fox, *1893 Report*, p. 18.

or on behalf of the said John, Baron Tollemache, namely on the 11th October, 6th January, 6th April and the 6th July next after the date hereof.

And the said George Stockings undertakes and agrees as follows, that is to say:

1st Not to plough any part of the said Allotment land but to cultivate it with the Spade, leaving one half wheat, and the other half Peas, Beans, Potatoes or other Vegetables, and not to have any Turnips or Beet-root growing for seed without the consent of the said John, Baron Tollemache, or his agent.

2nd To attend some place of worship once on each Sabbath Day.

3rd To keep the Glass and Windows of the said Cottage in good repair.

And Lastly it is Agreed that if this tenancy shall be determined on the 6th January, 6th April or the 6th July, the said John, Baron Tollemache, or his Heirs shall pay or cause to be paid unto the said George Stockings the value of all the Manure, Tillage, Corn, Vegetable, Seeds, and for sowing the same, that may be growing in the Garden and Allotment Land for the sole consumption of the said George Stockings and his family. The value of such Corn, Vegetables, Manure, Seeds etc. to be ascertained by a licenced valuer to be named by the said John, Baron Tollemache, and any Rent or Arrears of Rent to be deducted from the Amount due for Valuation; and should there not be sufficient on the Premises to discharge the Amount due for Rent and Arrears of Rent the remainder shall be recoverable by Action at Law.

As Witness our Hands this fifteenth
day of March, 1884.

George Stockings | his X Mark

Postage

6ᵈ

Witness:

Stanhope Tollemache

It will be noticed that this is more than an orthodox agreement between owner and tenant, relating solely to the use and management of the property rented. It has moral or ethical clauses: a man must go to church at least once every Sunday, and he is not allowed the soft option of hiring or borrowing a plough to cultivate his half-acre. He and his family must dig the land with a spade and look after it according to definite rules, chief of which appeared to be the Biblical injunction: 'In the sweat of thy face thou shalt eat thy bread'. But oral testimony discloses other, unwritten, rules which the tenant would know and well understand before taking up a tenancy. If, for instance, a tenant's daughter had a baby before marriage she had to leave the village; and her parents had little say in the matter: 'I recollect there was one girl who became pregnant, and they told her to leave the village. Her parents had to turn her out of the house. If they didn't they themselves and the whole family would have had to go—and would probably have finished up in the workhouse. This went on for many years until someone higher up made a mistake. Nothing much was heard of the custom after thet.'

The agreement—plus the other unwritten clauses such as the one quoted and the commonly understood rule that the boys should touch their cap or forelock to Lordship or Ladyship and the girls curtsey[1]—shows the nature of the social relations in the closed villages of the beginning of this century before the 1914–18 war had caused the break-up of many of the big estates. In essence the relation was feudal, not of course in the legalistic sense, but in the commonly accepted social usage of this term which had its positive as well as its negative side. Paternalism at this stage meant, as the name implies: 'I'm Father. I'll look after you. But you must do as I tell you. Father knows best!' And at its best it did, indeed, still hold the old feudal overtones of *noblesse oblige*—rank involves obligation; and privilege carries with it the duty of service to the community. It was in both senses a noble ideal and was much preferable to the calculating coin-directed ethos that grew up with a full development of a money-economy. A Helmingham comment is relevant here:

[1] It is remembered that during John Tollemache's time, after a girl had omitted to greet his wife in the expected manner, she was caned at school next day.

'John Tollemache used to say he wanted only two sorts of people in the parish: the rich and the poor. He didn't want any in between.'

We must beware, however, of ascribing the present-day standards of what social relations ought to be to a Suffolk village of a century ago when a Victorian authoritarianism was the dominant pattern, certainly in the rural areas. It is possible that some of the inhabitants of Helmingham did not feel the paternalism of the squire in any way oppressive and would blithely sing of 'the rich man in his castle and the poor man at his gate'. Some, too, would probably feel—as some still do—the cosy warmth of aristocratic contact. Like the lady who was in a very distinguished line, and through her forebears had shaken hands with Doctor Johnson who had been touched by Queen Anne and so on and so on, they felt that they, too, were in touch with the great who in their turn were in touch with the Great of the Land. And this gave them the assurance—even if it was only illusory— of leading a much fuller life than their neighbours in less favoured villages where they could not drop the casual but distinguishing remark: 'Her Ladyship called this afternoon, and she said, etc., etc., etc.'

Yet there was alongside this an underlying, smouldering resentment whose depth and intensity can be gauged by the fact that it has lasted until the present when the overt conditions which gave rise to it have to a great extent been removed.

'You were under and you dussn't say anything. The old Lord used to come round to look at the house, the garden and the allotment just as he did the farms; and the farmers were as afraid of him as we were.'

'You had to go to church on Sunday and the farmers had to see that you went, too.'

This appeared to be the rule in most Suffolk villages up to 1914. Herman Biddell, a Suffolk farmer,[1] used to proceed down the aisle at the end of the service while the rest of the congregation still remained seated. He cast an experienced eye over the pews and if there was a gap in the pew of one of his tenants he leaned

---

[1] *H.I.F.*

over and asked: 'Where's Charlie? How is it he's not in church this morning?'

Dress was also controlled in Helmingham; and this had its positive and negative sides. If a family was in need the Tollemaches helped them with the provision of boots and clothes. But it would not do for an estate tenant to have his own ideas about dress. 'You had to dress according to your station. If you didn't *they* soon let you know about it.' This strict sumptuary law is confirmed in other parts of Suffolk. Farm-workers had to go to church and had to shine up their working-boots, the only pair they possessed, on a Saturday night; and they went in corduroys. If they wore anything but *cords* they were considered to be getting above their station and there was trouble. A young girl working in a big house in West Suffolk went to church on a Sunday morning with two feathers in her hat. Not even one feather was allowed. Her mistress told her that she must dress more seemingly or else she would have to leave. The girl, having an independent nature, left immediately and went into domestic service elsewhere.

The farm horseman in Suffolk dressed well, and he seems to be an exception to the dress regulations. But the horseman was paid two or three shillings more than the 'day man' who got ten shillings a week at the beginning of the century: the horseman who was also foreman got fifteen shillings. His dressing well did not contradict the sumptuary rules but merely confirmed the hierarchical structure of the village at that time, especially the closed village. Like the gamekeeper and the gardener whose suits were provided for them by the estate, the horseman did not excite comment if the quality of his suit was as good as the farmer's. Everything was in order if there was no danger of his being mistaken for one.

Many of the stories that are still told in the village of Helmingham about the John Tollemache regime can be classified as gossip. But, as has been said, a writer who proposes to glean more than just the surface material of a village would do well to listen to gossip. Although it can easily be faulted as a most unreliable signpost in his pursuit of the truth it does reveal one thing infallibly—the attitude of the persons retailing the gossip, the undersurface reaction which can well be the true reaction where conditions preclude any overt comments.

John Tollemache was a keen driver of a four-in-hand, and drove round his estate and to the neighbouring towns himself, his coachman sitting beside him. He was very proud of his skill as a driver of a four-in-hand; and at that time there was great rivalry among the *quality* concerning their driving skills and especially their ability to take a coach through the narrowest of openings without touching the gate-posts or the walls.

'John Tollemache had the reputation in the county of being a man who could handle horses. He claimed he was the only man who could drive to Ipswich and turn his coach and four horses straight into the *White Horse Inn* yard [a difficult right-hand turn in a narrow street] without his horses being led. When he found out that one of his coachmen could perform this he gave him the sack.'

When he wanted a new coachman he interviewed the candidates himself; and his own experiences in driving, and possibly his own rather dangerous pretensions, prompted the question he asked each of the five or six applicants for the post:

'How near can you take the carriage to a post without hitting it?'

He got various answers, each designed to illustrate the coachman's extraordinary skill, for example: 'I can stick a match into the side of the post, my Lord, and hit the match without hitting the post.' But one man gave the answer the Lord had been waiting for:

'I don't know about being near to it, your Lordship. I reckon to keep as far from the posts as I can.'

'Right. You're the man! You're the man for the job.'

12 Cottage Economy

The cottages at Helmingham show a pleasing variety of design, but they all have features which have earned them—along with many public houses—the name of Tollemache Tudor. Of these the heavy capitals of the chimneys and the steep pitch of the roofs are most noticeable. But the cottages were very well built; and the present Lord Tollemache has followed the progressive policy of the first in bringing them up to date with piped water and modern amenities including bathrooms. In the 1850's when they were built they were far in advance of the farm-workers' dwellings elsewhere in the area and they were undoubtedly the most manifest proof of John Tollemache's reputation of being a model landlord. But their design bears the mark of the period,[1] making in some of their features too great a concession to the current antiquarian fashion. The bedrooms, for instance, in most of the cottages are disproportionately small owing to the steep pitch of the roof; and they offer a symbolic illustration of the dangers in a wider context of emphasizing historical continuity at the expense of function.

[1] Helmingham School illustrates how the mid-nineteenth-century estate planners tried to achieve a unity of design by duplicating features of the Tudor part of Helmingham Hall in the new buildings.

But one old survival that was included in the design served a useful purpose for many years after the cottages were built, and it is not without its uses even today. This was the building of an outside kitchen or outhouse where most of the domestic work was done. Such an outside kitchen, similar in purpose to the kitchen of the medieval hall, existed in the village of Blaxhall in Suffolk.[1] It contained *back-stocks* or open fire-grate, brick-oven, a two-pail copper for heating water for domestic purposes and pig-killing, and a six-pail copper used for the home brewing of beer. At one time it was probably shared by more than one cottage, but its original siting was no doubt due to a need to lessen the fire-risk to a timbered and thatched dwelling. The intent of the designer of the Helmingham cottages, however, appears to have been to increase the living space in the cottage itself by arranging to have most of the domestic work done outside it.

The Helmingham outhouse or kitchen was shared by the two families in the *double-dweller*. One of the main activities in the shared kitchen was the weekly baking of bread. One Helmingham householder told me how they used to manage when the baking of bread in the brick-oven was the usual custom:

'We baked our own bread up to the First World War, and some families carried on long after it. Baking day was always on a Friday: it was the same day all round here, and in most parts of Suffolk I believe. It was the custom. We heated the brick-oven with bush-faggots—whitethorn and blackthorn branches kept from the trimming of the hedges. To light the oven you cut the faggot in half—crossways. I laid it across a block of wood we kept for the purpose. After cutting it you fed the top part of the faggot, the twigs, into the oven first; and when it was properly alight you put in the thicker sticks of the bottom half.

'I often laugh when I think about it. There were rows in some of the double-dwellers on a Friday morning. The rumpus was usually over who was to bake first. If you baked in the morning you'd have to heat up a cold oven; and that would take at least one and a half faggots—maybe two. The woman who baked in the afternoon needed only one faggot as the oven was partly hot

---

[1] At Mill Common; the cottage owned by Mr. Stowe.

when she came to it. I recollect that often there used to be a commotion, shouting and swearing, about who should go first. Of course, there was no fence separating the two cottages and the kitchen as there is today; and this made it worse. The women used to throw buckets of water over one another in one particular double-dweller; but on the whole I suppose they got on quite well in sharing the kitchen. But it wasn't as quiet then as it is now. You take this road: at that time of day there were large families in most of these cottages: ten children sometimes in one family. Today there are not more than three or four children in the whole road going to Helmingham school. At one time there used to be thirty.'

The most interesting side of the Helmingham cottage economy is the way it was linked with the old methods of farming. In some of the cottages—whether designed specially or not—there was a downstairs bedroom. This was a feature of those cottages occupied by farm horsemen: by sleeping downstairs he could get up in the early morning (4 a.m. during the summer)[1] without disturbing the rest of the household. In many of the cottages the rooms no longer needed for this purpose have been converted into bathrooms. Other indications of the old horse-regime on the farm still exist in some of the cottages and their half-acre. Joe Thompson, who lives at 102 St. John's Row, Framsden, pointed out to me a horseman's herb, elecampane,[2] a huge, large-leafed plant that still flourishes in his garden.

Another building design in the village of Helmingham shows a feature which has an accidental link with the past when the high pitched roof was truly functional (it was evolved to prevent undue *thrust* on the timber walls and also to ensure that the rain-water ran smoothly and quickly off the thatch). This is the smithy. John Tollemache built it at the same time and along the same lines as the other buildings; and it lies in a good position roughly at the centre of the villages comprising the estate and at the boundary of the Park. The smithy itself is built to a traditional design, with the forge roughly in the centre of the shop, separate *trav'us*, and half-hatch door to the shop. Over the forge itself there is the usual large canopy to guide the smoke into the chimney. But John

---

[1] *H.I.F.*, p. 21.   [2] Ibid., pp. 232–3.

23. Stradbroke, c. 1864. Tree-fellers with timber-jim. The children are having their lunch in the midday break from the school which is just out of the picture

24.
Young girl,
Halesworth (Suffolk) district,
c. 1890

25. Servants from the big house

Charles Knight (born 1883), the Helmingham smith, found that while he was working the smoke curled outside the lip of the canopy and collected up under the steep pitch of the roof, some-times making working conditions uncomfortable. He, therefore, got the Estate to open up a hole in the roof and cover it with a louvred frame (Plate 17a) to take off the excess smoke. This is a modern example of the medieval arrangement where there was a central hearth in a dwelling but no chimney: there was at that time a similar device to get rid of the smoke. Some smiths solved the problem by having alternate ridge-tiles raised a few inches, providing a series of vents along the ridge of the roof. There is an example of this in the village of Brooke, Norfolk.

From the cottage tenants, who according to their agreement with the landowner worked their own holdings, I got direct evidence of farming methods and processes that were little affected by modern improvements or mechanization and were substan-tially the same as the methods that had been practised from earliest times. Older tenants like Caleb Howe (1886–1967), Dan Pilgrim (born 1882) and A. W. Lankester (born 1893) described to me the old processes they had used: the sowing of corn broad-cast, with dibbles and with a hand-drill, the cutting of the corn with the sickle, the bagging-hook,[1] scythe and cradle or bale, the harvesting of the corn and the threshing of it with a flail on a *tilt* or tarpaulin cloth behind their cottages. As the agreement implies John Tollemache kept as strict a watch on the farming of the allotments as he did on the farms themselves. The crops the tenants grew, the rotation of the crops, and what they did with the crops were carefully governed. The diagram (page 130) shows the crops that were grown on each side of the dividing path in John Tollemache's day: they were changed over each year in a kind of 'two-field' rotation. The evident design was for each cottager to be as self-supporting as he could. The cattle-beet or mangel-wurzels were fed to the pigs, and the rest of the produce was consumed by the family: selling anything was frowned upon. The land on each side of the centre-path was manured with pig

[1] Or badging-hook: a hook to cut corn, peas, beans, etc.; probably derived from Low Latin, *bladum, bladus* or *blada*—corn.

manure each year. Caleb Howe described how they used to farm their half-acre during his father's time and this is included elsewhere.[1] He also told me: 'We dug in the pig's manure. Everything was dug with a spade. They reckoned the spade was a wonderful implement in those days, everything by hand. The farmer you

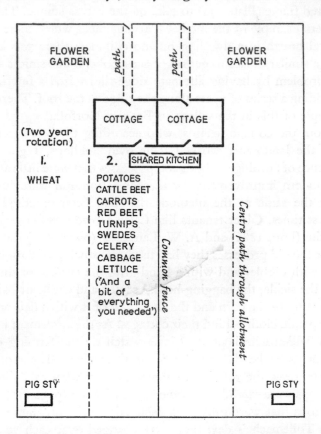

worked for supplied the straw for the pigs if you didn't have enough of your own; and in return he carted away the manure you'd got spare. The owd Lord came round to look at the allotments. They had to be kept well or else you had to go. You had to farm your land right up to the *dick*. The farmers were as much afraid o' the Lord as we were.'

[1] *F.A.V.*, pp. 70–3.

Dan Pilgrim and Anthony Lankester confirmed the thoroughness of the inspection: it appears there were regular inspections on more or less formal occasions but John Tollemache kept his eye open as he went round the villages on day-to-day business:

'He used to drive a coach-and-pair, sometimes a coach-and-four when he went round the villages looking at the farms and the allotments. At that time o' day all the rows had to be pointed inwards from the road so the Lord could see the rows were straight and properly weeded. There had to be at least one pig in the sty and nearly every tenant had to have a couple. There was a workman at Pearl Farm years ago and John Tollemache went round his allotment and found he kept no pig.

"Where is it?" he say.

"The farmer won't give me one."

'John Tollemache went straight to this farmer and he say: "Give this man a pig"; and he had to, of course.

'He treated farmers and cottagers alike. There was a farmer down at Gosbeck; he had a bough hanging over the road not far from his farm. John Tollemache drove down that way one day, noticed the bough was dangerous and mentioned it to the farmer. The next time he passed the bough was still there.

"Get that bough down before sunset!" he said. And the farmer had to send a man immediately to cut it down.'

But later on after John Tollemache's death many of the strict regulations about the cultivation of the cottage holdings appear to have been relaxed. William Sherman (born 1902) told me: 'Sometime in the 'twenties my older brother and me grew six combs of oats on our quarter-acre. We sold it to Mr. Thompson, the schoolmaster and we got thirty shillings a comb for it. Mr. Thompson used to have a pony and trap: he used to go to Ipswich and so on. About that time, too, I recollect there were prizes given for the best allotments. One year the judges came round to inspect the allotments and they praised my brother for using up every bit of his land. He had tomatoes growing round his pig-sty. The judges were mostly local farmers. The first prize was thirty shillings, the second twenty-five—and five shillings less as you went down. They had different prizes for the gardens

which were chiefly flowers. This was in connection with the
flower show held at the Hall. Six parishes took part; and the
Tollemache family owned either all or part of the land in these
parishes: Helmingham, Framsden, Gosbeck, Ashbocking, Pettaugh and Otley. The flower show was held in July and they
had a furrow-drawing match the same time.'

Joe Thompson's account of his dibbling the Helmingham half-
acres and of his later acquiring and using a drill illustrates the
special feature of the Helmingham allotment holders. They were
in a sense a group venture, and in theory at least each individual
tenant had the help of the landlord, his farmer, and his fellow-
tenants. Joe Thompson's account of his dibbling has been given:[1]
later he acquired a drill:

'In the late 'twenties I bought this two-coulter drill [Plate 18]
you are now looking at. I bought it off a man called Jim Rose of
High Row, Framsden. That was before the cottages up there were
pulled down. That was about forty-four years ago. I paid £1 5s
for it and it cost between £3 and £4 for the wheelwright to fit a
new wheel and get it ready again for use. Jim Rose had used it
for about forty year himself; and he'd bought it from the two men
who'd made it. They worked at Red House Farm, Framsden. At
that time Red House was a big farm and they had carpenters and
so on of their own. A man named Mutimer was the one who owned
it first. So that will give you some idea of its age.'

Henry Mutimer's (born 1861) daughter, Mrs. Edith Fox (born
1891), remembered the drill. Her father was bailiff at Red House
Farm; she recalled his using it but could not confirm that he had
made it: 'A man always pulled the drill; and although they used
to put animals to strange uses then I don't recollect them ever
using a donkey in the shafts. I know my brother once had a
nanny-goat that pulled a little four-wheel cart. It used to amuse us
children very much.'

Joe Thompson added: 'It's a lever coulter drill built on the
same principle as the Smyth drill. A neighbour borrowed it this
spring (1968) for one of the Helmingham half-acres to sow horse-
beans as a break-crop for corn. It looks a bit of a museum-piece

[1] *F.A.V.*, pp. 36-7.

but it works as well as ever. I used to hire it out regularly to people around here at a shilling a time. I recollect one short Saturday afternoon four of us drilled an acre of wheat.[1] There were two pulling: one in the shafts of the drill, another hitched up like a trace-hoss, the third walking behind the drill to see it was running right, and the fourth raking over.

'We used the drill to sow various kinds of seed. It has three sizes of cog-wheels connecting the driving wheels to the corn-barrel—that is, three gears that controlled the rate of sowing. The greater number of cogs the slower the rate: the first wheel has fifteen cogs and sows oats, peas or beans (small horse-beans). The second wheel has twenty cogs and is used when sowing barley. The third wheel has twenty-four cogs and sows wheat and cattle-beet. The two coulters are spaced equally between the two driving wheels. In drilling cattle-beet we used only one coulter because beet is set with an eighteen-inch interval between the rows. To keep the rows even, as we came back after one run of the drill we ran the near wheel of the drill in the end coulter marks. This mark of the wheel was called the *wheeling* and it was the aim of a good driller to finish his work so the wheeling couldn't be seen.'

Joe Thompson mentioned High Row Cottages in Helmingham where he bought his drill. This was an inaccessible part of the village, some distance from the school and the main road; and in later years it was not a much sought-after place to live in. Eventually the building was demolished, and the size of the timbers that still remained on the site showed that it was originally a substantial farmhouse, like some of the neighbouring 'Halls' such as Bastings Hall. But it had long ago been converted into three cottages. 'At one time there were three tenants there called Fox, Cockerell and Gosling. And that was the only time I know that a fox laid down between a gosling and a cockerel.'

[1]*F.A.V.*, pp. 39–40.

Market Square, Norwich

13 The Norwich Drovers and the Cattle Trade

During the latter part of the nineteenth century and up to the Second World War large numbers of Irish cattle were sold at Norwich market. The cattle landed at Holyhead, Birkenhead, and Fishguard; and they came by rail to Norwich. The Irish cattle-dealers who shipped the cattle and followed them over employed local drovers to receive the cattle at Norwich. The drovers disposed the cattle, tended them until the sale-day, and when they were sold delivered them to the farmers who had bought them. Irish cattle were very popular at Norwich market because they were ideally suited for the coastal marshes in Norfolk and north Suffolk. They fattened up quickly and were ready for re-sale at Norwich within three months.

James Moore, born in Norwich in 1896, is one of the local cattle-drovers. He was employed by the Irishmen for the greater part of his working life: 'I'm known as Pinny Moore—that's what I go by. My father who was a cattle-drover too went by the same name. I recollect him taking me down to Trowse when I was a young boy to meet the cattle as they came in. Mr. O'Connor was there (he was one of the biggest of the dealers—he and Tom Rooney) and Mr. Rooney said to my father:

"Is this your boy, Pinny?"

'My dad said "Yes", and Michael O'Connor put one hand in

one pocket and the other in the other pocket and pulled out two coins. In one hand he had a shilling and in the other a gold sovereign.

"Which would you rather have?" he say.

'I remember I chose the shilling; and my father say:

"You're a bad judge, boy!"

'But I didn't know any different. I'd never seen a gold sovereign in my life, and I didn't know what it was. But I'd seen a shilling.

'I started droving with my father in 1908 or 1909. The cattle came from the ports by railway to Trowse station in Norwich. D'you know, they'd take only about fourteen hours from Holyhead? That was good going. Most of the local drovers used to be around Orford Place in Norwich at mid-week, and the Irish dealers would send telegrams, perhaps to the *Orford Arms* or another pub, telling a drover to meet so many head of cattle at Trowse station. The cattle arrived on a Thursday and before the time of their coming you'd often see a drover flourishing a telegram around Orford Place, as much as to say, "I'm fixed up". He'd just received it to tell him to meet a couple of hundred head of cattle down at Trowse.

'About thirty to thirty-five wagons of cattle would arrive at Trowse on a Thursday. We would meet them and feed them until the following Saturday. The cattle came from all over Ireland: Roscommon, Waterford, Derry, County Meath, Clonmel. Mr. Rooney, I recollect, had two places, one in County Meath and the other somewhere else. We fed the cattle wherever we could, in the paddocks by the river down at Trowse, alongside the road, too (you could in those days). Then on Saturday morning we left at 6.30 to get to the place the owner was entitled to on the market which was right by Norwich Castle in those days. Each Irishman had his allotted place for taking his cattle on the market. I remember the order they went: Mr. MacGinney, Mr. Tom Dolan, Mr. Horgan, Mr. Shanden, Mr. Michael O'Connor, Mr. Tom Bell, Mr. Cussens, Mr. Clancy, Mr. Rooney.

'We'd often drive about 1,300 cattle on a Saturday morning. They'd be going in one continuous line through the streets.

When we got to the market and the cattle were in their places the dealing would start. No Irishman had cattle in the auction sales. They sold all their cattle by private arrangement. Each dealer dealt with the farmer who wanted to make a bid for some of his cattle. But even before the farmers had come up to the market someone had probably met them at the station, because each dealer had a tout—a local man. He used to go to the station and watch the farmers coming in; and if he saw a likely one or one he knew, he used to approach him and try to get him to a pub to have a drink and talk things over. Then when he'd softened him up he would take him up to the sale and introduce him to the dealer he was touting for—on commission, of course. They would then perhaps try to get him to another pub near the market—*The Jolly Farmer* or *The Golden Ball* (George Mutter of *The Jolly Farmer* used to lodge three or four Irishmen regularly). They'd then give the farmer plenty of Scotch and try to get him so he didn't care if he was giving £24 or £25 a head for bullocks.

'The way they made a sale was very interesting. After talking for a long time, even going back to one of the pubs and then coming back again to the market, they'd begin to reach an agreement; and the farmer held out his hand: '£20!'. The dealer, if he took this price for each head of his cattle, brought his hand down and slapped the outstretched palm of the buyer. As soon as this was done the deal was over. Then up went the Irishman's hat or up went his stick with his hat on top of it, and as he twizzled it round he and his helpers shouted out: "Sold again! Sold again!"

'Each Irishman had a little way of his own. One always wore his hat covering his eyes; another always had his umbrella up, rain or shine; another would keep on spinning a coin to see if he was going to be lucky. Of course, they never made any money! I'd ask one of them: "How did you get on?" He'd say: "Bad. Bad! I lost a lot o' money. You won't be seeing me next week, Pinny. I won't be bringing anything at all!" But the next week you may find him bringing twice as many cattle as he had the week before. But it's a fact that none of them seemed to die rich. Even the big 'uns like Mr. Rooney and Mr. O'Connor didn't leave much money.

'I recollect one dealer who brought over a hundred head of Welsh runts—small, black cattle—and we were trying to sell them to a farmer. Another farmer came up to me and offered me £12 10s. But, of course, I couldn't do anything and I had to get the dealer out of the pub. I didn't think he'd let him have 'em for that price, and when I found the dealer I could see I was right: "I can't sell 'em for that," he say. We went over to the market, but the farmer wouldn't budge: he was sticking at £12 10s. Then the Irishman asked him suddenly:

"Now tell me: how many grandchildren have you got?"

"Twenty," the farmer say after he'd counted up a moment or two.

"Right," said the Irishman taking out a wad of notes, "here's a pound each for your grandchildren. And may God bless 'em!"

'And he counted out the notes into the farmer's hand. The farmer was wholly surprised: "Well, I've never met a man like you before. I haven't . . ."

"£13 10s!" the Irishman said quick.

"Right," said the farmer; and down came the hand and the deal was finished.

'Of course, it left the Irishman about £80 better off than he'd been if he'd taken the first bid.

'The big men like Mr. Rooney and Mr. O'Connor would never bring less than 200 head of cattle; and I've seen Michael O'Connor and Tom Rooney bring a 1,000 cattle between 'em. They'd have most of the wagons. Then there'd be a lot o' little men who had, say, one wagon with twenty or twenty-four cattle in it—little calves, *sucks* they used to call 'em. They made about £6, while the bullocks made £11 or £12. This was before the First World War—about 1912 I'm telling you about now.

'Mr. Tom Rooney was a fine gentleman, a religious man, a Catholic. He didn't drink and he stayed regularly at *The Royal Hotel*. He was greatly respected and the other Irishmen used to give him the touch of the cap. He used to sell cattle to Mr. Slater of Somerleyton, a fine old gentleman. I've seen the train wait for Mr. Rooney on a Sunday morning. I've run down Prince of Wales Road to Thorpe Station to tell them he'd be a bit late; and they've kept the train back for ten minutes for him. Mr. Tom MacGinney used to lodge with Mr. Grix in Red Lion Street. *Grix's Café* they used to call it. He used to have a bottle of whisky sent up to him in bed every night and he'd always have a bottle of whisky with him on the market. He weighed twenty stone, and he didn't move about much: the farmers had to come to him.

'All the second-class Irishmen stayed at the pubs; and Friday night was the drovers' night in the pubs round about the market. It was amusement night. The pubs would be full and there'd be plenty of singing and dancing, with the Irishmen joining in. Of course the drover chaps liked their drink. I remember once at Trowse a dealer had one of his bullocks queer. So he say to the drover: "Get half a bottle of whisky from Perry [the landlord of *The Pineapple*] and mix it with a drop of water and give it to that bullock." They were both in the pub at the time, and the drover got the whisky and went out to give it to the bullock. As he didn't come back the dealer went out to see what had become of him. There was the drover lying half drunk in the bullock's manger. He wondered what was happening when the dealer's stick hit him square across the back.

'Each dealer knew well the cattle he'd brought from the Irish villages. One of them used to walk round with me up at the market pointing out his bullocks: "These four belong to the policeman; these four I bought off the publican; these belong to the baker." They used to bring some good cattle from Mullingar. Meath, Mullingar and Roscommon were the main places where the Irish cattle came from. At the end of the day the cattle market closed. At 5 o'clock[1] three Corporation attendants with a policeman would turn everyone off the market; and they had to take the cattle they hadn't sold with them. The Irishmen, if they had any cattle left, used to drive them into the street; and they'd carry on bargaining with the farmers under a street lamp; and when the police came along they'd move further on to another lamp until they'd sold all their cattle. York was another big market for the Irishmen. The market there was held on a Thurs-

[1] Signalled by the market bell which is still in position.

day and they'd ship cattle from Ireland on a Monday for the York sale on a Thursday.

'Our job after the sale was over was to walk the cattle to the farmers who'd bought them; and we'd have up to 200 cattle on the road of a Sunday morning delivering so many to each farmer. We used to go out to North Walsham, South Walsham, Dereham and so on. Each drover had a certain district. I used to walk to Somerleyton and I'd perhaps deliver some cattle at Loddon and again at Haddiscoe. Mr. Slater of Somerleyton would buy a lot o' *drapes*—cows that had had two or three calves. When we drove them out they looked like a bag-o'-bones going along but they'd fatten up faster than bullocks. When we walked the cattle then, of course, all the fields alongside the roads had hedges, and there were gates everywhere. There had to be. I recollect once I was driving some cattle and I saw a gate open along the road in front of us. I ran past the cattle and closed the gate quick. The farmer could see what was happening and he came along shortly after and gave me a shilling. I had a dog for the job—and a good dog took a lot o' training. I had some trouble with a man from Brooke Hall once. A car belonging to him killed my dog as I was driving cattle one Sunday morning. There was a court-case over it; and the judge said, "The dog was essential for this man's work and was valuable." I got £10 awarded for it.

'The farmers round here used to fatten the cattle within about three months. Then they'd bring 'em back to Norwich market. There'd be a train of about 120 wagons; and the farmers were allowed at that time to ride in the *brake* at the back of the train along with the guard. They'd sell the cattle up on the market to dealers from all over England—Manchester, Sheffield, all round the north and London. They were special buyers, and the cattle would never go through the auction. Each farmer would sell his own beef.

'But the big shipments of Irish cattle more or less finished at the outbreak of the 1939 war. They couldn't get the boats to bring 'em over. A few of the big dealers got permits but the smaller men were cut out; and the whole trade went down. After the War the Irish got too clever: before, they had only one outlet for their cattle—England. But afterwards they got a wider outlet, and they sell cattle now to France and Germany and so on. They fatten the cattle themselves. If you had a thousand Irish cattle here at Norwich market tomorrow they'd sell like fire-brands, because the Irish bullock is the one bullock that does well down on the marshes near the coast.

'I'm still working at the same job. I was at Ipswich today [22.5.69], and I go off to King's Lynn tomorrow. They come and fetch me in a car. But there's no walking cattle now, of course. They're all moved by lorry.'

Mrs. Margaret Meek (born 1909) is the daughter of Jonathan Slater (1866–1941) of Somerleyton, Suffolk, son of William Slater (1841–1914), 'the old gentleman' James Moore referred to. As a young girl during the First World War she spent a lot of time with her father on and about the farm; and as she was a delicate child she did not go to school at the usual age. Although she was young she did more than accompany him around the farm; she gave him active help:

[T] 'I went everywhere with my father. I didn't start school until I was nearly eight. So whatever I did I did with him. We used to go round in a dog-cart, and he had Park Farm, Somerleyton which was good arable land, with marshes in various places where he fattened cattle during the summer. These were at Blundeston, Somerleyton, and Haddiscoe. He would sometimes buy these cattle at Norwich market on a Saturday; but I didn't go to Norwich with him so I have no memories of that. But he would meet the Irish dealers and sometimes buy cattle there. I remember chiefly the cattle coming to our local station at Somerleyton. We could meet them at Somerleyton station: they had obviously come direct from Ireland because they were often in a bad state. My memories are vague about this, but I certainly know there were deaths and there were wounds on the cattle—often. They were very fierce and had lived very poorly in Ireland. But when they were transferred to the marshes they thrived very quickly on them without any other food for most of the season. But of course to get these cattle to the marshes they had to be driven: there were no other means of transport.

'I went round with my father as a very young girl; and my father having come from Cumberland we went on living in the Cumberland style, I suppose—which was not the East Anglian style. For instance, when I was eight I went to school for the first time; and I wore clogs. I was certainly laughed at. They were a very cheap style of footwear because my father got the *clinkers* from Cumberland and the special nails, and he put the clinkers on himself. I was the laughing-stock with these clogs. But I got my own back when it was frosty because the clinkers are absolutely splendid for sliding on ice. I did go about with my father a lot and helped him with the animals; and this was considered unusual. Continuing this, actually in 1942 when we returned to Suffolk after being in Oxfordshire, it was not thought the thing at that time in the middle of the war—although there were land-girls—it was still unusual for Suffolk women to work on the stacks and so on. It was taken for granted in Cumberland that the farmer's wife worked—looked after the poultry, helped with the cows—and she had a very, very hard life indeed.

'When I was still a girl I helped in taking the cattle down to the marshes. We had a Cumberland sheep-dog always with us which we used to have sent down by train from Cumberland. I wouldn't have liked what we did then without this dog. He would know the route—which we went many times. He would go on ahead through the hedge and stand in a gap and put the cattle back on the road if they attempted to go through a gap. This was all right if the cattle were quiet. But of course they'd been in trucks and they came out very wild sometimes. And, in fact, in some cases they were crazy. On some occasions we had some terrible drives with them. I remember there was one which ran amok on the way to Haddiscoe marshes. We would put our cattle on Pettingill's Level on the Haddiscoe marshes which was a very long drive from Somerleyton through to St. Olaves. The road was very similar to what it is today: it was first through moorland and then it came into wooded country. I think this must have been during the 1914 war because they had trench practice there. There were trenches that you could stumble into where they had been having rifle practice. And one of the cattle went in once: and it was summer and there was bracken everywhere—not very nice stuff to run through. I was ill after this: it was such a terrible chase after these cattle, but it had to go on to the end; and then we had to get them to the marshes. I was in bed for some days after that chase. That was one of the worst memories.

'Having got to St. Olaves we then went over the river on that bridge to Haddiscoe; and we had to drive them by the New Cut—the waterway—where there is now a new concrete bridge that goes over the New Cut and the railway. We had to drive the cattle along this roadway by the water—between the water and the dyke—and that wasn't a very easy thing to do with a spirited pony, at least if I was driving the pony. Then we turned into the marshes, and I believe there were twenty gates to open before we got to Pettingill's Level. (I haven't been there recently but I believe there's a roadway and you can drive right up now.) But it wasn't only opening the gates: you had to be careful your cattle wouldn't get mixed up with the cattle that were already in the different stretches of marsh. Although the road makes it different today the marshes are still there, and there are members of the Pettingill family still living there as they were in my grandfather's time.

'In Somerleyton we had to ferry the cattle across the River Staithe when we brought them from the station. We sometimes had fun-and-games on the boat on those occasions. It was a flat-bottomed boat with two or three movable rails that went in front and at the back. Somebody—often myself—had to go in front of the boat, against the rails that were in position; the others would then drive the cattle into this boat and *you* had to stop them from jumping over. This was not an easy job. When they were all in the boat the rails were put across at the other side, and it went across somehow on a chain. Someone on the boat wound a handle. When the boat had reached the other bank of the river someone would lift the rails and off the cattle would go on to the other side. But many a time they jumped into the river. Of course they could swim but they had to be guided to a shallow part where they could get out and start again.

'All this happened when I was between eight and fourteen years old, because at that age I went to Norwich to school during the week and I wouldn't be doing much at week-ends then. I liked being out with my father. Labour was very scarce at that time owing to the war. Not only did I help with the cattle but I helped on the farm—rode the binder-horse and also led the wagons and the tumbrils back and forth from the harvest-field to the stack-yard. The young men were, of course, away at the war, and my brother who was twelve years older than myself was also away a good part of the time—so everybody had to lend a hand. I didn't do much milking but I helped bringing in the root-crops; and a cold job that was, throwing the beet into the cart as it came along. And I did do jobs like collecting acorns which we fed to the pigs, mixed with other things. And I also picked stones off the fields which was done in those times, stones as metalling for the roads.

'Once we got the cattle to the marshes they were looked after by the marsh-man, who often lived in a very isolated place. He would send a message to my father if there was any trouble, and away we would go to deal with it. As well as these special journeys we could go for regular inspections of the cattle—because there were troubles. Some of them would be heifers or dry cows, and they would get what I suppose we'd call mastitis today but then we called it *gargut*. If we found a cow had a very bad *quarter* [teat] what sounds a cruel practice was the only one under those conditions: the cow had to be cornered and this quarter was cut, and the pus was got out in that way. More than once I have been the one who's had to hold the cow by putting my hand in its nostrils; and I was quite a young girl but my father insisted I should do it because the cow was in pain and this was the only way of relieving it at that time.

'I also have some happy memories. The thistles had to be cut regularly which my father used to do and I would go down with him; and while he was doing this I would fish in the dyke, and later on fish with a rod in the Waveney for roach, perch and so on. We'd have a picnic. Those were very enjoyable days. Another incident: this happened when I was quite small. We went across the marsh and the dyke was rather wide for me to jump so my father would throw me across. But on one occasion I landed in the middle of the dyke! We hardly dared to go back to Mother that day because the dyke was very muddy, and I was covered. My father was also interested in wild flowers; and we were always looking for flowers and unusual birds. And—well! I didn't want to go to school when school-time came.'

William Rogers of Boundary Farm, Ilketshall St. Margaret, confirms that the Irish cattle were wild. 'They were collected from all over the country, from different places: two here, four or five there and so on. They'd never been together as a herd. They were horned cattle, too, and that didn't make things any easier.'

John Edward Page (born 1895) who worked on Boundary Farm for many years, contributed an interesting note on the Irish cattle trade:

[T] 'Owd man Sadd—Owd John Sadd we called him—who lived at the Grove Farm, Ilketshall St. Margaret, he always used to go and buy a drove of Irish cattle—this was well afore I went into the 1914–18 War—and he wouldn't buy unless they'd got the foot-and-mouth disease[1] or had had it. And they had a meadow outside of Norwich which they used to call *The Foot-and-mouth Disease Meadow*; and they used to turn the cattle on there one night or 'haps two, and then bring 'em hoom here and then take 'em up to a long shed up the top o' thet long field—the Long Meadow we used to call it—and here they used to dress these cattle with Stockholm tar and salt. Then they used to *do* [get fat, prosper] like an owd house a-burnin'—after they got over it. Thet cured 'em. Now, d'you see, they kill 'em all. That's why I argue about it. Yes, yeh; that's when I was a boy before the First World War. They wouldn't buy the cattle unless they had foot-and-mouth disease at the time or had had it before. It had to be either one of the two: it got to be along o' him. Because I remember he went up there to Norwich one Saturday and he told a neighbouring farmer, Mr. Jimmy Tibbenham, that he couldn't buy any because they hadn't got the foot-and-mouth disease and they hadn't had it.' Of course he was a proper owd-fashioned

[1] Undoubtedly a different strain of the virus from the modern one.

26. The gamekeeper

27. Suffolk sailor or fisherman, *c.* 1890. Note *whole-fall* trousers

28. Group of Suffolk malsters from the Barking-Battisford district. Burton-on Trent, *c.* 1906

29. The three Suffolk malsters and their landlady, *c.* 1901. James Knights is on the left, wearing a braided belt

farmer: he niver larned it out of a book. No fear! They put the Stockholm tar and the salt—all on the nose and all round their mouths and on their feet now where they picked up the clay. They used to dab that in there. Stockholm tar! That's nothing about thet. That's lovely stuff, ain't it? I suppose they put the salt in with it—helping. I'd like to take you to the shed where they used to put 'em. I will do if I can one of these days. We'll go down there and see the man what's on the farm—Mr. Geoffrey Murray—and we'll ast him if we can just go up there.

'When I was with Mr. Rogers's father his brother bought some cattle up there at Norwich and he couldn't stow 'em. I suppose they got dropped on him in the sale and he had to hev 'em. He made a bid and they got dropped on to him. Well, they come to Billy Rogers while I was there. And do you know it was weeks afore they'd eat beet and corn and chaff—all good food. All they'd want was water and hay. When the food got stale in the manger we used to take it out and put some fresh in. But once they did get hold of it—my word!—they done, like an . . . they did! You could stand and see 'em do! You'd never believe. (I don't know why they kill all these cattle with foot-and-mouth disease. I've been about here now—yeh, I'm seventy-four. I couldn't be above nine or ten at the time.) They came on very quickly: I had been told that they did by these owd people. And once they got a start they do like an owd house a-burnin'. They would. I can see 'em in the yard there now, when they first got there. And they wouldn't come! And thet's a rum 'un when there's all thet lovely corn and stuff and they won't come for it. It make you say suthen. Yeh. They say you can lead a horse to the water but you can't make him drink—and thet's just how it were with their food in their bins. It were!'

14 The Marshmen

The coastal marshes where the cattle were fattened illustrate an economy and a way of life that are apart from, though necessarily linked with, the arable farming of the region. The cattle were either 'walked' down to the marshes direct from market or were brought to the nearest point by train: today they are transported by motor-lorries, and in recent years a rough road has been built right across the marshes to enable lorries to have direct access. But apart from this difference and the inevitable presence of the tractor on the marshes, the marsh way of life does not appear to have been greatly affected by the recent revolution in agriculture.

This at least is the impression one gets from visiting Haddiscoe 'Island'—the 2,000-acre stretch of marsh that lies between the lower reaches of the River Waveney and the New Cut, the canal that was constructed by Samuel Morton Peto, the railway contractor who bought Somerleyton manor in 1844. The 'Island' is looked after by marshmen who are responsible for a definite area of the marsh. The Pettingill family, for instance, have been linked with the marshes for at least a hundred and fifty years; and their sector of the marsh—an area of about 430 acres—is known to farmers all over East Anglia as *Pettingill's Level*. The house where the family lives stands alone on the marsh, a short distance from the dyke on the west bank of the Waveney. Alongside the house is the ruin of an old tower windmill which once pumped water from the marsh into the river. A small electric power-house has in recent years made the windmill obsolete.

The Pettingill family live in a house that probably dates from the seventeenth century when Jan Piers Piers 'the master of the dykes' drained this part of the region. Mrs. Pettingill, the ninety-four-year-old head of the family, told me:

'This house used to be known as *The Seven-Mile House* a long time ago before our family come to live here. A man named Dowson lived here in those days. It is seven mile from Yarmouth and used to be a kind of pub or lodging house for wherry-men when the wherry traffic was the only kind on the river. There was another place farther down which is now *The Bell*, at St. Olaves. That were the same kind o' place: they called it *The Six-Mile House*.

'I was born Rose Mary Brooks at Belton on the 16th November 1876; and after I married George Edward Pettingill (1871–1928) we lived away from the Island. Then my husband's father, George Elliott Pettingill (1833–1923)—Grandfather we used to call him—was left alone on the Island, living here by himself. He was an owd man well over eighty and he wanted to end his days on the *mashes* where he'd allus been. So me and my husband come to live here with our children. We had eight boys and two girls. My husband recollect when they used to climb up the stocks to put the owd canvas sails on the mill. The trouble there was to do that when the wind was rising. They used to put the cloth on for the winter and take it off during the summer. We've got to cross the river to get to the nearest shop which is about two miles away; and in the winter when the weather is bad we're more or less cut off. So we always have to lay in stores that will last us a month or six weeks—a sack, or perhaps two, of flour, and groceries and so on. One of the worst winters we had was at the start of the last war, in 1940, when the river was frozen over for six weeks right to the end of March and there was two feet of snow. Of course, during that time we run out of flour and had to get water and groceries. Archie, my eldest boy who lived at

Haddiscoe Marshes

Belton, used to bring the groceries down to the cart-shod at the other side of the river. We got the dog and give him a couple of rope ends in his mouth and he take them across the ice. And Archie tied one of the ropes to the box of groceries and we pull it across; and then we tie the other rope to the empty box and he pull it across empty ready to fill it up again. When we got the rope tied across, Ivy my daughter, she walk across the ice to see if it hold her. She was the first to go. When you stand in the middle of the river, a hundred and twenty feet wide, and look each side of you, it's a rum 'un. You want a rope. Ivy was the first to go across. But we niver did walk across the river before or since.'

The economy of the marshes is more like Wales and the West Country than the rest of East Anglia. Grass is the only crop and the only harvest is hay. The grazing season starts in the early days of April when the cattle come down, either from the farms or direct from the local markets. The grazing season ends on the 31st October, the traditional date when the cattle are brought down from the hill pastures to the homesteads in Wales (the Celtic Hallowe'en). Leslie Harry Pettingill (born 1913), one of Mrs. Pettinghill's sons who still work on the marshes, said:

[T] 'The cattle should be all gone by 31st October. If they stay longer they make a lot o' mess and spoil the marshes for another season. If it get too wet like last season (1968) they jam all the grass up and there's no grass and feed for another year. It's a long while a-getting over it. The owners of the marshes can please theirselves when they take their cattle away, but I'm talking

148

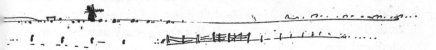

about the hirers. We look after the marshes for different owners. Mr. Slater who farms at Somerleyton; he owns up to sixty acre, Mr. Sidney Cole used to have about sixty, Mr. Carr another farmer—and so on. We charge them marshmen's fees for looking after the animals. They pay for the material for the fencing and the gates and the dykes, and we do the work. Looking after cattle means keeping an eye on 'em, getting them out of the dyke if need be. If they're ill in any way—mastitis or anything like that, or calving; if a cow calves you have to see to it and let the owner know. We are on the marshes nearly all the time during the day; and in the meantime we look after our own bit as well, getting hay off the *rands* when we can, and that sort of thing to help us out. So we do the lot together. What we keep really is enough to help get us a living. We aren't farmers in no sense: we just keep a few *things*[1] to keep a-going. It wouldn't be a living otherwise.

'We take between four and five hundred cattle during the season, an average of about one an acre. Sometimes you get small cattle and you can take more than one an acre. The cattle are a bit smaller[2] than they used to be years ago. In the winter we see to the dykes and the pumping.

'When we had sheep on the marshes they used to have the shepherd come down and look after them because they were so much trouble. Sheep allus got to be attended to: there's the flies and the foot-rot. Us boys would never eat a bit of mutton be-

[1] Animals; a word frequently used by the East Anglian farmer of the old culture. Tusser used it in the same sense.
[2] The cattle are not smaller in breed but are younger when they come down to the marshes for fattening.

149

cause we'd seen so much of the sheep. My father used to cut their feet when the shepherd wasn't there and cut them when they were fly-blown. We saw enough. We don't wany any mutton. A shepherd used to lodge here with us. Mr. Brundell come here. We haven't got many sheep here now. We had some down here for poor old Mr. Clement Gaze, and we had about a hundred and thirty down here the year afore last. But we really can't deal with sheep and cattle the same time. The sheep want too much attention. We never had many cattle in the dyke. It used to be horses that got in the dyke most. There was one got in there on one occasion we all recollect. We found him at half past six one evening and we didn't get him out till nearly one o'clock in the morning. We had to go up to St. Olaves and get Basil, another of my brothers, to come and help us. He had a motor and could show us some light. We used to have *blocks*, pulleys to haul 'em out. We'd first cut a slope down into the dyke like a ramp to get him up. But this owd horse wouldn't help himself. He'd plunge past to another part of the dyke and we had to dig another slope— it takes about an hour and a half to dig a slope through—and it got thick with fog so we had a real night of it. He were a two-year-old, a big owd farm-horse.'

The *rands*[1] (pronounced *ronds* by the Pettingill family) are an essential part of the marsh economy. They are the strips of land that lie between the natural riverbank and the artificial embankments (the dykes or river walls) which usually run parallel to it. The *rands* on the *Pettingill Level* are about sixty yards across on each side of the river. Leslie Pettingill said:

[T] 'The *deeke*[2] [dyke] was built well back to give the river some room if it overflows the banks. The *wash* of the boats has taken a good six yard of the banks—pushed the rands back—during our time. It's a good twenty feet less on this side to what it used to be; the river is getting wider. At one time wherries and a few sailing boats were the only traffic. We used the rands for hay up to the 1939–45 war. The last time we took hay was on the *Nine-Acre*

[1] O.E.; Dutch: a border or edge, brink; Icelandic, *rönd*.
[2] O.E., *dic*, properly a ditch, but it is used in East Anglia for the bank of earth thrown out of the ditch or dyke. The ditch itself was called the *deeke-holl*, or simply the *holl*.

Rand. But all the hay come down on the tide and set up against *Dashwood's Deeke.* They dropped a stick o' bombs here and two on 'em fell in the river. The bombs blew a hole eighty feet through in the bottom of the river, two big holes together. Nine feet high reeds were flattened just like a steam-roller been over 'em, the blast from the bomb, and everything levelled down for 300 yards round it. It pulled the land down, too, down for 300 yards around it. After that the rands were always flooded. Of course, we got bigger tides now than we used to have years ago in Grandfather's time. They never had no water come out of the river then. But now since they opened the bridge and increased the depth of the harbour—they dredged it and widthened it and dredged the harbour-mouth to get bigger ships in—got rid of the bar to get bigger ships in, that let the water in. That's the reason we can't git hay off the rands now. If we'd go back to the olden days and block the harbour up, there wouldn't be so much water come up here!

'We had an owd flat-bottomed boat—an owd horse-boat we used to call it; you could take a horse and cart across the river on it. It was anchored down along the dyke here. We used to cart the hay with the hoss-boat, run it up to the rands. Took it down the river. We loaded the hay straight on to the boat. We put a few planks across and pulled it on. We used to take about seventy hay-cocks on the hoss-boat at the same time. You'd see it floating in the river in the 'thirties with its load o' hay. Sometimes we had to wait till the tide come up to get it off the dyke when it was loaded right up. I don't know how she'd fare now with all these craft. There used to be a lot o' pleasure craft then, but times have altered now to what they used to be. My mother'll say there niver used to be any boats only wherries. The holiday craft— pleasure-craft, cruisers and so on—have multiplied twenty times to what they used to be.

'They used to cart manure away in the wherries and the reed, too. Nearly all the wherries are off the river now. Barges, *Billy-boys*, London barges we used to see going up and down the other river, the New Cut. But we do take a bit of rough hay off the rand even now. There's an acre of rand-grass between the mill and the house. That's where we were when you come down. We carted it—it was only cut yesterday—we been a-carting it off. That's the only way of holding it, to get it. If the wind get round to the north-west it would be all afloat tonight. You can't do anything with it then. When there's a tide you could set in here and see the water level with the wall. In the big tide in 1953 there were about three feet of water on the Island in thet year. February 2nd this year [1969], we had just as big a tide. This tide coincide with the north-west gales that blew around the Atlantic for a week, and I suppose that build the water up to such a pitch in the North Sea and it had to get out. You allus got to watch for the wind and the tide. It will leave the boats—they look as if they're out in the North Sea: you can see 'em in the distance.'

Just before one of my visits to the marshes (July 1969) there had been a succession of very bright, hot days when there had been no rain and rarely a cloud to disturb the almost tropical sunshine. But on the day of my visit the marshes were wearing their more usual apparel: the sky was grey and overcast and there was a lightish sea-mist hanging over field and dyke. As I arrived at the Pettingills' house, one of the brothers met me, but he looked preoccupied. He took me into the house and left me with his mother; and as I chatted with the old lady and her daughter, Ivy, I heard voices in the background and Ivy left us suddenly. It was one of those little crises, as Ivy told us when she returned, that frequently happen in the marshes. A north-west breeze had blown up suddenly. The brothers feared a higher tide than usual and they were concerned that the grass they'd cut the day before and was still lying on the rand would be washed down, as it is apt to be if the river rises only a little above its normal level. While this was going on and they were arranging to cart the half-made hay off the rand I talked to Mrs. Pettingill and recorded her on tape:

[T] 'This hay they're now a-getting come in for litter or any-thing they want in winter-time. Rough hay. They've done haysel; it's only this little odd bit. They grow reeds on the rands now. Reeds for thatching and the reed-merchants come and get them. The wind is the right way for the tides today, so they think when the wind comes up it will be all over the rands right up to the wall; you got to watch the weather and the tides very closely. We don't get no warnings here, you see. When they get the high tide at Yarmouth they get a warning. We get no warning here: we got to wait and see what come.'

The old lady then went on to tell me of an incident that happened on the marshes many years before. It was the day that Grandfather Pettingill fell into the *deeke*; and while she was telling me the story her daughter Ivy and Leslie, her son, came in:

[T] 'Mr. Slater, the grandfather of the present Jonathan, come down to get some sheep. He come down to get these sheep hoom. They were the last *things* to take hoom. They put them down in the *mashes* sometimes while they take the cattle away, you see: they bring some sheep. Well, he was then a-taking of them hoom and he got 'em up as far as the house. They had to *walk* them; they had to start walking them then. So he come up to the house and he said (I got a relation here from Yarmouth) and he say:

"There's one sheep missing, Mrs. Pettingill," he say.

"Well," I said, "there war'n't this morning, Mr. Slater," I said; "they were all there when the boys went round this morning."

'So he say: "Tell 'em to look when they come in."

'I say: "As soon as somebody come hoom," I said, "they'll go and look for you."

'He left and we arranged to get the sheep that was lost into the shod and they'd fetch it with the horse and cart the next morning.

'So I said to Grandfather—it was just after dinner; and Grandfather he say:

"Well, that sheep is there. It's a rum 'un," he say, "being missing since this morning," he say.

"Well," I say, "don't you goo!"

[But Grandfather, having a mind of his own, went out to look for the sheep; and in a very short time had got himself lost as well. When they missed him, Mrs. Pettingill and her relation went looking for Grandfather, without success:]

'As I say I'd an aunt here from Yarmouth, and she wanted to go hoom by the four o'clock train from Belton. She'd got to go to the station. The children were all at school except the baby I'd got at hoom, so she went. I got her over the river and she went hoom. She said:

"Send Archie," she said, "send Archie after him; send him down to see."

'We'd hunted high and low: went to the garden, down the mill—everywhere we could think of but couldn't find Grandfather. So when Archie come home I say:

"Archie, *hod*[1] on the owd mare's back," I say, "and go down and see where Grandfather is, in Slater's place," I say, "he's looking for Slater's sheep."

"Well," he say, "he won't have to look far for thet. There's one up agin the mill."

[That had gone round the windmill and the dog hadn't got it and the farmer went home without his sheep.]

"Well, he's gone somewhere," I say, "Grandfather's gone somewhere. We've looked in the river; we've looked in the garden and we can't find him nowhere."

---

[1] This word is not in the East Anglian dialect dictionaries. It means to *jog along*, the only instance of its use is cited in *The English Dialect Dictionary* from one of Robert Burns's poems.

'So Archie came and he hod on the mare's back and down to the *mashes* he goes. And when he got there he come back agin almost like lightning. He say: "Hurry up, Mother," he say, "he's nearly dead," he say. "I dragged him out, to the end of the dyke."

'It war'n't the water he got into. It was the mud. Of course it was clay and mud down there, you know. Thick! Thick! He couldn't get out and he couldn't git up. Of course he were an owd chap, over eighty. So I dragged him up against the gate. I asked him if he could ride on the mare if I tried to git him on; and he couldn't. I propped him up against the gate there.

'So when the others came home from school I went up to Mr. Fisk at the gate-house, and I say to Ivy, I say: "Don't you light the lamp till I come back." Of course we had paraffin lamps then. So I said: "Don't light the lamp;" I say, "have the candle till I come back." And so I went to Mr. Fisk; and then Mr. Pettingill was coming up against the cart-shod at the other side of the river, and one of the boys, Cyril, was with him. So we called to him:

"Hurry up," I say; "Grandfather's down here into a dyke."

'And so they had to cut a great owd sack open and they took that with them and they had the railway lamp—of course it was getting right dark. So they went off and carted him home; and they laid him down in the wash-house, and they thought he was dead. Mr. Fisk he say: "There'll be an inquest tomorrow!"

'Howsomever, they cut these leggings, you know, these buskins. He had them on. They cut them off and they got him into the other room and laid him—I'd made the bed aforehand—on the sofa there; and I say:

"Have you got the kittle of water on, Ivy?"

'She say, "Yes;" and so I say; "Make a cup o' tea."

'So she made a cup o' tea and came in with it, and he drank that and you could see a little difference in him. I say:

"Can you drink another one, Grandfather?"

'So he say [she nodded her head]; and so I gave him another one and we let him lay there for a little while. Then Mr. Fisk, afore he went home, we got him upstairs to bed. He couldn't—well, we thought he was dead. Fisk say:

"Well, that's no use. We can't send for the doctor tonight. It's getting so late!" The doctor lived right up against Yarmouth hospital, Doctor Meadows. And he came over next day and he say:

"He'll be a lot wuss afore he's better," he say.

'But howsomever, as soon as the doctor had bin, he got up. And the next morning he was out there a-mucking out the cow-shod. He warn't no more trouble after that. He used to git up of a morning and go round to see all the cattle. Him and his stick. He was tough, and a very nice owd chap. He lived many years after that. He died on 24th March 1923, just afore his ninetieth birthday.'

Just before I left that afternoon Leslie Pettingill told me: 'When we've gone it will be the end of this way of things out here. They won't get any young 'uns to stay out here on the marshes. The cattle will have to look after theirselves, I reckon.'

Part Three

The Village

❦

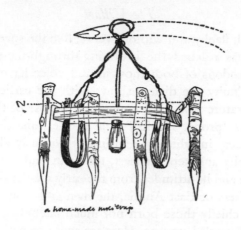

a home-made mole trap

15 *Dialect*

As the richer oral tradition is transmitted in demotic speech it is appropriate to discuss dialect as the main vehicle of oral testimony. The *Shorter Oxford English Dictionary* defines dialect as 'a variety of language arising from local peculiarities' or 'a variety of speech differing from the standard language, a provincial method of speech'. The dialect is this and very much more: it is a clear reservoir of spoken language which can enrich and purify the modern tongue. This may, at first glance, appear too large a claim to make for a form of speech that many people assume to be nothing more than slovenly English. But there is no more slovenly speech in the dialect than there is in standard English; and what advantages it has over the speech of most people today can be demonstrated by a comparison on recording tape of the speech of an East Anglian countryman, for instance, of the old, prior culture and the average, academically-educated speaker. The one is rich, virile, full of good concrete imagery and with an unconscious rhythm that—apart from an occasional unfamiliar word—makes for communication at its highest level: the other is undistinguished, already beginning to be standardized by the clichés of the mass media, and is often a medley of abstractions that has no discernible ground-base apart from the actual meaning. The comparison shows a great paradox: one is like the speech of a young man 'in his fair prime and pollen' while the other is tired

159

and battered, flabby and without verve, like the speech of an old man who has reached the breathing-through-the-mouth stage when the tendons of both thought and voice have sagged.

The continuity the dialect shows with the earliest period of English literature is in itself enough to dispose of the statement that it is not 'proper English'; and at the same time it argues that the society in which it remained vigorously alive also had that continuity and kept, at least, the main outlines of its structure, its lore and its attitudes from the early medieval period. The dialect speakers of East Anglia, the men and women of the old generation, chiefly those born not much later than 1885, spoke much of Chaucer's language. Here are some examples:

A word in the *Miller's Tale* describing Alisoun, the carpenter's wife, had a curious ring to it which I found hard to identify:

> *Fair was this yonge wyf, and there-with-al,*
> *As any wesele her body gent and smal.*

Alisoun was lithe as a weasel but how did *gent* come to mean slim which is the meaning the glossary gives for it in this context? It is clearly derived from *gignere* (to beget) and it is connected with *generosus* the medieval Latin equivalent to *gentleman*, a well-born person. But how is this derivation linked with slim? An old Suffolk neighbour, Mrs. Tom Jay of Blaxhall, gave the clue. Two years ago I called on her while she was recovering from influenza. I asked her how she was. She said she was much better but mentioned she had lost a lot of weight. Then she bent over and lifted up the hem of her skirt:

'Just look at my ankles. They're right *gentle*.'

This was Chaucer's word in its identical usage and the word was linked with the old country belief that any woman with slim ankles had *gentle* blood. I came across a similar belief in Cambridgeshire where a high instep was also thought to be a mark of breeding.

Long talks with East Anglian farm horsemen were for me real journeys into the past. In discussing their craft, the processes, the beliefs and practices connected with it, they often referred to words that are not in the local dialect dictionaries, and even when they are they have not been satisfactorily annotated. Such a word is *hayt*, given in the Chaucerian glossary as *a command or exclamation to a horse: Come up.* It occurs in the *Frere's Tale*:

> *The carter smoot and cryde, as he were wood* [mad]
> *'Hayt, Brok! hayt, Scot! what spare he for the stones?'*

But the dialect speaker shows that the word has a much more specific use; and one old Suffolk horseman has given full evidence for its early meaning. Here is a page from the notebook of William Tracey of Tattingstone: it is dated 1893.

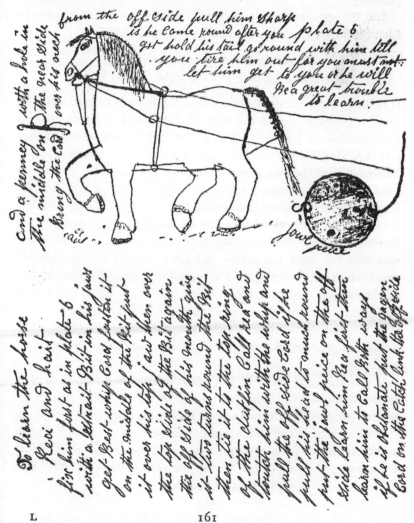

It is clear from this that *hait* means *go to the left*, and *rea* (or *ree*) *go to the right*. Chaucer's couplet is now much richer in meaning. The image is of a horse shying or stopping at the sight of some big stones in the road, and of the carter urging him to pull round them—to the left. Joseph Wright[1] relates the word hait to a Swedish dialect word *hajt*—a cry to an ox or horse to turn to the left. He also quotes the saying: *He will neither hait nor ree*. (He will go neither to the one side or the other. That is, He's a wilful person.)

Scot, it appears, was a name frequently given to a horse in Chaucer's day: the *Reeve* also had a horse so called:

> *This reve sat up-on a ful good stot,*
> *That was all pomely grey and highte [called] Scot.*

It is likely that *Scot* does not refer to the horse's origins, and the word is probably connected with the Old English *scot* or *scott*—a contribution or payment, a meaning still in use in the phrase *scot-free*. But Scot was also the name of many farmhorses in Suffolk before they went from the farm ten or fifteen years ago. One Suffolk horseman I knew had a horse called Scot and he frequently used another Chaucerian word, *wang*, meaning a molar-tooth. When he noticed that one of his horses was getting thin he first of all inspected his manger. If he saw that some of the food was still left after the horse had been treated he immediately suspected a condition known as *wang*—or *wolf-tooth*. That is, one of the horse's molar-teeth had worn to a sharp edge, and eating had been so painful to him that he would prefer to starve rather than to endure the pain of the tooth fouling his cheek. The horseman told me the cure, and he had his *tongue* in his cheek while doing so:

'I get someone to hold the horse's jaw open, either with a farrier's gag or by holding his tongue out at the other side of his mouth (or perhaps I'd put a rope round his upper jaw and sling it over a beam in the stable and get someone to hold him there), and then I file down the wang-tooth with a rasp. And I got a bucket o' water by the side o' me to stop the rasp getting red hot!' (He

[1] *The English Dialect Dictionary.*

certainly used a bucket of water but not to cool the rasp but simply to clear it of the filed pieces of tooth that still adhered to it.) 'A wang-tooth,' he went on, 'was a rum business.'

A short while after talking to the horseman the couplet from the *Reeve's Tale* came up. It refers to the two students who said they had come to the Miller of Trumpington for him to grind corn for their college bursar (or manciple); he always had his feet under the table and his teeth were always busy:

> *Our manciple, I hope he will be deed,*
> *Swa werkes ay the wanges in his heed.*

The richness and depth of the language spoken by the people of the prior society also inheres in the implements they used and which have become obsolete since the passing of the methods of farming associated with the ox and later with the horse. It would clearly be advantageous to preserve and annotate these expressions as fully as possible with the aid of the old dialect speakers who have preserved the lineaments of this long culture in such an unselfconscious way. *Trav'us* is a word they often used for the annex to the blacksmith's forge. It was here the horse was shod, and it was particularly important for a young horse to be clear away from obstacles against which he might injure himself while protesting at being shod for the first time. Many people, including myself, used to think that the word was a development of *traverse*, the partition that divides some trav'us buildings from the smithy itself. But the word undoubtedly derives from *trave*, the wooden frame-work built specially for shoeing unruly oxen or horses and trav'us was formed on the analogy of *buck'us* or *wash'us*. 'The trave (O.E. *travois*) disappeared in England[1] when plough-bullocks were no longer brought to be shod. But the term survived longer in France because bullock-traction lasted longer there. Hence Larousse, *c.* 1900, could still produce a picture of a *travail.*'[2] How much more fully can we appreciate Chaucer's image after we have heard an old horseman describing how a young

---

[1] Though there was a trave standing outside the smithy in the Suffolk village of Belstead in 1951.
[2] Personal communication from A. A. Dent.

horse reacted to his first visit to the trav'us. Chaucer is describing the same lady, Alisoun, in the *Miller's Tale*:

> *And she sprong as a colt doth in the trave.*

Another implement often used by the older East Anglian countryman was a beetle. The tool is included in the fourteenth-century compotus already mentioned (page 88): *1 batellus pro marra*, one beetle for timber. A beetle is a heavy wooden mallet with two round faces each reinforced with metal bands to stop the wood from splitting. The wood from which the head was made is usually elm in East Anglia, though George Sturt[1] preferred apple-wood or beech. The phrase beetle-headed (wooden-headed or stupid) was used by Shakespeare, and Langland in his *Piers Plowman* used the phrase beetle-browed. The image here is also taken from the wooden mallet whose main purpose was to drive iron wedges into timber in order to split it cleanly: it was used in more recent days for try-your-strength feats at country fairs or for driving in heavy tent-pegs and stakes at village fêtes. The edges of the much-used beetle-head tend to split and curl over, thus providing for a man with a pronounced superciliary ridge the ancient description beetle-browed.

There is, in fact, hardly an object linked with the old prior culture, either through the work or the home-life, that is not without some celebration either in literature or the oral tradition. A Norfolk reed-thatcher, Sam Blackburn of Salhouse, recently showed me a piece of bramble-stalk he had taken out of the roof of a thatched cottage: it was in the attic amongst the debris of former thatchings. He had previously found a similar piece in a thatched cottage. 'The owner sent it to Cambridge for dating, and they reckoned it was 400 years old.' The thatcher explained that bramble used to be employed in the old method of tying the thatch to the rafters; later they used tarred string; today he uses iron thatching-spikes or pegs which he drives firmly into the roof's timbers.

After talking with the reed-thatcher I went to visit a Suffolk neighbour, Sam Friend. I asked him about the bramble:

[1] *The Wheelwright's Shop*, Cambridge, 1963, p. 194.

'You mean a mulberry stalk.'

'Well, it looked like a bramble to me.'

'Yes, yes. We allus call blackberries mulberries. A bramble, I reckon, is the same as a mulberry.'

Then he went on to explain how he used, when he was a boy, to help a bee-keeper make his skeps. The bee-keeper made them from wheat-straw tied with mulberry stalks. He prepared the stalks, taken out of the undergrowth in winter, in this fashion:

'First he took off the thorns; then he split the stalk down the middle with a sharp knife. After he did that I used to take the pith out so you could bend and twist the stalk more easily.'

While Sam Friend was describing the process, his wife said: 'I've often been out a-mulberrying when I was a girl. We used to gather mulberries at sixpence a peck.'

It is difficult to explain why people of the old culture called blackberries mulberries. It is true that a certain species of bramble, often growing low down in a hedge, has bigger fruit than the average blackberry and that some East Anglians even today call this variety the mulberry. But it is also clear that the older generation called all kinds of blackberries of whatever size by this name. It is probable that this is another instance of the ironic subtlety of the dialect.

The mulberry was very fashionable in England during the seventeenth century. 'King James had the idea of turning the whole of England into one vast silk factory.'[1] His scheme, however, did not prosper although Cecil, James's Secretary of State, tried vigorously to promote it, bringing over from France at least a million trees each year and ordering the Lord Lieutenant of each county to announce their periodic distribution at the county town, at a cost of three farthings a plant or six shillings a hundred.[2] Some of these trees are reputed to have lasted until this century. But only people of substance would have access to the mulberry fruit. The less favoured had the bramble; and

[1] Mea Allen, *The Tradescants*, London, 1964, p. 54.
[2] Shakespeare had a mulberry tree at Stratford-on-Avon. James Boswell, in his *Life of Dr. Johnson* (A.D. 1776, Aet. 67), recorded how a local crank who owned Shakespeare's garden cut down the tree to 'vex his neighbours'. The poet Milton's mulberry tree at Stowmarket in Suffolk lasted into comparatively recent times.

it was probable that they referred to this as the mulberry because it was the poor man's fruit, free for the taking. There are a number of analogies for this kind of irony in the dialect. In Suffolk country people used to refer to the small pony or even the donkey they often used in ploughing their *yards* or allotments as *the poor man's Punch,* that is the modest counterpart of the heavy farmhorse, the *Suffolk Punch.* In south Wales, too, the ubiquitous elder was referred to as *the Welsh Vine.* This attempt at a derivation is pure conjecture but we can be sure that *mulberry* in the above sense has a long-standing link with ordinary country people for the action rhyme: *Here we go round the mulberry bush,* is real evidence. Genuine mulberries grow on trees, therefore the mulberry bush must have been a bramble.

The use of the word *yard* in the sense of a cultivated area of ground is peculiar to certain parts of Suffolk. Chaucer's description of one kind of yard was to be seen in name and in reality in the Suffolk village of Blaxhall up to twenty years ago.

> *A yerd she hadde, enclosed al aboute*
> *With stikkes, and a drye dich with-oute*
> *In which she hadde a cok, hight Chauntecleer,*
> *In al the land of crowing nas his peer.*
>
> ('The Nun's Priest's Tale')

Unfamiliar, though ancient, forms in the dialect frequently lead many into thinking that these are mishearings or slovenliness of speech; and this gives some townsmen the comfortable assurance that their speech is more correct and therefore to be preferred. Correct speech is a difficult term to define, especially today, when to be too correct is often to be pedantic—but it would be profitless to take up this issue here. What is more likely is that the old, unlettered countryman will have the more interesting speech than the townsman not because of some mystic virtue he absorbs, as it were, from the soil of his native heath but simply because he is using a form of language which is in unbroken line with an ancient tradition. Here is an instance: an East Suffolk speaker will often use the word *dead* where the Standard English speaker uses *death.* This is not because he cannot tell a noun from an adjective: it is very probable that he could not but has been spared the toil or embarrassment of making the distinction, getting on very well without it. He uses *dead* instead of *death* because it sounds right to him, as in the sentence:[1]

'It's a good job some of these book-farmers weren't a-farming fifty years ago: most of 'em would have starved themselves to *dead*'.

This form is historically correct for the dialect speaker in East Suffolk, the only district in which I have heard it.[2] *Dead* used as a noun derives from a Norse root *død* while *death* comes from the Old English *deað*. *Dead*, therefore, is more than of philological interest: it appears to be valid additional evidence of the Norse influence along the East Anglian littoral.

An East Anglian will say *yeh* instead of *yes*, not because his speech is necessarily slipshod but out of preference for the form that is at least as old and probably older than *yes*. Tindale's *Bible* has: '*Let youre ye be ye and youre naye be naye*', a usage that gives the dialect speaker some support—if he needed it—for persisting in saying *yeh*. It has been said that the real and natural life of a language is in its dialect; and even the villages today, much battered as they have been by the repeated assaults of the new culture, still remain reservoirs (admittedly not as full to over-flowing as they once were) of the old replenishing culture.

Another province of the dialect which has potential interest for the folk-life or history student is the varying names given to farming equipment. These differ even in one county or district. The curved bars of wood or metal which fit between the roll and the body of a horse collar and take the pull of the traces are re-ferred to in some districts of East Anglia as *hames* (Low German *hams*; Dutch *haam*). In other districts the bars are known as *sales*. This is the older native word and appears as *seles* or *selys* in fourteenth-century East Anglian farm documents,[3] and has been spelt variously as *sales* or *seals*. The word comes from the O.E. *saelan*, to fasten with a cord; and the old farm horseman in Suffolk

[1] *H.I.F.*, p. 49; also see p. 266.
[2] Joseph Wright lists Scotland and Ireland and at least eight other English counties where *dead* is thus used.
[3] See p. 34.

tied or lashed the top of the *sales* together with a leather thong—
his *top-latch* or *lash*. It might be possible through plotting the
differing terms for this piece of horse equipment in the counties
of East Anglia to show a pattern; but it would have to be done
very quickly before the older generation of horsemen has gone
completely.

Frequent references have been made to the aid the dialect can
give to a student of English literature. The East Anglian dialect
is full of echoes, often unrecognized, of some of our earliest
literature. But the whole temper of the speech of a good dialect
speaker, his concrete, tactile imagery arising mainly from his
powers of acute observation; his expressive diction that has not
been blunted by an attempt to handle imperfectly apprehended
concepts; his instinctive feeling for words, formed by long oral
usage, recapture some of the best periods in English literature.
And a sympathetic, though not sentimental listener, has the feeling
that here is some of the speech of Chaucer, of Spenser, of Shakespeare, of Tusser and of Clare kept wonderfully alive right into the
twentieth century. But language does not exist in a vacuum; as
already suggested, the old language or dialect in East Anglia has
persisted because the material culture that was its matrix lasted
in comparatively unchanged form until the first quarter of this
century. It was based on the historical work of East Anglia—
arable farming—and while animal- and man-power remained the
chief motive force of that farming its structure and its cultural
ambience remained intact. But once the character of the work
changed, as it did with the coming of the tractor and the motor-
car, the character of rural society (and it is not an exaggeration to
say the *millennial* character) also changed in a revolutionary way
within a couple of generations.

'Our language thinks for us': with no one is this more true
than with a survivor of the old culture; and once these old people
have gone it will not be easy to recapture this correspondence
between speech and its underlying attitudes or to compare
language with that of a much earlier period; although some of the
temper of the period and a great deal of the speech itself will be
preserved in the recordings already made on tape. Yet as Sir

George Stapledon pointed out,[1] once the old material culture has
been displaced both in the actual farming and in the memory of
men themselves, students of English literature will have practically no points of reference to some of the richest provinces of
their heritage; and this lack will decrease their understanding of it
and diminish their enjoyment.

One of John Clare's lesser known poems, 'The Mole-Catcher',
will illustrate this point:

> *When melted snow leaves bare the black-green rings,*
> *And grass begins in freshening hues to shoot,*
> *When thawing dirt to shoes of ploughmen clings,*
> *And silk-haired moles get liberty to root,*
> *An ancient man goes plodding round the fields*
> *Which solitude seems claiming as her own,*
> *Wrapt in greatcoat that from a tempest shields,*
> *Patched thick with every colour but its own.*
>
> *With spud and traps and horsehair string supplied,*
> *He potters out to seek each fresh made hill;*
> *Pricking the greensward where they love to hide,*
> *He sets his treacherous snares, resolved to kill;*
> *And on the willow sticks bent to the grass,*
> *That such as touched jerk up in bouncing springs,*
> *Soon as the little hermit tries to pass,*
> *His little carcass on the gibbet hings.*

The true understanding of this poem and an appreciation of its
imagery presupposes a knowledge of the technique of the old
mole-catcher. But how did he catch moles—here in East Anglia
as well as in Clare's country in the East Midlands? He first made
the trap himself, out of wire or horse-hair and a rather crude
looking wooden framework. He took this trap with him into
the field and dug out a place for it in the mole-run: into this he

---

[1] 'Yet children born today in the towns cannot enjoy our great heritage of
English literature because its background amid the countryside is quite outside
their experience. With industrial towns we have sacrificed a great part of our
traditional poetry.' *Human Ecology*, edited by Robert Waller. *The Soil Assocn.*, 1968,
pp. 157–8.

fitted the trap, covering it up with soil but leaving a loop of wire or horse-hair showing above the surface. He used a *spud*, a small chisel-like spade to dig out the hole. He next took a willow- or hazel-rod, about four feet long, and thrust it firmly into the ground near the buried trap. Finally, he bent over the pliable rod until it engaged in the loop of wire to form a spring arch. The mechanism of the trap was so arranged that when the mole passed through the run he would disturb a little toggle of wood that held the sprung rod. It immediately straightened up, at the same time drawing taut the wire or hair below and holding the mole in it, trapped—in Clare's accurate image—as on a gibbet or gallows. Old countrymen, who knew how to make these traps, used them in recent years in East Anglia in preference to the later steel traps: the mole was killed immediately by the quick release of the sprung rod and the old home-made traps were easier to manage in the field. A mole-catcher could set a dozen of them in a particular field and from the bent or upright rods he could tell at a glance which traps had been sprung, and which were still undisturbed.

No one is able to speak with more conviction and authority about the language used by the people of the prior culture in East Anglia than the novelist Adrian Bell. His well-known trilogy[1] was written out of the impact made on him by his coming to the Suffolk farmlands fifty years ago and, as a farm apprentice, working with and listening to farm-workers whose language was a kind of revelation to him:

'I went out into the field with them, hoeing. But they took little notice of me and just went on talking one to another, talking all the time while they *singled* the young seedlings with their bright hoes. To them I was an incompetent lad, quite uneducated in their sense, hardly knowing one end of the hoe from the other. But I listened to them and I was amazed. Here they were speaking in a language I knew of but had not heard, nor even imagined could still be heard. I'd just come from four years in a public school; but no one there had told me that the language that was the real glory of English literature was still being used in the field by unlettered men like these.

[1] See *Bibliography*.

'About this time, when I first started as a farm-apprentice, I had to go out horse-hoeing, taking a horse carefully between the rows of tender young plants; and this is how one of the farm-men instructed me:

"You lead that mare as slowly as ever foot can fall." '

That short sentence had the mark, rhythm, and the substance of the old culture, as Adrian Bell recognized when he first heard it. It was tied firmly to the reality the farm-workers knew; it was concrete and clear because it was so full of the ordinary images of everyday life made wonderfully alive; it was the language of Shakespeare. Indeed, the phrase *as softly as foot can fall* occurs in *As You Like It*;[1] but the old horseman had probably not heard of Shakespeare. The consonance of the two phrases was due to his language and Shakespeare's having a common source. Adrian Bell gradually became aware of the provenance of the old farm-worker's language and this gave him the keenest sense of enlightenment and a corroboration of its worth: 'It was a privilege to me to listen to these men, to understand the true perception they had gained from a close regarding of the things they knew, and to admire their ability to give apt and concise expression to what they knew. I could say that I didn't begin my true education until I had this privilege of listening to the powers of expression of Suffolk farm-men who had left school when they were twelve years of age.'

John Bunyan had gone to the same source when he wrote *The Pilgrim's Progress*. *The Authorized Version* gave him the inspiration, and its language confirmed him in his instinct that the tongue he knew, the language of ordinary country living, was there to his pen. It was familiar; it was plain: he used it and did not falter.

Bunyan, closely following *The Authorized Version*, was one of the last to use this language directly and memorably; for during his lifetime the dominant consciousness, essentially medieval and undifferentiated, had changed. A divided society had as its reflex a divided consciousness, emphasized on one side by the class that was nourishing the ideas and experiments of the new science.[2]

---

[1] III, ii.
[2] Christopher Hill: *Intellectual Origins of the English Revolution*, Oxford, 1965, chapter 2.

A different consciousness clothed itself in a new pattern of language; and already by the beginning of the eighteenth century Dean Swift was satirizing the old 'homespun' language in his essay *Genteel and Ingenious Conversation*. By the end of this century the new idiom had so far advanced, with Dr. Johnson as the protagonist, for an American lady to remark after a coach journey with him to Oxford, 'The gentleman talks like an essay.' Dr. Johnson was himself a battleground between the old language and the new idiom. His first and natural thought: '*It* [a stage comedy] *has not wit enough to keep it sweet*,' became, '*It has not vitality enough to preserve it from putrefaction*.[1]' On the whole, *putrefaction, etc.* has held the day ever since, with the old language going underground and being kept alive in the dialect.

A quotation from one of Mrs. Leavis's essays adds another viewpoint to the discussion:

'The dialect, whether in its undiluted form as spoken by old Joseph or in modified forms such as Zillah's, Hareton's, and others, is full of life, not only in idiom but in intonation and vocabulary, above all notable for the independent and sensible attitudes it expresses so forcefully. The common people's speech here is so much more lively in general than that of the educated (just as in Scott) that it makes one feel there is some justice in Max Muller's dictum that "The real and natural life of language is its dialects".[2]

[1] Boswell's *The Life of Dr. Johnson* (*A.D.* 1784, Aetat. 75).
[2] Q. D. Leavis, *A Fresh Approach to Wuthering Heights* (Appendix), in *Lectures in America* F. R. and Q. D. Leavis, London, 1969.

reaper: Blythburgh

16 The Dialect and the Old Culture

In the last chapter an attempt was made to illustrate the uses of the dialect to the student of history, English literature and language. It was also implied that attention—particularly at this time—is due to it out of the simple consideration of local or regional piety. Yet it is probable that the most important reason for studying the dialect *now* is not among these. I write *probable* because it depends on whether the hypothesis put forward in recent years by Benjamin Whorf[1] and other American linguists is true or not. This hypothesis holds that the study of language has the potential to help 'initiate this Copernican revolution which . . .' as Claude Levi-Strauss writes, 'will consist of interpreting society as a whole in terms of a theory of communication.'[2] What the new studies in linguistics and anthropology appear to suggest is that all language has a masked or unconscious element below its obvious, expressed and universally recognized uses; and this unconscious pattern of language, by reflecting the structure of the society in which a man lives, does much of his thinking for him. And apart from this, the recent work of Noam Chomsky of the Massachusetts Institute of Technology has given a new importance to the study of language beyond that hitherto assumed.

[1] *Language, Thought and Reality*, Massachusetts, 1964.
[2] *Structural Anthropology*, New York, 1963, p. 83.

If this is so, the oral tradition and the taking of oral evidence assumes a new fundamental importance in a culture such as East Anglia's which has changed so quickly within the last two generations. Up to the present in taking evidence of past social conditions we have naturally paid most attention to the content of what our informants told us—chiefly the social conditions they had experienced and their reaction to them. Although, for my part, I was also interested in the actual speech, as outlined in the last chapter, it was chiefly in the words themselves and not particularly in the form or shape of the language. As the balance in the previous chapters shows, *what* an informant said took precedence over *how* he said it. But in the light of this new hypothesis increasing value will be placed by linguists and by anthropologists or students of folk-life on the *form* of a man's testimony. They will do this if only to test the hypothesis that the unconscious element in a man's speech will, to a certain extent at least, mirror the actual assumptions of the culture in which he lives.

It would be as well to define the word culture at this point. I quote from a symposium[1] which discusses the hypothesis put forward here: it answers the question, 'what does culture include?':

'A good statement of it makes culture "all those historically created designs for living, explicit and implicit, rational and irrational and non-rational which exist at any given time as potential guides for the behaviour of men." From this standpoint culture constitutes the set of the modes of procedure or the guides to living which are dominant in a group.' Claude Levi-Strauss gives an alternative definition: 'By culture, we mean the relationships that the members of a given civilization have with the external world; and by society, we mean more especially the relations men have with each other. Culture produces organization: ploughing the land, building houses, manufacturing objects etc.'[2]

It is obvious that the old East Anglian rural community which broke up at the beginning of this century had by either of these

[1] *Language, Thought and Culture*, edited by Paul Henle, University of Michigan, 1965, p. 2.
[2] G. Charbonnier, *Conversations with Levi-Strauss*, London, 1969, p. 40.

definitions sufficient claim to be considered a culture separate from the present one in this region. At one level just discussed—the vocabulary of the old horse-farming culture, if we can so call it—changes in the culture have already affected the language. But it is a fact, and by no means a newly discovered one that the structure of language reflects in some degree the culture of which it is a part. Early written language suggests this. For instance early Latin texts consist of short gnomic utterances: short, simple sentences, placed side by side, each a unit without any connecting particle. Each unit is a short link in a chain of meaning but each unit is disparate, being joined to its fellows by no 'physical' coupling. This early writing is analogous to the *pointilliste* style of painting where the eye of the observer builds up immediately and automatically a series of dots or islands of colour to form a continuous living line, just as the listener to the simple 'biblical' statements constructs the sense from the various but contiguous *points* of meaning. The grammarians used to call this the *paratactic* style where parataxis implies the arrangement of short sentences side by side: the sequence and the sense, owing to the very proximity of the statements, were self-evident.

In a people who are at the simple, undeveloped stage of their material culture there is a direct correspondence between this culture and their paratactic form of speaking and writing. At this stage, each separate activity of each member of the group is meaningful to the other; for example, preparation for the hunt, the ritual to ensure its success, the various tasks allocated in the hunt itself. Its meaning, the composite sense of the group activity, flows directly and automatically from the various separate activities themselves.

But at a more developed stage, a greater diversity of function has been reached. Society has become more complicated, and such polarities as slave-freeman, priest-layman, and later town-country arise. In addition, with the group's expansion in size there are necessarily separate *places* of labour as well as a finer *division* of labour. Then a more complex style of written language evolves—the *hypotactic* or syntactic where syntax implies a connected system of sentences built up into a characteristic *periodic* structure. It is as if language itself unconsciously mirrors the new complexity of the culture, recognizing the necessity of bringing together, of knitting its various units into a meaningful structure or sequence; just as within society a fragmentation and division of function demands inevitably a compensating binding together by administration and government.

It would perhaps be theoretically possible to postulate the steps from the simple gnomic writings of the early Romans to the full Ciceronian period and to relate it to the development of Rome from primitive Latium to the late Republic or early Empire. This, however, would no doubt be an impractical exercise because of the relative paucity of the earlier writings; but at least there would be no difficulty in the later centuries. There would be a strong argument here for stating that the full rhetoric of the Ciceronian period, the intricate and finely balanced Latin sentence could not have evolved anywhere but in a sophisticated and highly-organized culture that was marching to the founding of an Empire. Its periods rolled on with the assurance of breakers curling repeatedly in the same beautiful rounded ending[1] as they fell in ordered rhythm on to the shore. But this did not last for long. The culture of the later Empire was even less conducive to ordered rhythm than that of the Republic, and the rather uneasy rhythms of a Tacitus came nearer to the norm. Something similar happened in eighteenth-century England where in a new Augustan age Gibbon was a kind of English Cicero, building the model of a new prose. Like Cicero, too, he preceded the opening up of the state from a nation into an empire; and after him came a loosening and denigration of the tight classical rotundity which was heralded by Blake and pursued vigorously by the later Romantics.

But if it is permissible to compare small with large, there appears to be, much nearer home, a clear instance of the correspondence between language and the structure of the society that used it. This is between the old prior culture in East Anglia and the dialect which was the sole language of the ordinary country people. To them the dialect was an extra tool: it enabled them to do their work. They kept their ancient vocabulary because at

---

[1] E.g., *esse videatur*.

their level society had kept its ancient techniques: in most areas of East Anglia up to the end of the last century the farmer ploughed, reaped and harvested with men and animals as he had always done since the beginning of history. The names of the tools had remained the same for centuries, and social relations within this arable farming culture remained largely the same over a similar period. Although the old subsistence farming had been superseded centuries before by farming for the market and emphasis on producing and marketing a cash-crop (wool), the old subsistence ideal lived on, and the full force of the Industrial Revolution did not reach East Anglia until the present century when the self-propelled machines changed the nature of farming completely. In thus changing the nature of the work it made a large sector of the old language truly archaic.

All, or nearly all, of the old terms connected with the pre-machine farming in the region are no longer used and are already incomprehensible to the younger generation who have never seen a team of horses ploughing in an actual field. These are hames- or hem-gear, thill- or fill-gear; ploughing a-breast, at length, or overwart (athwart), pommel-tree, whipple-tree, middle-stead or middlestree, taking up the brew (brow), fleet, gove or goaf, bark-sele, barley-sele[1]—and dozens more in farming itself and in the numerous crafts and skills that have become obsolete now that the old horse-power farming has almost completely disappeared. In so far as the passing of the old pre-tractor economy has caused a great change in vocabulary, with a corresponding loss of many of the ancient words, this is a negative proof of the thesis that change in culture causes a change in language. But can it also be said that the form of the language itself has changed or is likely to change? As has been suggested, in the old prior culture the language of the ordinary unlettered people in East Anglia was singularly concrete, free of most abstractions. They would, for instance, rarely talk of early summer but of beet-singling time or haysel; and autumn would be Michaelmas-time, or sowing of winter-corn. Just as an old lady once remarked to me when I showed her some healthy-looking apples: 'Those apples will keep

---

[1] *Haysel* will remain.

till apples come again.' She avoided the abstract phrase *till next season* as though by instinct, preferring also to keep—again by instinct—her sentence's pleasing rhythm. The old dialect speakers relate all states or qualities to objects or persons; and this concreteness gives the dialect a poetic quality that is full of images which capture and hold the interest of the listener. After recording dozens of dialect speakers over the last thirteen years I have noticed that there is a distinct difference between the oldest generation now living—the men and women born between 1880 and 1890—and the later generation that came to manhood during the First World War. The language has lost a great deal of its tactile nature, and on the whole is much more ordinary and correspondingly less easy to listen to. This, I think, is because the younger generation have to some degree ceased to use the images that a listener finds so easy to translate and give visual form to as he concentrates on what the speaker describes.

There is another reason why the dialect, the language of the old community, is likely to change. It will lose a large area of its common ground with farming through the dramatic fall in the numbers of workers employed; and since the farm and the sectors of life connected with it were the main nourishers of the dialect it is bound to become in some measure attenuated. Again, the new farm-worker is much more of an individualist than his grandfather. On a two-hundred-acre farm he is often the sole employee. He and the farmer do all the work between them. He is on his own for most of the day and during his break periods he has no chance to talk with his fellows in barn or stable as did the farmworkers of a generation ago. The oral tradition and therefore its vehicle the dialect are bound to be the sufferers. Already the tradition of the old pre-machine farming is incomprehensible to the new generation of farm-workers about whom the older workers complain: 'They won't listen, and you can't tell them nawthen.'

There is, however, strong evidence for claiming that with the change in the social structure that is accompanying the new farming the language used by people in the rural communities is bound to alter in a more fundamental way than merely a change in the vocabulary. This is only a tentative analysis. There is little evidence for thinking such changes are happening. But the argument would not be worth putting forward if there were not strong grounds for believing that the language of the old prior culture in East Anglia had already a direct relation with the organization of rural society, with the many unspoken assumptions that kept that society together. It is suggested that as the relations within the newly-evolving community change, reflections of the change will permeate the language itself.

But in what way did the language of the prior culture in East Anglia reflect the organization within the culture itself? The following analysis is put forward as a provisional explanation of a peculiar use of language among the rural people of Suffolk. It is an aspect of the dialect that for many years struck me as being out of the ordinary. At the same time I had the feeling that it was in some way connected with the peculiar social conditions that obtained in many East Anglian villages (especially in the closed villages). But it was a feeling that obstinately refused to coalesce around anything that might be recognized as a fact. Then in recent years a reading of the new hypothesis of a close relation between language and social structure suggested a possible explanation. But here is the peculiar use of language noticed independently by a Suffolk farmer, Charles Kindred; and the fact that it had also been noticed by a Suffolk native emboldened me to look for an explanation:

[T] 'One of the things I've noticed is the funny little habit among farm-men of expressing themselves when they want to describe an opinion of theirs or rather when they want to *state* an opinion of theirs. They never do it *directly* but nearly always in terms of an imaginary conversation. They seem to be rather reluctant to commit themselves straight out. They say, *I said*, though obviously they haven't had any conversation on this topic. They are declaring an opinion of something but they like to include a third party somehow or other. This is a curiosity of Suffolk expression—of verbal expression—I've noticed for years and years. Very occasionally they'll say: "I should [have] said", but not very often.'

I have many examples on tape of the trick of language the farmer mentions: an intrusive *I said*[1] in a direct narrative where there is no question of reported speech. *I said* here is not logical because it is obvious that the speaker did not *say*: it is clear that the phrase is unconscious. But by postulating that it is unconscious one does not deny it a purpose. It is suggested that its purpose is to take the immediacy, the *pressure* out of the statement or opinion. The speaker, by including *I said*, is making the unconscious assumption that even now he is not fully committed: he has pushed or eased what he has stated slightly away from a *direct* statement. It is virtually a kind of masked *oratio obliqua*: it is as if the speaker is hedging and refusing to come out with a definite statement for which he can be held responsible. *I said* implies: 'You understand, I thought so at the time but I am still reserving a statement of what I now think.' This unconscious device is like introducing a third person—a rhetorical figment—into a dialogue; and it reminds one of the trick of speech I have come across more than once among the old community in East Anglia. This is when a speaker refers to himself or herself by name as though he or she were a third person, usually in a semi-jocular or even angry way. For instance, Mrs. L. says: 'Oh no! Mrs. L. is not going to do thet! Mrs. L. won't be there!' It is as if anger or a detached irony has induced the speaker to talk about herself as though she were someone else.

But the unconscious *I said* of the dialect speaker is not very different from the device of ascription used by some writers. Suppose, for instance, a writer does not want to declare an opinion as his own, by a half-conscious trick of the pen he will shift it on to a fictitious third person. He will write: '*A thoughtful man* may not believe this is the right course to take,' when in fact what he really means is: '*I* do not think it is the right course to take, but I don't want to get the reader's back up by saying so in so many words.' A writer or a public speaker will often, too, use a form of humorous ascription by which he neatly side-steps the charge that he has fathered a dismal cliché; that is, he safely uses it at one remove by imputing it to someone else, for example:

[1] See page 212.

'They forced it to *a damn'd near thing* as the Duke of Wellington said on a well-known occasion.' Or he will merely write, *as they say*, implying that *I* do not say it: 'The owner of the business was at the end of his tether, as they say.' Again, a writer or speaker will often prefer to use the boring and repetitive *one* rather than the more lively and personal *you* because it is safer, being in the third person at one remove away from the reader or listener. But, although in their form these devices of ascription are not very different from the dialect speaker's mannerism, their motivation is very different: in the one it is calculating and sophisticated and at most only half-conscious; in the other it appears to be entirely unconscious.

The Suffolk farmer also described another attitude which is relevant to the above:

[T] 'Then there's a dislike of being questioned. I don't think it's resentment exactly so much as a reluctance to come down definitely and make any kind of overt stand—unless they know you very well indeed. They won't do that. They'll shuffle and hedge. And that's not through any weakness of character or indecision on their part. I don't quite know what it stems from. They are very cagey and not at all eager to let anyone else know their business, especially if they have a bit of good fortune. They'll conceal that at all costs. I suppose that's the attitude of the peasant, really. When he gets a little bit of something—well! I include myself here. I'm a peasant! and I think you're frightened of tempting fate if you've got something good or had a bit of luck. Or on the other hand, the landlord may get to know about it and stick the rent up. That would be a lot worse!

'We do—all of us I think, Suffolk people, I mean farm-people— we shun the direct approach always. We hardly ever ask the direct question. Indeed, I loathe being asked the direct question, even now still. I've had people ask me: "Where do you come from?" That always annoys me somehow or other. I don't see why I should let them know where I come from. I know it's irrational but I usually give them a wrong answer if they do that. Well, I don't know, some of it may be courtesy. If one doesn't put the direct question, that gives the interviewee a chance to shuffle a bit without losing face. Old Charlie S.: he came here to work when I was three years old. He still works here, not very much, but he still comes and every year since I should think about 1938 he has borrowed my scythe, this little scythe; he's borrowed my scythe and my scythe-rub which is a little smooth-gritted carborundum. And he always asks first for the carborundum. He'll come up here when the nettles start getting knee-high. I know perfectly well what's he's coming for. He'll come round the shed there and say: "I suppose you ain't got an owd carborundum, Charlie?" He knows perfectly well I've got it. He knows perfectly well he can have it. You don't ever say: "Can I borrow your scythe and carborundum?" He always wants to give you the chance to refuse without . . . well, awkwardness, I suppose. That's what it is.

'He'd never ask a question. You'd never lay yourself open. At least I never did. I was never brought up to. One thing you avoided was the direct question. You found out things all right but you had to do it slowly and do it by watching more often than not; and then if you did ask a question finally when you were pretty sure of the answer anyway, you'd say: "I suppose that isn't so-and-so and so-and-so?" You'd never say: "Is it so-and-so?" '

Also related to this characteristic reluctance to come down un-equivocally to the committed judgement is the use by members of the old culture in East Anglia of the dialect word *fare* (O.E. *faran*, to go). This was, and still is to a certain extent, a very common word rich in associations and idiomatic usages; but one of its most interesting uses is in easing a statement slightly off the irrevocable as in: 'I fare (or incline) to think you've made a mistake, bor.' or 'You don't fare to hev any luck with the weather.' Allied with this and confirming the Suffolk farmer's observations about the direct question are the expressions an old Suffolk farm-worker will use if he does not want to answer a direct question: 'I don't fare to recollect anything about thet,' or, 'Thet were afore ma time.'

Linked with this also is another peculiarity of oral communication, not confined to East Anglia but particularly noticeable here among the old community because it is the rule rather than the exception: *A* relates to *B* an incident that has happened in the village and in which *A* himself may have been involved. *A* is pretty sure that *B* knows something about it; but in conversation *B* will assume ignorance of it and would even deny knowledge of it if he is tackled about it (which is unlikely to happen for the reasons already stated). *A* makes no judgement about it as he would do the same himself in the same situation. It is the convention in this social context and is not remarked on. It is the attitude of extreme caution, the semblance—but only the semblance—of minding one's own business, that was built into social relations in many East Anglian villages: it was the uneasiness of making an overt statement in public with the likelihood of its being brought home to you in circumstances that are directly to your disadvantage. Behind it was the attitude or frame of mind that had been sensitized by generations of intense social insecurity, of naked exposure to power that in the small world of the village was absolute. The evidence that this caution was bred *in* and *because* of the social structure in the villages is in my view inescapable; some of it is included in the previous chapters. But it can be repeated here that in the conditions obtaining at the end of the last century and for a great part of this—of a farming depression, unemployment, lack of an effective union, the evil of the tied cottage—did not contribute to free, untrammelled oral communication within the village itself: 'You had to be some careful what you said or else your words would catch up on you.' This caution is symbolized by the injunction sometimes heard in the villages, 'Keep it *squat* (secret)', and the people of the old community could not be blamed for this attitude. Their social environment had stamped it on them indelibly. Yet this pattern of caution must be very much older than the last century, for if the above hypothesis has any weight at all it is discernible not only in the content of their speech but in the very structure of the speech itself.

There appears to be some evidence that the social structure in an arable farming area, as opposed to a pastoral area, was inherently hierarchical. The ground has to be prepared, the crops have to be sown—often in a critical few days—and then they have to be waited on, harrowed, weeded, and watched and then harvested. Before mechanization all this was impossible without a disciplined body of men, especially at harvest-time. And some of this structure lasted well into this century and could be seen in the careful organization of the horsemen or ploughmen on the bigger farms. As well as their churches the Normans appear to have left their military imprint on the farming of the region. For they were unquestionably soldiers first and farmers second; and they demanded of farmers in an apportioned area that, in addition to producing enough to keep the population of the area, they should produce enough surplus to keep an armed knight and his entourage—squire, page, at least two horses, harness and equipment—ready for service in the field. One historian[1] has estimated that it took ten plough-teams to produce the equivalent value needed to keep one knight and his party operational. This military stamp remained in the arable areas in the pyramid structure of landlord or squire, farmer, farm-foreman, horsemen and day-men. In some areas the Industrial Revolution broke up this rigid structure or at least modified it by creating a side-effect to the establishment of an industry. Farm-workers had alternative employment on their doorstep, and many moved into the town, thus causing an improvement in working conditions and wages on the farms. But in so far as no large industrial complexes developed in the area during the nineteenth century, the Industrial Revolution by-passed East Anglia and offered no conveniently-placed industries to compete for the available labour. The result was that throughout the nineteenth century wages in Norfolk and Suffolk were lower than many other parts of England; and even today, according to a recent Government report,[2] the general level of wages has remained below the national average. Undoubtedly this is a factor that has contributed to the late survival in East Anglia of a social atmosphere that could justifiably be described as 'feudal'.

[1] Lynn White, Jr., *Medieval Technology and Social Change*, p. 29.
[2] *East Anglia, A Study*, East Anglia Economic Planning Council (1968), H.M.S.O. See also: *East Anglia; A Region Survey*, E. Anglia Consultative Committee (1968). *East Anglia; A Regional Appraisal*, E. Anglia Consultative Committee (1969).

That, at least, was the first impression I gained after moving into Suffolk; and twenty years' living there has done little to modify it. At that time I was reading Ivan Turgeniev's *A Sportsman's Sketches*,[1] and I was struck by the similarity between the social attitudes and the responses of the people he was describing and those of the people of the old culture I was meeting in Suffolk. A great deal of this social atmosphere would not be easy to describe, and could not be attempted in a small space. Turgeniev attains his telling effect by writing discursively about a hunter who had moved around the country visiting various communities, apparently in search of sport. He avoided tackling his real theme—the state of the peasantry—head on, and his most vital comments are unsaid and remain as a muted but clearly-heard undersong to his stories. Occasionally, however, he does make a direct comment, and the following is one of them: it appears to confirm the special speech mannerism (discussed above) that people of the old culture sometimes used in East Anglia. He is discussing the taciturnity of the peasants and the difficulty to get through to them; then he makes this qualification:

'... but I have noticed that some peasants, when things are going really badly, speak out unusually calmly and coldly to every passing "master" on the subject that is close to their heart, just as if they were talking about someone else's problem—save that they may occasionally shrug a shoulder or suddenly drop their eyes.'

The question was raised above whether or not the speech pattern will change and reflect the new attitudes now that there has been a technical and—at least on the surface—a social revolution in the East Anglian countryside. As suggested, the dialect has lost much of its character by the shedding of the working vocabulary of the old culture; but it is unlikely that the ingrained speech habits will change as quickly. Some of them will probably die out with the survivors and some will still remain. For although theoretically there has been a reorientation of power within the region it has not yet made itself fully effective. It is true that the

[1] Recently published under a different title: *Sketches from a Hunter's Album*, Penguin Classics, 1967.

old landowner class has, by and large, ceased to have the great
power it had at the beginning of the century: they would not
be able to act as high-handedly as they once did. Their real
power has been diminished and public opinion is able to act as
a brake on the misuse of the power that still remains to them.
Yet a great deal of their former influence remains by the persistence of the structure, out of a kind of social inertia, long after
much of its reality has disappeared.

This tendency is assisted by two factors. First, the regard for
status shown by the 'new men' who are moving out into the
country from the towns—businessmen, professional men, and
retired military men who are attracted to the old social hierarchy
and hope there will be a place for them inside it. They are able
to enhance their own status by saying, as they often do: 'I was
talking to Lord So-and-So last night, and he . . . etc., etc.' Attitudes such as the ones implied in this remark though imponderable
are in fact real bricks helping to shore up a tumbling edifice.
Again, the scarcity of voluntary administrators in a rural area,
where only moneyed or leisured people can afford to spend up
to two days a week in local government work, ensures that the
power structure here will remain as it has always done unless it is
drastically reorganized as the Maud Report appears to propose.
Certainly local government is not democratic in East Anglia: only
very rarely is a wage-earner able to serve on either a county or a
rural district council. Where he does he is enabled (paradoxically)
to serve because his wages are made up by the big industrial
firm for which he works. By the nature of their jobs farm-
workers or small farmers are debarred from serving on these
two bodies. This is not to deny the ability or the integrity of
many of the voluntary administrators in the country districts.
They have given and do give years of dedicated service. But a
large proportion of them are retired military men and parsons
and inevitably perpetuate the old effete social structure in the
countryside, causing the frustration that arises from the working
of a system that functions not as it appears to do on the surface or
as one would imagine it to do from a scrutiny of its formal rules,
but largely through a masked or unseen dynamic which is the

most important single factor in all council deliberations either open or unspoken.

But the farm-worker is insulated against much of the treatment he had formerly, simply because he is in greater demand; and if a man is a good one a farmer knows that he cannot afford to lose him. Here is a description by a present-day East Anglian farmer of his relation with two of his men:

[T] 'You take Leslie who works here . . . you give him an order—well, in fact you won't give him an order; you'll make a suggestion more than give an order, all the time. You don't order a farm-hand to do anything; you tell him *you want to have him do* so-and-so. And, "*Mm, well, oh . . . mm,*" that's the response you get, "That'll be a rum job—'ont it?" In a case like George who's older than myself, more knowledgeable: give him an order about what you want him to do and if he doesn't agree he says: "That I aren't!"—"I won't bloody well turn 'em out there," if you tell him to turn the cows out somewhere, perhaps a little bit too soon, or the wind is up. You know they got this phobia about turning cattle out in a wind for the first time. "That I bloody aren't!" he'll say.'

17 Place-Names

Place-names offer another good example both of the age of the oral tradition and of its use in a scholarly discipline. They also illustrate how the survivors of the old rural culture are the unknowing though accurate carriers of a tradition which has remained, from this evidence, unchanged for centuries. This may seem a strange claim because it is notorious that popular interpretations of place-names are often ludicrous and show nothing except the creative imagination of country people who appear to have a built-in onomastic faculty and can invent explanations for names that would defy any poet's attempts at their improvement. But this skill only operates when they come to *think* about a particular place-name: where they use the name in a matter-of-fact way in their ordinary daily commerce they are in a sense transmitting true history and no fabrication.

Dr. Reaney, the place-name expert, once said: 'If you want the most interesting pronunciation of a particular place-name, the one that's nearest to the root meaning of the name, go to the ordinary villager whose family has lived in the village for generations.' There are many East Anglian place-names that illustrate this thesis. Here are a few. The village of Nayland on the Suffolk–Essex border is pronounced nowadays as it is written; but the survivors of the old culture in that area call it *Neiland* to rhyme with *island*. In fact the name denotes an island (it is on the River

188

Stour) and was written *Eilanda* in Domesday Book, O.E. *egland*—island, or river land.[1] 'The *N* has been carried over from the dative of the definite article: *atten Eilande* became *atte Neilande.*'

Another Suffolk village illustrates the same principle. This is Witnesham just north of Ipswich. Most people call it Witne*sham*, the last syllable of the name being pronounced as in Masham. But Percy Wilson, the wheelwright and carpenter who has lived in the village all his life and whose family had lived there for many years before him, always pronounces the name Witnes-*ham*. He does this meticulously, making *ham* a separate syllable. And his pronunciation, were it not so natural and unassuming, would seem a pedantic illustration of the roots of the place-name: *Wittin's HĀM*—the homestead or village of Wittin which is a diminutive form of Witta who was probably the founder of the original Anglo-Saxon settlement.

Groton, a village in West Suffolk, is another example. This village also illustrates what happened to names and words that were taken to America from East Anglia in the sixteenth and seventeenth centuries. The word or name has changed in this country while its old form is frequently preserved in the U.S.A. Today this village is usually pronounced with a long vowel in its first syllable: Grōton. But the older generation in the district used to call it Grŏton; and members of the Winthrop family returning from the United States have expressed surprise that the village their forebears emigrated from should be called anything but Grŏton. The element is *grot* (O.E.) meaning a particle; *sandgrot* is a grain of sand, and the name is probably derived from the O.E. *Groton -ea*, sandy stream.

In Norfolk the village of Smallburgh offers another example. The first element in the name is pronounced today, almost inevitably as being synonymous with little, and it immediately invites a fanciful derivation. But, here again, the pronunciation of the old dialect speakers[2] in the district could immediately correct it. They call it *Smaalburgh* which is very near the root meaning of the name: Domesday *Smaleberga*, the *bearg* (O.E. bank or mound)

---

[1] E. Ekwall, *Dictionary of English Place-Names.*
[2] Personal communication from Geoffrey Taylor, Yarmouth.

on the river Smāle which is the old name of the present river Ant.

But there are a number of interesting place-names in villages, the names for instance of farmhouses or hamlets that rarely figure in standard dictionaries. They are worth investigating, for even a wrong or fanciful derivation has sometimes drawn into its net a piece of authentic history. There is such an example in the Suffolk village of Creeting. A farmhouse on the edge of the village is called *Hungercut Hall*. It appears that its original name was *Hundred Court Hall*; and local evidence seems to support it as there is a legend that a moot used to be held at the nearby cross-roads. This junction is overlooking Bosmere (O.E. Bosa's Lake), a natural stretch of water which probably gave its name to the old Hundred of Bosmere. The element *mere* (lake) often appears to be synonymous with *meare* a boundary, not necessarily because of any etymological connection but probably because constant water-supply such as a lake or pond, in a dry area like East Anglia, was shared by neighbouring units—parishes or hundreds —and to save dispute local boundaries abutted on the mere.[1] Therefore the derivation *Hundred Court* is eminently reasonable.

But some of the older local people will have none of it. They say: 'The name is *Hungergut*; and when a long time ago they had a plague in Needham Market (a nearby town) they shut them all up inside the place to stop it spreading. And they brought food to the parish boundary just near the farm there and left it. Then all the hungry-guts came from Needham to get it. It stands to reason that the right name for the farm is *Hungergut Hall*!' Reason will stand for the seventeenth-century plague in the town, and it is well-documented, but it will hardly stand for much more. Linked with inventive derivations like this are the ironic names given to local spots or hamlets in a parish: these, too, show accretions of history contemporary to the time of their naming. Instances are the calling of outlandish parts of a parish[2] *Van Dieman's Land* or *Botany Bay*. I myself remember an instance of this mythopoeic naming in south Wales during the 'thirties.

[1] David Dymond (*East Anglian Studies*, Cambridge, 1968, p. 25) has drawn attention to Rymer Point in West Suffolk. This is the site of a shrunken mere where nine parish boundaries converge.

[2] *A.F.C.H.*, p. 204.

About the time Mussolini was making his questionable imperial experiments in Africa the depression in the industrial areas had at last spurred the Government to action. They founded the Land Settlement Association[1] which proceeded to set up small-holdings in various parts of Britain. In the south Wales valleys some miners were given holdings away from the valleys up in the hills. A group of these between the Aberdare and the Rhondda valleys was referred to, inevitably, as *Abyssinia*.

Mention of Wales prompts an observation which though not connected with the theme of this book is worth making because it is relevant to the study of place-names. This is the occurrence in East Anglia of names with Celtic roots and it is probable that there are many more than are listed: Ekwall's derivation of the element *Bran* from O.E. *brōm* (broom) in such names as Bran-caster and Brandon, is far from being proved and it could well be the Celtic element *bryn* (hill) or *bran* (crow or raven); and Yare, the name of the East Anglian river, which he derives either from the Celtic *gair* or *ger* or *garan*, a crane, is more likely to come from *garw* rough, referring to the river's once comparatively turbulent estuary. But the Celtic roots are not confined to place- and river-names in East Anglia. It is perhaps a little ironic that the name of the nearest approach to rock in Suffolk—crag—is a Celtic word *creag* in Gaelic, *craig* in modern Welsh. Although the mass of shelly sand which is crag is not a true rock, the corraline crag which occurs between the Stour and the Alde hardens after exposure to the air and is usable as a building stone as in Chillesford and Wantisden churches. Not very long ago crag used to be called by its recognizable Celtic name; a Suffolk farmer, J. G. Cooper, gave evidence before a *Select Committee on Agricultural Customs* in 1866,[2] and in answer to a question concerning marling of the land in south-east Suffolk towards Orford he replied: "That is a neighbourhood I know very little of; I have understood that the farmers in that district cart a good deal of loam and *craig*.'

There is also an old farm tool which is typically East Anglian but whose name has a Celtic root. This is the *crome*—the fork

[1] Sir Arthur Richmond, *Another 60 Years*, London, 1965, chapter X.
[2] *British Parliamentary Papers*, 1866, vi, p. 84.

with bent or crooked tines. It was known to Tusser by that name, and is occasionally used today to rake manure out of a tumbril, and we still hear its old name *muck-crome*; I have used one in recent months to rake deep-rooted weeds like twitch- or spear-grass out of a garden. *Crom* is the Welsh for crooked as in *cromlech* and as it is in the Gaelic *caschrom*, the crooked foot or breast-plough.

Earsham Church

18 The Church

Much of the oral testimony circulating in a village under the old culture was in the form of stories. Many of these appear on the surface to be negligible, but it is often worthwhile noting and investigating them if this is possible; or just waiting—perhaps a more rewarding practice—until an explanation turns up. Even the most fantastic story sometimes has relevance to the village's history. An example is the story of the donkey grazing on the church roof at Long Itchingham, Warwickshire. It was a well-known one in the village in spite of the unlikelihood of its being true. For how could anyone looking at the church's steep, pitched roof believe it was not a fantasy? Yet a local historian[1] traced the story to its roots and found it to be true. The church was being restored and some of the villagers who had long noticed the crop of grass that had been growing on its flat roof thought it was a pity to let the crop waste. They therefore decided to give a donkey a free run of it. Ropes and tackle were conveniently at hand, and one morning the people of Long Itchingham stared in amazement as a donkey looked down at them from the top of the church. The incident was worth recording in itself but it also

[1] Archibald Payne, *Portrait of a Parish*, Roundwood Press, 1968, p. 153.

served to fix the date—sometime in the 1860's—when the church exchanged its flat roof for a pitched one.

Stories like this also emphasize an aspect of the old culture that is often neglected in the more formal accounts of village history. This is the sense of fun and the persistent retailing of an incident out of which a laugh can be rung. To record these stories in East Anglia is not to imply that this part of England was particularly *merrie:* for the majority of people it appears to have been exactly otherwise—at least during the past couple of centuries. But it was probably just for this reason that the amusing, the bizarre or the exciting incident was seized on, cherished and retailed, claiming for itself like ordinary gossip a therapeutic importance—something to fill in and lighten the long dreary hours of routine work. As many people of the old culture have told me: 'At that time o' day there were few amusements: you had to make your own fun.'

It is natural that the church should be the centre of many of these stories because down the centuries it has been the main focus of village life. Many stories concern the sidesmen or *questmen*[1] who kept the congregation alert and in order in those days when many were reluctant listeners who would much rather have been elsewhere. I first heard about the office in the village of Blaxhall where the parish clerk[2] had a *wand* or long stick for keeping unruly boys in order during Sunday school. But in some East Anglia villages the questman with his wand was kept busy during most ordinary services. He was called the *waker-up*. This was during the period when most churches still retained the old box-pews with doors separating them from the central aisle, a useful device to prevent draughts in an unheated building. In the early days a good deal of activity went on under cover of the box-pews, as readers of Pepys will know. But in East Anglia, as far back as memory extends, the main extra-spiritual activity appears to have been sleeping as the name waker-up implies. It was his job to keep an eye on the congregation from some vantage point in the rear; and if during the sermon someone's head started to nod he sidled up quietly, leaned over and tapped the sleeper on the shoulder with his wand or long cane.

[1] W. E. Tate, *The Parish Chest*, Cambridge, 1951.   [2] *A.F.C.H.*, p. 132.

On one occasion in a church in the Stowmarket area of Suffolk the waker-up inadvertently caused a commotion in the middle of a sermon. He noticed a man whose chin was on his chest and who was miles away from the sermon. How far away he was the waker-up revealed when he tapped him on the shoulder. He shot up out of the pew like a rocket and bawled out: 'Haughley! Haughley! Change for Finningham, Mellis . . . and all stations to Norwich,' before he realized where he was. In his more active hours he was a porter at the nearby railway junction. In the same district the waker-up nearly got into a fight with a man who resented the indignity of being *tapped* when he was virtuously listening to the sermon. It turned out that the waker-up had not been to blame: 'Some mischieful boys had hit him on the shoulder with an apple-core.'

The Torlesse manuscript[1] from Stoke-by-Nayland in Suffolk describes the pews in the church at the beginning of last century: 'The pews were high and lined with green baize. They lent themselves to various quiet amusements during services, and the mouseholes in the corner were a great source of interest and pleasure. The pews were appropriated to the different families and were looked upon as private property. Naturally, that of the squire was the most impressive. It had a large table in the middle in addition to a fireplace. When the squire thought that the sermon had lasted long enough, he poked the fire. If the hint were not sufficient he rattled the door-handle. "Twenty minutes is long enough for one gentleman to keep another," was the verdict on the length of the sermons. The rest of the congregation did not consider they had sufficient value if the sermon was under three-quarters of an hour. Two questmen walked up and down the aisles during the sermon, carrying long wands with which to wake the sleepers.'

The Unitarian meeting house (built 1699) at Ipswich has many examples of well-appointed box-pews. The original pews were symbolically aligned as they are in many Quaker meeting houses, facing inwards to form a square in order to enhance the feeling of a

[1] Frances Torlesse, born 1839, daughter of Charles Martin Torlesse, curate and rector of Stoke-by-Nayland for fitfy-eight years. *Reminiscences* transcribed by her cousin, Susan Liveing.

corporate and 'equal' worship. There are family pews in the corners of the meeting house with seats on three and even four sides; and in one or two small stools on which children could stand to look over the high pew while they were singing hymns. In some pews in the galleries there were a few wig-holders, small wooden pegs on which to hang wigs, taken off for comfort during hot weather.

The stories concerning church pews and benches lead to a consideration of their place in the Church's development. In the early church the congregation either stood or knelt but there were, it

unitarian Chapel, Ipswich

seems, stone wall-seats in some churches. They were built into the side-walls and were used by old or infirm people, which use is said to have given rise to the saying, *The weakest go to the wall*. The placing of benches in the nave came much later;[1] 'it is certain that benches in our [Suffolk] churches were rare before the end of the fourteenth century and it was not until the fifteenth century that they became common.' The evolution of the church benches and pews from the fifteenth century onwards is a natural reflection of the changes that were much more wide-spread than the church itself; and the continuing division of the church-nave into bench-spaces and pews was a symbol of a new system that was growing out of the communal social order of the Middle Ages. A glimpse of what this division tended to and to what it reached at its climax has already

[1] H. Munro Cautley, *Suffolk Churches and their Treasures*, Ipswich, 1954, pp. 149–64.

been given in the excerpt from the Torlesse manuscript. But no-where is this more clear than in a seventeenth-century book (actually written down from 1700–06), Richard Gough's *History of Myddle*[1] (Shropshire). Gough chose quite naturally to write about his native parish on a plan that shows dramatically the structure of the post-medieval social order. After giving a general account of the parish in the orthodox manner of the local historian he devotes a whole section to *Observations Concerning The Seats In Myddle And The Familys To Which They Belong*. He gives a plan of the seating of the parish church as it was in 1700 and writes about the occupants of each pew as he knew them. He first gives a definition: 'A Peiw is a certain place in church incompassed with wainscott, or some other thing, for several persons to sitt in togeather.' At that time the pews were in the holding of the occupiers of the various farms and tenements in the parish; and in the same way as the ownership of a farm or property was not identified by bricks and mortar but the title-deeds or documents which constitute in law the title to the land, Gough's definition shows that it was the actual area in the church not the wooden structure that was implied by the word pew. As a later definition shows the pew was not loosely linked to the farm or dwelling house in the village: 'A seat, or the prioryty in a seat, may bee claimed by prescription, at common Law and action upon the case lyes for it at common law. If a man sell a dwelling-house with the appurtenances, the seate in church passes by the word appurtenances.'

It is instructive to observe how far this fragmentation of the church nave was removed from the communal ideal of the Middle Ages. The same tendency had already altered the dwelling house. Instead of the open hall type of dwelling where most of the house-hold lived and slept in one big room or hall the house became more and more compartmented. Most of the old halls—*open* from ground to roof—were *ceiled*, a floor was inserted and private rooms and *upstairs* sleeping chambers became the fashion. This in itself was no doubt a commendable development, even if only from the stand-point of hygiene, but it was also a part of the movement away from communal living and a counterpart of the early enclosure move-

Centaur Press, 1968. With an Introduction by W. G. Hoskins.

ment whereby a man ceased to be a *champion* or open-field farmer, tilling the land in common with the community in which he lived, but instead became an individual farmer, farming in *severalty*, that is on his own separate holding. He was a new pattern of man who was heralding a new era. The idea of individual property in land and the break-up of the medieval commonweal of producers was undoubtedly necessary and inevitable. The Tudor enclosures and the rise of the great individualists, the wool *entrepreneurs*, broke up the shell of the system that that had become almost innocent of its old ideal. The new men—uncouth and uninviting as many of them undoubtedly were—were needed. They enclosed the land and the same impetus led them to embrace and alter the Church. The Reformation was both their stimulus and their justification. As individualists they wanted direct communion with God without the mediation of priest or Church, though they recognized that the temporal Church was part of God's plan. But they would worship only on their own terms; and one of them was separate pews in the church for themselves and their families. Their ideas of property were, in fact, whole and very logical: having divided the land they proceeded to divide the nave of the church as though by their taking of the idea of private property to the very threshold of the kingdom of heaven they could thereby sanctify it for all time.

The oral tradition gives plenty of evidence that in the long run it did the Church great harm and helped to estrange many of her best sons. For the dividing of the church into *closes* was an affront against the symbolism of the church fabric (a very real symbolism) and gave the lie to the spiritual profession of the Church as one family under God. The pews themselves, in spite of the beauty of many of them, are as much an affront to the architecture of the church as they are to its spirit. They clutter up the base of the columns in the nave and aisles like irrelevant undergrowth crowding round the roots of a once noble avenue of trees. It is impossible to see a church's true interior proportions when its nave is full of fixed pews; and the examples of churches which are altogether or even partially free of these—Thaxted in Essex and Blythburgh in Suffolk—show how an unencumbered nave enhances the church's form. It acquires a sense of uncrowded space which lightens the atmosphere and at the same time suggests the organic fluidity that is the mark of a healthy community.

Although the sense of property in church pews has lessened, the dead hand of the old order still remains in many country churches in East Anglia. A country rector, Canon H. K. Florance of Stradbroke in Suffolk, told me that in his church the best places in the nave are still nominally reserved, through a kind of prescriptive right, for the successive occupants of certain houses or farms in the parish. These may seldom attend, but when they do the churchwardens always try to put them into the pew with which their property goes. It sometimes happens that they cannot do this, for the person who has previously occupied the house or farm continues to occupy the pew. The new occupants are, accordingly, put into a nearby pew that happens to be vacant. The nave is thus reserved mainly for those who have some kind of business, professional or property qualification. The cottager or council-house dweller keeps strictly to the side-aisles or the back of the nave. So thorough has the conditioning process been over the years that they truly 'know their places' and are loth to change them. 'I have sometimes discussed this with members of my parochial church council and have tried to point out how anachronistic is this old precedence in seating; but I don't seem to make much headway.'

A sincere parish priest would naturally wish to change the old order of seating because he is bound to be aware of how vulnerable the church—any church—is to the charge that its structure is merely the reflection of the dominant social order. And in many country districts the old social order—mainly it is true through a kind of inertia—still gives its imprint to the structure of the church; and still gives emphasis to those aspects of church doctrine which, as the cynics imply, are merely a projection into heaven of that form of government that our betters would wish for us on earth: an omnipotent authoritarian presiding over a host of complaisant and properly accoutred villagers—some more properly accoutred than others.

These, the natural assumptions of the old rural governing class, still alive in residual form, induce one to sympathize with the puritans whose revolt was as much a social as a religious one; and a discussion of religion with ordinary country people has confirmed my belief that, in the main, the proliferation of sects was not due primarily to differences in doctrine or dogma but to the differences in class and social groupings. In this respect it is significant that here in Britain, where there has been a greater movement towards an egalitarian society in recent years, the discussion towards forming a universal or general Church should become possible only now after there exists a better social basis for realizing it.

Village tradition is able to give many examples of the intimate link between the social hierarchy and religion, and to demonstrate in the end—materially, at least—which was the more powerful. Here is one of them. John Tollemache of Helmingham got into conflict with the incumbent who held the living, John Charles Ryle an evangelical priest with strong puritan leanings: he was a big muscular man—captain of the Oxford cricket XI for three seasons and also a rowing blue—and he was at least as strong minded as the squire himself. Ryle adorned the nave of Helmingham church with coloured gothic texts—some of which still remain—and it is clear there was a dispute over doctrine between the two men, a difference that probably had its confirmation if not its origin in the different social strata they had each sprung from: Tollemache the landed aristocrat and Ryle, the son of a wealthy Cheshire banker who had failed. But whatever were the underlying reasons the dispute came to a climax over the length of Ryle's sermons: 'Why they quarrelled is not known but, I suspect, that the length of Ryle's discourses had something to do with it. Tollemache would stand up in his pew and hold his watch in his hand if he thought the sermon was too long.' J. C. Ryle moved to Stradbroke in the same county, and after a drastic restoration of the church there, threw out the old Jacobean pulpit, had a new one installed and caused the following text to be carved on its ledge so that the officiating priest could not but see the legend:

Woe unto me if I preach not the Gospel

But even this was not sufficient for Ryle; and on one occasion when he had doubts about the strength of the injunction he had taken out his pocket-knife and underscored *not* with a deeply incised line.

J. C. Ryle left Stradbroke in 1880 and was shortly afterwards made the first Bishop of Liverpool.

Other gleanings from village tradition relating to the church could be included under the heading folklore. The first is the tradition among the older generation of country people in East Anglia that presence at a Confirmation ceremony when the Bishop visited the church was a good cure for rheumatism. Men, and old women especially, who suffered from this complaint made a practice of repeated attendance at Confirmation ceremonies in the hope of relief if not an outright cure.

Blythburgh

The other concerns the children's custom of visiting the parish priest on Valentine's Day and singing him a traditional Valentine song. Sister Emma of All-Hallows Convent at Ditchingham in Norfolk was born at Tuddenham St. Mary in Suffolk in 1882. She remembers as a child walking through the snow to sing at Tuddenham Rectory on St. Valentine's day. 'The Rector had a big bag of pennies, and he gave us a penny each out of his bag. One of the songs we sang was *Good Morrow to your Valentine.*' Sister Emma's song is a version of the one recorded in Essex at the end of the last century:[1]

> *Good morning to your valentine;*
> *Curl your locks as I do mine,*
> *Two before and two behind,*
> *Good morning to your valentine.*

> *I only come but once a year,*
> *Pray give me some money as I stand here,*
> *A piece of cake or a glass of wine,*
> *Good morning to your valentine.*

Apparently, too, it was the custom in East Anglia on this day to leave small presents on someone's doorstep, to ring the bell violently and then run away.

But the singing custom was well established in the region during the eighteenth century. James Woodforde, the Norfolk parson, recorded his Valentine gifts over many years. His first entry on Valentine's Day was in 1777:

'Feb. 14 To 36 Children being Valentine's Day and which is customary in these parts this day gave o. 3. o, being one penny piece to each of them.'

The numbers coming to Parson Woodforde for their pennies increased over the years, and by 1795 he had to be more selective:

'Feb. 14 This being Valentine's Day gave to Children that were under 14 years and could speak at one penny to each, 56 in Number, o. 4. 8.'

But, in spite of the introduction of this new principle, by 1799 he had 'a great Number of Young Visitants', in fact a record and his bag was lighter by 76 pennies or 6s 4d.

---

[1] *Old English Customs*, P. H. Ditchfield, London, 1896, pp. 55–6.

Helmingham school house

19 The School

The oral testimony of the oldest generation of country people now living can do a great deal to fill in some of the earlier stages in the development of State education. They can, moreover, testify to the differences in country schools, depending on whether the village was a rich one or a poor one. For most schools in the country were *National* or Church schools; and although these schools had been Government assisted since the foundation of the *National Society* in 1811, voluntary assistance played a great part in the founding and running of a school, and it often contributed twice as much money to the school's upkeep as that obtained from Government grant. If a village was a closed one, having a well-disposed squire, the school was likely to be a good one, well maintained and usually well staffed. Such a village is Helmingham in Suffolk where John Tollemache founded a school in 1853. He built the school at his own expense; and he—and later his family—contributed generously to its upkeep until the county council took it over. There were two sections to Helmingham School at its foundation: the Upper School and the Lower School. The distinction was not an academic one. The Upper School was for the sons of farmers and tradesmen or professional men: the Lower was for the children of the farm-workers. The Upper School had places for twenty boarders during its first years, but the number of boarders trailed off after the foundation of Albert College, Framlingham in 1865. Pupils in the two sections of the school used separate entrances. It is certain that J. C. Ryle, who held the living at Helmingham from 1844 to 1861 had a great influence—chiefly through John Tollemache's wife—in determining the dual nature of the school. Here again his actions conform to the picture of the seventeenth-century Puritan: his segregation or dividing off of the chosen, the *Elect*, from the mass; and his quarrel with the squire (mirrored in John Tollemache's remark, already recorded, about not wanting the *middle sort* in his village) appears as a late recrudescence of the classical conflict between the emergent middle class and the old landed aristocracy. This seems to be confirmed by what happened after Ryle went to Stradbroke. There was no dominant squire in that village and he more or less had his head. In 1863 he set up the National or Church School at a cost of £1,300, but he also attached to it a private school which he called *The Middle School*. He got the money from this venture from private subscribers like Sir Edward Kerrison. The Middle School was part of the National School and the Trust that Ryle formed paid for a classroom in the building. In the playground was an iron fence dividing the area used by the *Middle* (boys only) from that used by the *National* pupils. The Stradbroke schools have long since been taken over by the county council. But there is still a rather embarrassing sequel to the old venture: the East Suffolk County Council still pay to the Trust a pound a year as ground rent for the old Middle School which they took over.

Much of the following chapter comes from men and women who went to Helmingham school at the end of last century or the beginning of this: it can be judged against the accounts from men and women from schools in open villages where voluntary subscription was not as generous and as regular. In many respects the closed village of the mid-nineteenth century in East Anglia was like the medieval manor: no one was likely to starve as long as he remained under the Lord's protection, but freedom, where there was complete economic dependence, was little more than a legal fiction.

Dan Pilgrim was born in June 1882 and started school at

Easter 1887. He remembers his first school-room where he sat in the infants' *gallery* or raised platform. He was a very bright pupil; yet, although the 1880 Act compelled school authorities to enforce attendance up to the age of fourteen, Dan Pilgrim left two or three years before he reached this age. His leaving was quite legal as he had passed an examination and had been given a Labour Certificate testifying that he had reached the required standard of education. The Labour Certificate legislation of 1876 arose out of the difficulties experienced in many areas: they are typified by what happened in East Anglia. The 1870 Education Act had given the Government powers to compel local authorities to build schools and enforce attendance; but social conditions were weighted against the Act, especially in rural areas. By 1880 in East Anglia an acute farming depression had started, and it lasted with brief intermissions until 1914. This meant that farmers more than ever wanted cheap child-labour, and parents were in no position to refuse. For most of the farm-workers were day-men, that is they were paid by the day; and often in the winter season they took home only three or four days' wages. As their full week's wage at this period was ten shillings (and even nine in some districts) families were often in real need of food and clothing; and any money the children could earn would help to buttress the starvation wages. Therefore, children had to work with or without permission during school hours and out of school hours as well; and they left school at the first opportunity.

The schoolmaster was under pressure from two sides—parents and employers; and as some of the employers, the landowners and farmers, were also school managers the pressure was acute. The Labour Certificate appears to have been an attempt at a compromise and to have continued in operation after the 1880 Act; but for the schoolmaster of the time it meant that he lost most of his brightest children almost as soon as they began to show academic progress. They sat the examination and were away. I have found that the most vocal and intelligent of my informants in the oldest generation were men and women who had passed the Labour Certificate examination and had left school at the age of eleven or twelve. Henceforward they were committed to a culture

that was almost entirely oral because few of them read to any extent
or used their writing ability after they left school; and perhaps this
accounts for the fullness of their memories, trained unconsciously
to forgo a reliance on written or printed aids, and for their outstanding skill in clothing these memories in spare and vivid

No. 350

FORM 146 (a).

EAST SUFFOLK COUNTY EDUCATION COMMITTEE.

LABOUR CERTIFICATE No. 1 (for Total Exemption after 12 years of age).

I Certify that *Annie May Moyes*

residing at *Ashfield.*

Age.

is not less than **TWELVE** years of age, having been born on the
22nd day of *April*, 1900, as appears by the Registrar's
Certificate [or the Statutory Declaration] now produced to me, and has
received a Certificate from *G. H. Grindrod Esq.*

Proficiency.

one of His Majesty's Inspectors of Schools, that he (or she) has
reached the **FIFTH STANDARD.**

Dated this *31st* day of *March* 1913.

Edwd Wilson.

Chief Attendance Officer.

EDUCATION OFFICE,
COUNTY HALL,
IPSWICH.

language. Whether this is true or not, it does not affect the question
of their intelligence and I have often been struck by the wastage
of educational potential—if one can use a modern phrase in this
context—represented by these early leavers.

Henry Orchard, the Helmingham schoolmaster at the end of the
last century, appears to have been well aware of this although the

circumstances prevented him from being able to do much about it. But he tried as well as he could to prevent the younger children from being exploited.[1] Charles Stewart Thompson (born 1883) succeeded Henry Orchard as headmaster of Helmingham school in 1915; and he recalls that during his first year as headmaster a group of children sat for the Labour Certificate and none passed. The schools' inspector who came from the town to examine them agreed with him that it was 'a jolly good job' that no one had been successful. But by this time social conditions had changed slightly for the better: it is certain that farm jobs were no longer as scarce with so many of the young men away in the armed forces. The jobs too became better paid and the farm-worker was given at least a temporary charter in the Corn Production Act of 1917—a time when Fordson tractors were being imported from America to help step up food production in order to beat the German submarine menace. It is a strange modern paradox that awareness of the social conditions of the mass of the people and a concern for their education appear to come to Governments only when the country goes to war and that their most decisive actions towards improvement are taken when the fortunes of the country are at their lowest.

It is true that some of the boys who left school early returned for *evening classes*; but few appear to have persisted in the rural areas. There was not the same inducement to pursue further education in the country districts as there was in the towns. But there is evidence that in the 1890's there was a real desire among older men to acquire the basic skills of reading and writing that their sons had been taught in the schools. Dan Pilgrim recalls:

'I went to night school after I left school. I attended for three or four years and I won four or five prizes there. They gave me a game of draughts once, I remember. The school was held in the Mission Hall at Helmingham. I had to help teach my father to read and write so he could go there. He took a farm and he wanted to learn to read and so on. Forty to fifty old people used to go to the Mission Hall at that time o' day. It used to be full. Half the old people at that time couldn't read nor write their own name.'

[1] *F.A.V.*, pp. 54–60.

It was because of this that *Penny Readings* were popular in the country districts and also, probably, because of a scarcity of reading material. The following letter relating to these readings was found in a Suffolk horse stud-book and had a horse-pedigree on the back of the letter:

Framlingham,
20th Sept., 1881

Dear Sir,

I am requested to ask you to attend a Meeting to be held at the Crown and Anchor Hotel on Friday evening next at 8 o'clock for the purpose of forming a committee to arrange for a series of Penny Readings to be held during the coming Winter months.

Yours truly,
Edw. Maulden

The readings were of the kind popularized by Dickens and belonged to the period of the Working Men's Institutes and of the Victorian ideal of a controlled enlightenment of the masses. They were so called from the price of admission to the reading.

Arthur W. Welton (born 1884) also helped to teach his grandfather. He had gone to school at Blaxhall where he paid twopence a week, and a penny for the slate and a halfpenny for a pencil: 'When my mother had got the money we went, and when she hadn't we didn't go.' Later, when he was about fourteen, he moved to another Suffolk village a few miles away.

[T] 'I can remember the time right well. I was living with my grandparents at Benhall. My grandfather was John Edwards, *Owd England*; my father, John Welton, married his daugher in 1855. She was called Hannah Edwards and was my mother. I reckon Owd England was born around about 1830. Anyhow he was getting very old when I knew him as a young lad but he thought he would like to write his name. He wanted to write his name. So I writ it down for him and he copied it; and after a bit he started to write so he could make out his own name. That was over seventy year ago. I remember him well. He was rather a big man. He couldn't get down to trim his feet. I used to cut his corns. Many a time I cut his corns and his toenails. Yes, and I learned him to write his own name; and he could read a little as well.'

As already suggested the living conditions of the school children varied from village to village. William Spalding, a stallion leader (born 1896), knew some of the worst:

[T] 'There were nine of us and we had a very hard time to get enough food to live. We had to work very hard after tea, after we come home from school, doing various jobs like carting wood and so on. I had no boots in them days. And I know what it was like to fling a crust of bread and dripp'n' away one day and go looking for it the next because I was so hungry. I was often hungry. And I used to pick the oats out of the bowl—what the horses had to eat from—plenty of times.'

At Helmingham during the lean times no children went as hungry as this. Mrs. D. Manning (born 1900) recalls: 'During the worst part of the winter—that would be just before Christmas or just after—Lady Tollemache used to provide soup for the poorer families. We used to fetch the soup from the Hall when school finished. It was venison soup from the deer in the park. They used to kill so many deer a week and then boil up the venison in a big copper. *Buck-soup* we used to call it. The bigger boys and girls, if the mothers couldn't go, used to bring their cans to school and then they'd be let out at half-past eleven to go up to the Hall and fetch it—which they could do and leave it until they went home from school. And sometimes the lids came off the cans and two sticks went in to fish out a piece of meat before we reached home.'

An entry in the Helmingham school log book for December 1899 confirms that the family at the Hall gave a great deal of direct help to the village:

'$61\frac{1}{2}$ stones of Beef and 508 lbs of plum pudding were given away at the School to the Cottage Tenants of the Estate. 75 lbs of plum pudding were also sent to the Allotment holders.'

Charles S. Thompson said in this connection: 'The Dowager Lady Tollemache took great interest in the village clubs. These were started to encourage thrift, and they consisted of a coal club for both Helmingham and Framsden, and a clothing club for these two villages. There were a children's clothing club, a children's boot club and a coal club as well. The children had cards and I received their weekly contributions and entered them on the cards. The cards were totalled in October of each year and a bonus was added to each card by her Ladyship [3s to the clothing, 6d to the boot, 1s 6d to each coal club card]. Some of the boot and coal club cards were passed to local shops in Debenham and Coddenham. But—this is the interesting part—to save holders of clothing cards the fare to Ipswich, a "shop" was opened for the whole of one Saturday in the school and it was stocked with two van loads of goods. The vans were drawn by horses and came out from Fish and Sons of Ipswich. Generally, four assistants from the shop were in charge. All clothing cards were redeemed during the day and the full account was returned to me and the cards. I know the firm's assistants enjoyed their day in the country—as well as the beer which was included in the load. The advent of the bicycle—and later the motor-bus—tempted people to visit the Ipswich shops themselves, so eventually our school "shop" was closed.'

Mrs. Manning remembers that the shop opened at 9 a.m. on the chosen Saturday:

[T] 'Mothers went to the school with their perambulators, and they'd take out what they called the *Club*. We used to go home with the pram full of material. Mother used to make all our clothes, and the Club came in very handy. It was just what she wanted. Later we had a Christmas celebration at the school. Lady Tollemache used to come down and certain boys and girls used to have a nice present for attendance and also for being the best boy or girl in the class. Mr. Orchard, our schoolmaster, would allow us to come on the morning of the Christmas celebration with our hair braided up to make ourselves smart for the afternoon. But he wouldn't allow what we called *hodmedods*[1]—that would be hair curled up at the bottom with either rag or paper.'

Mrs. Priscilla Savage (born 1881 at Blaxhall) told me how school children managed for clothes in an open village:

[T] 'My mother used to make us underclothes. They had a brown colour. What we called quilted stays which had three but-

[1]East Anglian dialect for snails.

tons down the front and of course button-holes: we had brown calico chemise and knickers made from the same stuff. They were all made from the Garthwayte[1] calico that was given to the parish of Blaxhall. Every year each family had a sheet and a yard of calico for each child. They gave it out in the church porch. There were two shopkeepers. Mr. Mannall would see to half the village: Stone Common and up to Stone Farm and the Church Common; and Mr. Gibson used to have Mill Common and the Ship Corner —this end of the village. They'd have two tables on each side of the church porch and they'd have their rolls of calico there and they'd cut it up and give it out. Arthur Gibson's calico was better than Mr. Mannall's. It was two-pence-halfpenny a yard, but still that was good calico. That was the underclothes made from calico. And you had red flannel or pink flannelette petticoats; and your little dresses—well, they were made out of what your mother left off. For my own boys I used to make little wool jerseys and little cord trousers, and we used to knit a kind of fisherman's socks for them to go to school with.'

Boots were one of the most difficult problems; and the farm-worker of this period always tried to fit out the children with boots out of the money he got from the harvest. But Mrs. Savage gave me an example of how dearly a pair of boots was prized in a family; and, incidentally, how well-made were the boots ordered from the village shoemaker. She left school to go into domestic service:

[T] 'I went when I was eleven; and my father wasn't a strong man so, of course, my mother couldn't afford to buy things. She took the bottom of two of his shirts and the odd sleeves; and out of the best parts of the shirts she made me two print dresses. One was a blue and white plaid and the other was red and white which in them times was called the *Oxford shirting*. And she made me two print dresses to start with. And my poor old father said, well, he would get me a pair of boots—which of course were made by our village shoemaker, Mr. Newson. He made me a pair of high kid-topped button boots. They were buttoned halfway up the calf of my leg, and I wore them for years and years. And I didn't dispose of them not till two years ago. And they were in there in the cupboard and I said to one of the boys: "I'm tired of seeing those old boots about," I said, "I'll dispose of them." But the buttons! I've really got some of the buttons now. You know the buttons. There were no end of buttons on them!'

Sam Friend of Framsden, Suffolk, has been a farm-worker all his life apart from his war service during the First World War; but he has become a kind of rural philosopher with an earthy wisdom and an apt word—usually a dialect one—for most aspects of the old culture. He points out the main difference between the conditions affecting the children of his 'young time' and the position today:

[T] 'Some of 'em didn't have enough to eat; though, of course, at that time o' day what you did have you had to *stay*. I mean they used to bake the bread in the oven and brewed—home-brewed beer; and some of the ones who were better off they'd have pork in the pot. But if there was a family of five or six children what could they have with wages as they were? Ten or twelve shillings a week!

'It's like this: those young 'uns years ago, *I said*, well—it's like digging a hole, *I said*, and putting in clay and then putting in a tater on top o' thet. Well, you won't expect much will you? But now with the young 'uns today, it's like digging a hole and putting some manure in afore you plant: you're bound to get some growth, ain't you? It will grow won't it? The plant will grow right well. What I say is the young 'uns today have breakfast afore they set off—a lot of 'em didn't use to have thet years ago, and they hev a hot dinner at school and when they come home most of 'em have a fair tea, don't they? *I said*. These young 'uns kinda got the frame. Well, that's it! If you live tidily that'll make the marrow and the marrow make the boon [bone] and the boon make the frame.'

It was the children of the day-men who were the worst off because at the winter season when good food was so essential to keep warm their wages were often halved. The farm-workers who missed no time because of bad weather—the shepherd, the horseman and the stockman—had a shilling or two more than the day-man but, more important, they had their twelve or fourteen shillings regularly every week. Moreover, they often had perquisites. Mrs. Tom Jay's father was shepherd to John Goddard of Tunstall, and she remembers going out to him into the field during lambing time, over seventy years ago: 'I used to go out to my father's hut early in the morning. He had a little stove in his hut—I think it's still here in the house—and he used to warm the milk for the lambs on this little stove. Then came the time when he used to cut off the lambs' tails—he used to burn 'em off with a hot iron. Then he'd skin the tails and bring 'em home. And Mother used to stew 'em a little; then she used to take 'em out of the saucepan, cut them up and make a lovely lambs'-tail pie with potatoes and so on. It was delicious. I can taste it now. Delicious. But they have some other way of doing lamb today: they don't burn their tails off as they used to.'

An Ipswich man, Harry Frank Bloomfield, who was born in the same year as Sam Friend (1888), suggests that many children in the town were no better fed at that time:

[T] 'They were hard times. Children often went hungry and they were glad to get anything they could pick up. I remember when I was about five they used to have a candle-factory in the alleyway in Fore Hamlet in Ipswich—at the back of the *Earl Grey* inn. They used to make candles there, and they used to boil the mutton fat and then the candles were dipped. They made them by dipping the wicks into the mutton fat. Well, on a Saturday evening when the factory was practically being closed the children used to come round and get the scraps from the mutton. They used to enjoy that because they were very good to eat.'

The town also reveals another custom connected with the school, a custom that from its nature would rarely be met with in the country itself. Mrs. Susan Mullenger, born in 1878 in Bungay, Suffolk, went to St. Edmund's Catholic School when she was a girl and recollects the custom they had there of taking children to the gas-works:

[T] 'Yes, at certain times in certain months a teacher would come round the classes and get those children who had whooping cough and take them to the gas-works. They used to go there of a morning and they'd sit around in the gas-works for about half an hour. I never had whooping cough myself but one of the children from my class used to go. It cured them: the fumes from the gas-works, I suppose. Another remedy they had for whooping cough was fried mouse. They fried the mouse up—I suppose with something else, bacon or something like that—and they gave it to the child to eat.'

Nothing, however, I have collected about the social conditions which were the background to children's attendance at school before the 1914 war reveals the true position better than the accounts of catching sparrows for the pot. For the food many of the children ate, as well as being insufficient, was greatly lacking in protein. Meat was too expensive to buy, and if a family had no pork in the pot there was likely to be a grave imbalance in the diet. Many families were able to correct this by the poaching of rabbits, game and hares. But there was also a widespread and more legitimate custom of catching sparrows. At Tunstall, Mrs. Tom Jay recalls, there was a *Sparrow Club*; and members of the Club used to go round the stacks of a well-disposed farmer, John Goddard, netting the birds—usually at night:

[T] 'My brother used to bring them home and I'd skin them and open the breasts and stew them; and if we'd got a piece of pork it went into the stew with them. Sometimes I'd put the sparrows in a pie with different things to flavour it.' Her husband, Tom Jay, added:

[T] 'Those were hard times, they were: get what you could get and eat what you could eat. There was no picking this and picking that like there is today. I used to work at Snape maltings. I worked there for over twenty year; and at the time of year when there was snow on the ground (we seemed to get more snow then than we do now) the sparrows would come into the maltings for food, picking up grain and so on. And I'd trap as many as forty and bring 'em home and skin 'em. We used to boil them up in a saucepan or a boiler: we'd make a soup out of them.'

Sam Friend has also caught sparrows:

[Y] 'Yes, I've been round of a night after sparrows. We used to have a lot of fish-netting, and we'd arrange and leave it hanging at the front. Then we'd hev a bull's-eye lantern and we'd shine it on the net, and they'd go in and you'd see them bright and then you'd trap 'em. We used to flay 'em—take their clothes off—and cook 'em in a basin with a crust on top. We used to call it *sparrow dumpling*. A lot o' people never tasted meat, and that were better than no meat at all.'

We can understand the schoolmaster's dilemma about school attendance when he could see that it was necessary for the children to work in order to get enough to eat. If we can judge from the school log-books of the period in Suffolk, the various Education Acts were widely interpreted. Time during the school term was frequently allowed to children to carry out jobs on the farms. Sam Friend:

[T] 'They let such as me, say about ten or eleven years old, they'd let you go to the haysel because on the farm where my father worked there used to be five men; and there used to be a boy and a girl behind each man as they *mew*[1] the grass; and you used to pick it up as they mew it. You'd keep about a yard or two behind, and you used to take up the grass and sprinkle it all down the middle, kinda make a grass floor.

'Then at different times like *beet-singling*[2] they'd let a boy have a week off to single beet. That was the time when they used to plant beet on the *flag* [furrow slice]. I used to work with an old man. He'd have a big wooden dibble,[3] and there was a girl working with us, and she had a little hod full of beans, and she'd drop three or four beans, as near as she could, in each hole—about a foot to fifteen inches between rows of holes. And I had to come with a hoe behind her and give a chop forward with the hoe and then one back and then give the soil a tap to cover up the seed.'

Harry Denny, born in 1895 at Wetheringsett, Suffolk, remembers weeding in the field and stone-picking:

[T] 'We had an old weeding hook with a three-cornered hook on it. I've got an old hook at hand now that we used to have when we were boys. We used to go into the corn and cut out the thistles, and weeds like that. We went stoon-picking too with a

---

[1] Cf. *shew, snew, hew* (hoed), *gnew, shruck* (p. 219)—all forms of the old 'strong perfect tense' used by people of the old culture.
[2] Thinning out cattle-beet (mangold) plants.
[3] A dibble frame that would make three or four holes at a time.

man called One-Arm Chapman [a gang-master]. He used to hev an owd *dickey* [donkey] and cart. There would sometimes be about twenty-eight boys and his wife: "Well, boys," he used to say, "them that work the hardest I'll give a penny extra at the end of the week." We used to get fourpence to sixpence a week—working all day, during the Easter holidays.

'I went *keeping* crows, too. But when I went doing this I had to pick stoons as well. We had a pair o' wooden clappers or an old pail. You'd hit the pail with a stick. It would do just as well. The old rooks wouldn't come very near you. But I once had an old boss. He was pretty sharp. He used to catch an old rook in a trap. He'd set eggs in the middle of the field to give them a bait, and he set the traps right over the eggs. If you'd got an owd rook in a trap in the middle of a field you'd have no trouble with rooks. That you wouldn't. It would keep all the other rooks away.

'We had to shout and run to the other end of the field like when I was frightening linnets off seed. I did a lot of that when I was a boy. Linnets used to be more trouble for seed than anything I know. Grey linnets used to get into the kale and swedes and turnips. I used to think that time o' day the swede were very precious. They used to fold the sheep on the roots. They were good food, too. I mean, me and my wife—my wife she set there now bless her owd heart—we used to have potatoes and swedes or turnips nearly every day for dinner.'

There is a mention in a nineteenth-century Government Report on the effect of *crow-keeping* or *bird-tending* on some children:

'I found in the school [Drayton School, Norfolk (St. Faith's Union)] an example of the physical ill results that sometimes are produced by early employment. Asking a question of a little boy I could not hear his answer; when enquiring I was informed that the boy had been sent "to keep birds" when he was only six years old, and lost his voice by shouting at them. He is now nine years of age, and it is considered questionable if he will ever recover it.'[1]

George Garrard (born 1891) is the son of a Suffolk farmer but he went stone-picking:

---

[1] Rev. J. Fraser (Commissioner), *Report on the Employment of Young Persons and Women in Agriculture*, British Parliamentary Papers, 1867-8, p. 203.

[T] 'We used to pick the stones and put 'em in heaps on the field, but you had to watch out to make big heaps and place them close together; otherwise when the men came round with the tumbril to pick up the small heaps the stones would shake down and you'd want another bushel of stones to bring the level up to the chalk-line they'd made in the tumbril. They picked the flints to place on the roads. Of course, in those days there were no motor-cars. There were quite a few bicycles but they had solid rubber tyres at first. The roads were very bad at this time. They were unlevel, and the mud used to churn up in the winter-time, three or four inches deep. When I was a lad my boots would be in a dreadful state by the time I got to school. In the summer it was dust. If a flock of sheep went along the road in the summer you couldn't see for half an hour afterwards. I remember the first motor-car coming out in this district: you couldn't see for almost as long after it had gone by—couldn't see for the dust. One old man near us lived in a house facing the road. It had a very high hedge, and if he heard this motor-car he'd come hurrying down the path and he'd say: "I know . . . I know. I shall niver see one of these *modus-mokus*!" It went so fast it had gone before he got to the gate; and of course he couldn't see after it because of the dust. I don't know whether he ever did see a motor-car before he died.'

One of Mrs. Jay's out-of-school jobs was *keeping pigs*, a task that boys and girls in East Anglia had been doing at least since Shakespeare's time, calling it by the same name as he had done. It was a lonely job and the child had to be very vigilant to keep the pigs in the field. Mrs. Jay once went keeping pigs on a wheat stubble in Tunstall, but the pigs stampeded and she lost them: 'When I went after my money on the Friday night to the office Mr. Goddard was angry and asked me why I'd let the pigs run home: "Well, sir," I said, "they were after the acorns and I just couldn't stop them." '

But there was a light side to the country children's school days, not all were dark and earnest. There were, for instance, the games. Pamela Holmes (1905–68) gave me an account of some that were played in the Suffolk village of Bramfield before the 1914–18 war:

[T] 'Even before we went out into the fields in the spring we would start games. The earliest game of the season was hoop-bowling—for both boys and girls. Girls often had wooden hoops, boys metal ones; girls driving it with a wooden stick, boys with a most majestic sort of bent iron rod. We, as a family, had a whole set of iron hoops made according to our size by the village blacksmith; and each of them had our initials stamped on them. They hung up for many years in a certain place on the buildings, all one within the other and really waiting for the next season. Following hoops would come hop-scotch. Then came tops. The boys had *Flying Dutchmen* and we girls the more sedate *carrot* tops. This was all done in the village streets. We hadn't anything to bother about. Every now and again a horse would come slowly trotting by, but this was our sports-field. And then later on after we'd gone through our skipping—both kinds of skipping either with double skipping-ropes or single ones—as the ropes worked we sang rhymes as we played together.

'And then would come flowers—the early spring flowers. Now I can remember very clearly how a little gang of us girls would go off down the lanes and we would know exactly where to find the earliest violets: white ones in a corner next to old Goodings Lane, the blue ones up on the sloping bank of a pond, up on my own father's fields. Later on away we would go round Kensal Wood where there was a special little meadow which was always covered with most beautiful cowslips. These were more *get-at-able* than those that came quite early on the railway line; and we used to have to dodge Mr. Sturgeon's eye because he wouldn't let us gather them from there. And then this lovely cowslip meadow became full of pale mauve and deep purple orchids. And then we would finish, going round by Kensal Wood through the other fields, and on one bank were gorgeous wood anemones. I can remember quite clearly. A quite interesting thing happened to me even this spring. I was out walking and I thought I would come round by the wood; and I was thinking about all these little flower spots; and I thought I'll call in and look at every one on my way home. And I found to my utter amazement that the fields had all been turned into one—the cowslip meadow was one with the primrose bits and the orchid bit. And I could go in a straight line from the one farm practically to the end of the footpath by walking over the one big field where about eight or nine had been previously. The purple violet patch was down by the pond, but now even the pond had gone. Finally, down in my own lane I peeped through old Gooding's hedge; and sure enough there were still some very early white violets in a little patch there—the only remains of all the little flower patches from the time when I was very tiny.

'Marbles came later. There were separate games for the boys and girls. The boys played *Long Johns* which they did as they walked along the road throwing the marbles ahead of them. Or they played *Taps* which was hitting them up against the wall, the marbles bouncing back; and then seeing if you could span them with your fingers. You played *for keeps* sometimes, in other words all the marbles you won became yours. The girls played *Dibble Hole*. You had a small hole in the ground; and you stood a yard or two away. Then you bowled either two, three or four marbles towards the hole—according to the number you'd agreed upon. Then the person who was first—that is got more marbles in the hole on the first throw—finished by hooking in with her finger as many marbles as she could to the hole; and those were hers *for keeps*.'

Arthur Welton remembered the lighter side of schooldays by an incident that could have ended unhappily:

[T] 'During our schooldays we were always up to tricks, and one of our favourite little games was to take an old jam-jar and go down to the meadows and fish for *tan-tiddlers*. And there was a time when my oldest brother, he was laying out trying to catch these tan-tiddlers and he overbalanced and fell into Snape River: he went in head first and there were his feet just sticking out of the mud and the water. But luckily there was a man about a hundred yards away walking on the railway, and I *shruck* out and called him, and he knew there was something wrong. He came running, and he just managed to grip his feet and haul him out, and he laid him on the side on the bank. Of course there was plenty of mud and water coming of his ears and mouth. We got him home and my mother got him to bed; and that mud was a-working out of him for weeks afterwards. But he got better eventually.'

Another delight for the boys was to go with their fathers on a wagon to visit the town for oil-cakes or to go to the miller's. Anthony Lankester remembers his first trip to the town on a wagon from the farm where his father was horseman. He had also spent much of his boyhood catching birds:

[T] 'We'd make a trap cage at certain times of the year: we made wire-netting trap cages if we got no money to buy one. We'd catch a bird and put it into the bottom portion of the trap. And we'd go down a lane and set it on a hedge or hang it on a tree. The top portion of the trap we used to set so if another stray bird came to the cage and peep in it, it dropped on a little platform. As soon as it did that, that used to spring the lid and the bird was caught. Bullfinches, chaffinches, red linnets or goldfinches—the mavis [thrush]—it didn't matter what sort. We used to keep these birds in cages at home and we used to go to the corn chandlers in the town and get hemp seed to feed 'em.'

Even school had its lighter moments. Charles Thompson, the Helmingham schoolmaster, told this story against himself to show that country children are much shrewder than they appear to be at first acquaintance:

[T] 'My wife was a teacher with me in the school; and she was giving a lesson on fractions to her class one day. She was trying to impress on them the fact that the larger the denominator the smaller the fraction. I happened to walk into the classroom, and I could hear the lesson going on and I thought I'd chip in for fun. So I started to ask a few questions to see whether these children had actually taken in what was being taught. I asked the question:

"Now then, which would you rather have—half a cake or a fifth of a cake?"

'Up went all the hands and I pointed to a boy I knew was not any too bright. He said:

"Please, sir, I'd rather have a fifth of a cake." '

'So I thought the teacher's effort had been more or less wasted, and I went off the deep-end a little bit. But I said to the boy:

"Well, now then, just tell me what made you say you'd rather have a fifth of a cake?"

'He said immediately:

"Please, sir, I don't care a lot about cake." '

Charles Thompson also tells another story which shows how deeply the old Helmingham cottage economy had penetrated. During the First World War he had the task of vetting the applications for exemption from Home Defence duties. He received a form from one of the Helmingham cottage-holders who in answer to the question *On what grounds do you claim exemption?* had put down unfalteringly *On Half an Acre.*

20 Archaeology and the Oral Tradition

The link between archaeology and the oral tradition may at first sight appear too weak to bear the strain of any serious examination. It is true that oral testimony is of first importance to the archaeologist who is working among a primitive people who have no epigraphic or documentary material. But what relevance has it in Britain? It is suggested that the evidence that it can offer is not negligible. But before discussing this it is worth referring to recent examples of the value of the oral tradition in helping us to interpret aspects of two of the most outstanding of world civilizations—the Greek and the Chinese.

At the beginning of this century a Cambridge classical scholar, John Cuthbert Lawson, completed a two-year research tour in Greece and the islands. His purpose was to investigate the customs and superstitions of the modern Greek peasant and to test whether or not his findings might illuminate the religion of the ancient Greeks. Lawson, in the introduction to the study he wrote on his return,[1] made the same tentative appraisal which any investigator in this field is constrained to make today—so little headway has this approach made in those departments of learning where it might be supposed to have some relevance:

'Just as we speak of ancient Greek as a dead language, and too often forget that many of the words and inflexions in popular use

[1] J. C. Lawson, *Modern Greek Folklore and Ancient Greek Religion*, Cambridge, 1910.

222

at the present day are identical with those of the classical period and even of the Homeric age, while many others, no longer identical, have suffered only a slight modification, so are we apt to think of Greek paganism as a dead religion, and do not enquire whether the beliefs and customs of the modern peasant may not be a direct heritage from his classical forefathers. And yet, if any such heritage exist, there is clearly a fresh source of knowledge open to us, from which to supplement and correct the lessons of Art and Literature.'[1]

Lawson recognized that there was little in either Greek art or literature that would give him an infallible guide to reconstructing the central spirit of the ancient Greek religion. In the first the problems of interpretation were too great to permit any sort of confident assertion; and in literature there was little beyond a Hesiodic theogony or some Orphic hymns to exhibit. From the very nature of the religion there was little direct reference to it in the literature. Religion, in fact, permeated the whole of Greek writing: it had no founder, like Christ or Mahomet: 'It was a free autochthonous growth, evolved from the various hopes and fears of a whole people.' It was his confidence that the ancient Greek religion was a popular and not a particularly codified body of belief that persuaded him to study modern Greek customs and superstitions. He recognized, too, that the Greek Orthodox Church had not displaced or stifled the old pagan religion but in many respects had been politic and merely incorporated it into a more unified framework. This must have deepened his conviction that the ancient beliefs and practices had lasted right up to this century.

Instinctively, Lawson appears to have gone straight to the only source of evidence that could prove his hypothesis was a valid one —the ordinary peasantry. His observations here are worth quoting because they emphasize that it is the ordinary country people —in Britain as in Greece—who are the source of the most reliable evidence about old beliefs and customs; and his words are as pertinent today as they were sixty years ago:[2]

'In pursuit of my task I followed no special system. I have

[1] Ibid., p. 1.   [2] Ibid., Preface, viii.

known of those who professed to obtain a complete knowledge of the folklore of a given village in the course of a few hours' visit, and whose method was to provide themselves with an introduction to the schoolmaster, who would generally be not even a native of the place, and to read out to him a formidable *questionnaire*, in the charitable and misplaced expectation that the answers given would be prompted not by courtesy and loquacity, which are the attributes of most Greeks, but by veracity, which is the attribute of few. The formal interview with paper and pencil is in my opinion a mistake. The "educated" Greek whose pose is to despise the traditions of the common-folk will discourse upon them no less tediously than inaccurately for the sake of having his vapourings put on record; but the peasant who honestly believes the superstitions and scrupulously observes the customs of which he may happen to speak is silenced at once by the sight of a note-book. Apart however from this objection to being interviewed, the country-folk are in general communicative enough. They do not indeed expect to be plied with questions until their own curiosity concerning the newcomer has been satisfied, and even then any questions on uncanny subjects must be discreetly introduced. But it is no difficult matter to start some suitable topic.'

The amount of material Lawson collected and the light it throws on his subject are a monument to his strangely up-to-date manner of approach. It is also a remarkable demonstration of the truth that there is no backward limit in historical time to which it is not possible for the oral tradition to refer. More specifically it shows the use of present-day country beliefs and customs in interpreting ancient ritual practices, and since much of archaeology —in this country as elsewhere—is concerned with ritual and cult objects the usefulness of the tradition in this discipline should need little emphasis.

An example of the remarkable persistence of tradition comes also from the early civilization of China. C. P. Fitzgerald in his book, *China: A Short Cultural History*,[1] discusses the deification of rivers and mentions the human sacrifices made to the Yellow River: 'The barbarous custom was not suppressed until the very

[1] London, 1942.

end of the Chou period [the third century B.C.].' The custom was suppressed but the belief and its counterpart in a kind of negative practice lived on until the lifetime of the author of the book:[1] 'When living at Hankow I observed that the idea underlying these sacrifices is still alive today [in the 1940's] among the boatmen of the Yangtze. They are very unwilling to make any effort to rescue someone who has fallen into the river. It is believed that if they do so the god of the river, cheated of his prey, will take the rescuer himself in revenge. A charitable society at Wu Ch'ang in Hupei on the Yangtze had had to offer a high reward for such rescue work. Moreover it was necessary to double the reward if the victim was drawn out living, for the boat people were more inclined to allow the river god to have his sacrifice and then rescue the corpse for burial. Similar beliefs are entertained by other river dwellers in north China.'

Anne Ross has also investigated similar beliefs in connection with sacred rivers and wells in Britain in an important study[2] which has used tradition in interpreting pre-Celtic, Celtic and Roman-British archaeology. Much of the study—certainly the most absorbing part of it—is concerned with the Celtic cult of the head. This theme goes right through Celtic religious tradition; and human skulls, pottery and animal bones are frequently found in once sacred wells and pools.

'The human head was regarded by the Celts as being symbolic of divinity and otherworld powers. The motif of the severed head figures throughout the entire field of Celtic cult practices, temporally and geographically, and it can be traced in both representational and literary contexts from the very beginning to the latter part of the tradition.'[3]

It was also a powerful apotropaic symbol, on the same principle as the eye-symbol[4] but it was probably considered even more effective. Placed in the waters of a well or pool it was a symbol of fertility or the life-force: it would strengthen the healing and life-giving properties of the water as well as helping to keep away evil.

To show that present-day tradition in eastern England still has

---

[1] Ibid., pp. 50–51.
[2] *Pagan Celtic Britain*, London, 1967.
[3] Ibid., pp. 61 fol.
[4] *P.U.P.*, chapter 18.

a bearing on these ancient beliefs and practices I quote a recent archaeological discovery at Martell's Gravel Pit, Ardleigh, Colchester. Archaeologists found a shallow well or votive pit and at the bottom the hollowed-out trunk of an oak which contained bones and sherds of the Second and Third centuries. Among the bones was the skull of a young horse. While I was discussing the find with David T.-D. Clarke, Curator of Colchester Museum, with reference to Dr. Ross's work on wells of the same period, he remarked 'You've reminded me of something—an incident when I was a boy. My family farmed at Hemel Hempstead, at Wood Lane, Leverstock Green, on the site of the present New Town. We were deepening a well, and an old farm-worker who was helping said: "They may find a horse's head down there." '

The farm-worker's remark argues an empirical acquaintance with a very long tradition. There can be no question of how old the tradition is for, apart from Dr. Ross's findings, the practice of sacrificing an animal in a well or votive pit is celebrated in one of Horace's best known Odes:

O fons Bandusiae, splendidior vitro, etc.

O fountain of Bandusia that glitters more than brightest glass,
You are worthy of sweet wine—and flowers too;
But tomorrow you will be presented with a young kid
Whose horns are about to break through its forehead.

It is also particularly relevant to the Essex find to mention the traditional tale, *The Three Heads of the Well*,[1] better known as *The Three Kings of Colchester*, and apparently referred to in the arms of that town.

That it is a horse's head in this case and not any other animal's may be explained by reference to the sacredness of the horse among the Celts and by a specific instance in Wales: the well of Abergeleu:[2] 'Penant tells us that in olden times the rich would sacrifice one of their horses at a well near Abergeleu to secure blessings upon the rest.' And Anne Ross has given an instance[3] of

[1] W. Gurney Benham, *The Essex Review*, Vol. IX, p. 202.
[2] Charles Squire, *Celtic Myth and Legend*, p. 415.
[3] Ibid., pp. 324–5.

a little votive bronze horse found in Coventina's Well in Nor-thumberland. The oral tradition in my own experience[1] is so strong in connection with the horse in Britain that it would be well to listen to the most trivial-seeming piece of information that comes spontaneously from the right source, that is from members of the old culture, notably the farm-worker who is able to give splendid examples of the continuity of the tradition in Britain.

But many legends which have been kept alive through the word of mouth have been later substantiated in one form or another by archaeological finds; and some archaeologists, alert to the useful-ness of the tradition, have examined them critically and have in-vestigated sites apparently referred to in the legend or story. L. V. Grinsell, author of *Ancient Burial Mounds in Britain*,[2] states that there is not as yet[3] 'a published corpus of folk-traditions con-cerning prehistoric barrows and other ancient sites in Britain, although one exists for France and the French colonies'; but he himself has done a great deal to lay the foundations of such a work by publishing a map of ancient burial mounds and barrows, marking those which have a corresponding legend about their contents. One of the best known examples of the tradition relating to a site, which later revealed an outstanding archaeological find, comes from Wales. This is the well known *Bryn-yr-Ellyllon* dis-covery near the town of Mold. A mound near the side of the road between that town and Chester was broken into at the beginning of last century. The perpetual overseer of the Mold highways, John Langford, rented the field where the mound lay, and 'he set ten men to dig up the Tumulus for stone to mend the roads; towards the lower part they found some very large bones—a skull of greater than the usual size of man—a bright corslet with 200 to 300 amber beads; the bones became dust on being exposed to the air.'[4]

'The bright corslet'—now in the British Museum—turned out to be pure gold but later examination has established that it was not a corslet but a tippet or cape that fitted over the shoulders of

[1] *H.I.F.* and *P.U.P.*   [2] Second Edition, London, 1953.
[3] 'Barrow Treasure in Fact, Tradition and Legislation', *Folklore*, Vol. 78, Spring, 1967.
[4] Ellis Davies, *Prehistoric and Roman Flintshire*, p. 259.

a Bronze Age chieftain whose burial place the mound is assumed to be. Numerous stories were told at the time of the discovery of how local people had been frightened on different occasions by a *Golden Spectre* or the ghost of a *Man in Golden Armour* which appeared on and near the mound while they were passing on the road to or from Mold. Many of the stories can be discounted as vague memories that had been coloured and stiffened by the discovery itself. But Dr. H. N. Savory of the National Museum of Wales has looked at the evidence critically and has written:[1] 'I think it is fair to say that it seems to be established that the local people believed in a ghost at *Bryn-yr-Ellyllon* long before the gold "corslet" was discovered, but one cannot really be certain that "golden armour" etc. did not come into the stories about it until *after* the discovery of the corslet.'

Yet apart from the stories of a ghost connected with the site, the place-names themselves, *Bryn-yr-Ellyllon* and *Cae-yr-Ellyllon* (The Hill of the Goblins and The Field of the Goblins), would be sufficient to interest an alert archaeologist. C. W. Phillips, formerly archaeological officer to the *Ordnance Survey*, recalls a very similar though less spectacular instance: 'I may perhaps have mentioned the fact that when I was doing field-work in Lincolnshire I read in Peacock's work on the folklore of the area that a little man in a red cap was said to appear on a certain defined spot. When I identified this place in the field it was clear that a barrow had been ploughed down there.'[2]

But why should an ancient burial place be linked so frequently with ghosts or goblins and a kind of generalized superstition? Apart from its natural association with the ghost of the dead person, the explanation may well be that it was of the utmost importance to the builders of the grave-mound or tumulus that it should remain undisturbed, both for their own peace of mind and for the benefit of the inhumed person whose chances of survival in the after-life might hinge on the order and ritual of his burial and to his being undisturbed in his grave. Therefore, out of policy the whole place was surrounded with a carefully induced sanctity which inhered not so much in the grave itself but in the

[1] Personal communication.   [2] Personal communication.

minds of those people who took part in or witnessed the in-
humation rituals. To all these the ceremony communicated that
this spot was sacred to the gods and would be guarded by the gods
and was therefore taboo to mortals. It seems likely that many
barrows or tumuli were subjected to a secondary burial for this
reason. Such a place, already made secure by the numerous
apotropaic rituals that had been performed at the first burial, was
the obvious spot to lay another important person; and there was
a double assurance that the place would not be disturbed and the
valuable grave-goods would remain in the ground. This purpose-
fully-fostered awe was transmitted, through its strong initial im-
pulse, from generation to generation; but in the passage of time
the people in the neighbourhood would lose the original ap-
prehension of a sacred or taboo site; under the impact of a new
religion its purpose would cease to be rehearsed or transmitted.
Instead the spot itself would degenerate into a breeding-ground of
diffuse superstitions or imaginings and would become a credible
though perfectly irrational focus for what may be subjective
phenomena like ghosts. It is not, therefore, these phenomena that
mark the occasional archaeological site but the tradition which has
remained alive in folk-memory after many generations, being
metamorphosed by time into the universal currency of dwarfs,
ghosts and goblins.

But in the wider context of legends and stories concerning
archaeological sites, not necessarily linked with burial, there is
also a growing tendency to give attention to the folk-life material
which surrounds the site itself. Dr. Savory gives a good example
in his report on Dinas Emrys, a fortified site and dwelling, in
Caernarvonshire, of an excavation showing a peculiar structure
related to an ancient tradition concerning the site: 'It is, of course,
most remarkable that the excavation of 1955 should have revealed
a massive stone platform built partly in the peat filling of a silted-
up cistern. It is surely not unreasonable to see a connection between this and the first mystery revealed by the boy Ambrosius
Aurelianus to Vortigern's wise men: "What is the pavement of
this place?" . . . "I know, in the midst of the pavement is a pool,"
and to suppose that a north Wales composer of sagas, wishing to

give local colour to a story borrowed from a Powysian saga, introduced into it a reference to a curious structural feature well known in the district.'[1]

On a more general level still, C. W. Phillips has noted out of his long experience that where the word *black* occurs either in the oral tradition as a field name or part of a village (Blackland, Blackfield, Black Meadow, etc.) the site always repays close examination. Roman sites sometimes have this element in their name because of the much darker colour of the soil where there had once been a settlement. This was caused by the decay of organic rubbish, by the scattering of fire-ash and so on. 'In France it has also been suggested that *rouge*, as in *Maison Rouge*, often occurring where there is no red house today, and often along the line of Roman roads, recalls the former existence of a red-bricked building (posting-station, inn, etc.) which has long disappeared. It is certainly true there are many such instances across the Channel, but I know of no examples here—but they are worth looking out for. It is possible that the redness of brick was not the only factor, for there is reason to believe that the Roman equivalent of inns and pubs were painted over with a red wash to distinguish them.'[2]

But it seems to me that although tradition sometimes contributes much that is of direct use to the archaeologist, the main benefit it can offer him is a general one. It can help to prevent archaeology taking a wrong direction. Many archaeologists appear purposefully to avoid the kind of folk-life material discussed here because they see in it some threat to their lately acquired quasi-scientific respectability. This is an understandable reaction in a comparatively new discipline concerned to establish itself as more 'scientific' than history, the parent-body from which it derived. Indeed, some archaeologists see in the new technique a new surety and prestige, tricked out with an enticingly esoteric jargon—all the enviable marks of the natural sciences. But in spite of the new scientific techniques that archaeology is now using—the carbon 14 method of dating, palaeobotany, the proton-magnetometer and

[1] *Archaeologia Cambrensis*, Vol. CIC, 1960, p. 56.
[2] Personal communication.

so on—it cannot attain to the same degree of precision within a limited field that has served the natural sciences so well. Nor should it aspire to. Although science has extended the archaeologist's tools immeasurably it cannot help him in his most difficult task—the interpretation of his findings. Although the archaeologist, with the help of the new skills, can answer more accurately than ever before the two basic questions *How?* and *When?* he is still left with the most important one unanswered. For expertise and refined techniques alone are silent when he puts the final question *Why?* This is the vital question because it underlines the dilemma of the archaeologist; for to answer this question he has to go back to *History* even though he has moved away and become progressively estranged from it.

Archaeology like history is an art and although it uses scientific techniques it is taking a wrong direction if it attempts to go along the way of the natural sciences. The method of science is to isolate a part of reality, to construct a hypothesis and to prove or disprove the hypothesis by controlled, repeatable experiment. Archaeologists can experiment only in a very limited sense, for instance by constructing a model or working replica of an ancient boat, or by cutting down trees with a neolithic flint-axe; but even in these limited experiments they cannot hope to reconstruct fully the original environment as the scientist does in repeating his experiments in the laboratory. In the larger sense experiment is, naturally, impossible for the archaeologist. What scientific techniques have done for him is to refine his data; but he can get little direct help from these techniques in ordering and selecting the data to construct an all-embracing interpretation. When he comes to this, the question *Why?*, he is forced to look beyond the natural sciences, and his aids are more likely to come from anthropology, history, geography, ethnology, folk-life and even depth-psychology. For in the interpretation of his findings he is concerned with Man, not in one particular aspect of his activities but in the whole range of his living in time and space. His task here is no different from the historian's: to make a careful inference, a hypothesis that cannot be proved or disproved but has to be filed with the records of history itself. This is a hypothesis which in the last resort is personal and individual, in a real sense more like the artist's, and time alone can either fortify or demolish it.

The scientists may gain some satisfaction from the way the humanities appear to be taking over many of their methods; but the more perceptive of them see the limitations of science and there is some evidence of a movement in the opposite direction. Sir George Stapledon wrote the following after a long career as an agricultural scientist responsible for a revolution in grass-farming:

'. . . against the background of a life devoted to science I have plunged headlong into history, literature, and poetry. The result is that for the first time in my life I have been forced to realize to the depth of my being that facts and factors as such (either singly or in small groups) in the affairs of life (including of course agriculture) mean precisely nothing; it is their mass inter-relationships and interactions—and these for all practical purposes are infinite—that mean everything. In my view a first-class historian or a first-class literary critic tends to knock spots out of a scientist of equal calibre when it comes to a critical consideration of the all-pervading amplitudes of interactions and inter-relationships.'[1]

The dangers of too close a following of the methods of the scientist are obvious in the archaeological field touched on in this chapter. In excavating a burial mound the scientist can give the archaeologist tremendous help, but when he asks himself: 'Why did they bury this man in this particular way?' the archaeologist is left on his own and immediately has to widen his horizon of search. For here he is dealing with a universal question which has, as its corollary, a battery of questions that have concerned people of all periods of history, and pre-history from the time when Man first became aware of himself: Who are we? Where do we come from? Why are we here? and, Where are we going?

[1] Robert Waller, *Sir George Stapledon, F.R.S., Prophet of the New Age*, London, 1962.

Part Four

Migrant Workers

Sam friend's Burton teapot

Hall's Barn

21 On the Move

It has been suggested that the main use of oral information is to supplement and fill out evidence taken from other sources. But there are some aspects of the old type of East Anglian farming and the society which it nourished that are recorded chiefly—and in some instances only—in the oral tradition. These relate to migrant workers. There were three classes of these: those who moved about within the region, those who came from outside, and those workers who went outside the region to other trades during different seasons of the farming year. Documentary evidence of these movements is often small, and in one or two instances almost non-existent. But the oral information that comes from the oldest generation of farm-workers suggests that the movements were varied and in certain trades very considerable.

One of the movements which was undoubtedly of long standing arose out of the close link between East Anglian farming and the sea. Up to the recent past young farm-workers from the villages on the Suffolk and Norfolk littoral went fishing after the corn harvest and remained at sea during the autumn and the early part of the winter. They went mainly from Lowestoft and Yarmouth.

Eric Fowler of the *Eastern Daily Press* (Norwich) gave me an account of the latter part of this movement: 'They used to call them *joskins*—farm-workers who became unskilled members of fishing-crews after the corn harvest was over. The peak time of the movement was towards the end of September or the beginning of October. The finest herrings were caught at the time of the October full moon, and the first Scottish boats came down into East Anglian waters about that time. The special trains from Scotland bringing the fisher-girls used to arrive about the same time. These "girls"—a number of course were middle-aged married women—came down in crews of six with the most responsible member in charge. Their job was to gut and salt the herrings and pack them in barrels for export to Germany, Russia and elsewhere. I remember a day in the late 'twenties—I believe it was 1928 or 1929—I was at Beccles station when one of these special trains full of herring girls pulled into the station just as a local train was arriving. This was full of the joskins from East Suffolk and Norfolk. I've not heard such a combination of accents in my life as the fisher-girls and the joskins exchanged greetings. Many of the girls came from Stornoway in the Hebrides and from Wick and Fraserburgh in the north of Scotland—and there was a fair mixture of East Anglian accents as well.

'A great number of farm-workers went away from the Stalham area of Norfolk during the fishing season, but I believe the numbers that went fishing were greatest before the 1914 war. It was easy to recognize them: they wore blue jerseys and duffle trousers and they carried kit-bags.'

Many of the farm-workers in the Suffolk village of Blaxhall used to go fishing after harvest, some of them up to the period of the last war, but many more in the pre-1914 years when the demand was greater. These men, when they returned after Christmas, filled in their time until haysel by doing seasonal jobs on the land: bark-peeling, and ditching and draining.

The corn harvest was naturally the peak period of employment in this region, and during these few weeks many workers came into the region. Irish workers penetrated as far east as East Anglia though not in the same numbers as they went to the north of

England and Ayrshire, for instance, for the potato-harvest. Geoffrey Goddard, grandson of John Goddard of Kettleburgh and Tunstall, remembers his grandfather talking about Irish workers but more particularly about the harvest workers he took on from Lincolnshire: 'My grandfather told me about these men who came down to Suffolk from Lincolnshire *to take the harvest— take it to do,* as we say around Kettleburgh. These workers would get paid their *earnest* or *hiring money* of a shilling in the normal way, after the contract had been signed, and they'd immediately go out and drink it. For a shilling they'd get six or eight pints of beer—depending on the quality—or a half bottle of gin. I know that was the price because when my father was a boy, at the end of last century, the sheep clippers used to send him out to the pub with a half-crown for a bottle of gin, and he used to bring sixpence change. I remember my grandfather telling me once that on the first morning these travelling workers came in a gang to work (after spending the earnest money the night before) he'd lock the gate to the farm; and he'd be out there waiting for them before five o'clock in the morning. They'd still be more or less drunk from their spree, and he wasn't having them in that state. He used to stand in the yard, and he'd front 'em and say: "The first man who puts his hand on that gate, I'll hit it with this stick."

'To begin work he wanted them sober—as he meant them to continue. It was necessary to show these travelling workers who was master because he would not have the same hold over them as he would over his own local workers.'

It is likely that the Lincolnshire men came down into Suffolk and did a harvest on one of the farms there before returning to take part in a rather later harvest in their own county. This was not an uncommon practice with Suffolk workers at the beginning of this century. Some went first into Essex and took a harvest there before returning to Suffolk to do a second one. A Blythburgh (Suffolk) worker talked about this same period, sixty to seventy years ago; and about an earlier one: 'There was more money in Essex for harvesting. You could get over £8 10s there. My father, I recall, used to do two harvests, one in Essex and then another in Suffolk. This was before I can remember. But they used to say that south of Bourne Bridge in Ipswich you'd get more money working on the farm. If you came this way [well into the north of Suffolk] it meant a bob or two less a week. That's the reason I kept a-travellin' about. I kept going where I thought was the biggest money.'

This is an interesting and accurate observation. Nineteenth-century records show that the average wages for farm-workers in East Anglia were low compared with many other areas, especially with the Midlands and the industrial North; and the general level of wages in all industries in the region remains low to this day.[1] This is generally attributed to the region's being removed from any large industrial complex which would compete for labour. The worker in East Anglia during the Industrial Revolution and up to the present day sold his labour in a buyer's market: the nearer he was to London—'up Essex way'—the more likely he was to get higher wages; and apparently this still holds to a certain extent today. Harold Goddard, a Rendham (Suffolk) farmer, confirms the pre-1914 practice of workers taking part in two harvests, one in Essex and one later in Suffolk; and he adds the interesting note that at one time Essex farmers harvested early because they were not so particular about the quality of their corn. They got a good price for their corn-straw, selling in the London area for packing material and for the hat-making industry. James Seely, the Norfolk farmer, gave me some information about a migration —the extent of which is unknown—when a farm-worker actually penetrated into the Metropolis and sold his skills there, presumably at the highest rate of all: 'I knew an old man who worked on a farm near Hales—he'd be some bit over a hundred if he were alive today—and he once told me he used to go to London hay-making. The chaps on the farm used to laugh at him. But he was right. He was telling the truth. He used to make hay in some of

---

[1] *East Anglia; A Study*, H.M.S.O., 1968; para. 415: 'Table 30 shows regional differences in average tax case incomes for 1965–66 and indicates that East Anglian earned income falls some way below the United Kingdom average. East Anglia has the lowest average earned income from employment for all the English regions.'

See also: 'East Anglia Consultative Committee': *A Regional Survey, 1968. A Regional Appraisal, 1969*'.

the London parks. Before they had the machines they used to cut the grass with scythes. But at that time when there were no other transport except horses they could use all the hay they could get up in London.'

Sam Friend (born 1888) gave me an example of internal migration in East Anglia: 'A big farmer in Cretingham owned three farms, and at harvest there were allus three companies of men, eight men in each company. They took the harvest separate. Two

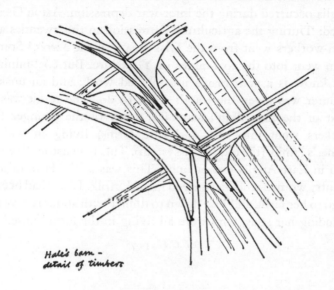

Hale's barn –
detail of timbers

of the companies agreed on the farmer's terms; but the third— the company from Doves's—wouldn't agree. They got taken on for harvests at other farms, and the farmer got eight men from Bungay to take the harvest for him at Doves's. The farmer came from Bungay, so likely he knew his way about up there. This was when I was a boy at school over seventy years ago. I recollect it well. One of the men from Bungay stopped me on the road one day and he ask me: "Where do Sam Friend live?". So I took him home, and my father he say: "Stannard! What are you a-doing down here?" My father had worked at Bungay and he knew the man well. Afterwards we went down to where the Bungay men

239

were put up. They had two huts on wheels put together. They were the sort of hut that was used with the traction engine. These men lived in these huts which they'd placed down there in the *Low*; and a ninth man, a cripple, used to cook for 'em. They used to start harvest 'arly at that time o' day, and I recollect 'em cutting wheat in Cretingham on the 28th July. Of course, the corn used to stand in stooks then: there were no waiting for it to git ripe like they have to now with the combines.'

One of the later small migrations of farm-workers from East Anglia occurred during the inter-war depression. Aston Gaze recalled: 'During the agricultural depression in the 'twenties a few farm-workers went from the Diss area into the *Sheres*.[1] Some of them went into the coal-mines of Yorkshire. But coal-mining as you know is a craftsman's job, skilled work; and an unskilled labourer was given the rough work to do. The result was that most of the men didn't stay. But some of the younger farm-workers went into the Yorkshire farms, living in with the farmer's family (the old bothy system). This is a custom I've never seen in East Anglia except once. This was at the farm of a fen-country woman who had moved into Norfolk. I once had occasion to go to her farm, and I sat down to dinner with about twelve men, including her sons, who were all living in the farm-house.'

[1] *A.F.C.H.*, p. 78.

22 Going to Burton

The records of one of these movements, involving a large number
of workers going out of East Anglia, is an example of the worth of
oral testimony. This concerns the migration of young workers to
the maltings of Burton-on-Trent over a period of at least half a
century. Documentary evidence for the migration is scant, and
what there is exists only through the stimulus of facts that had
been uncovered by old men's memories.

The search to collect evidence started after a chance remark
made by a farm horseman while I was collecting information about
his experiences on the Suffolk farms. I found that it was not the
first occasion on which a remark made on the margin of another
and totally different enquiry proved—when followed up—to be
more fruitful than the subject I was investigating at the time; and
I had come to recognize in interviewing one of the members of the
old culture that it was wrong tactics to keep to a rigid conceptual
framework, much less to a list of questions or topics to pursue.
It is often much more rewarding to let the informant have his
head, roughly within the area where you have directed the
enquiry, and to let him digress if the new subject promises to be
an interesting one. If it is of no importance at all it is always
possible to bring him back, after listening for a little while, to the
line you want him to travel. If he has opened up on what for him
is a vital section of his life and you divert him, it may be the last

you will hear of that, and moreover the smooth flow of communication is likely to be impeded. It is much better in an instance like this for the interviewer to return on another occasion to get the information he originally set out to obtain. For what the informant wants to tell the interviewer is more vital to him because he has given it preference in his own mind and it sometimes turns out to be more valuable than the answers the interviewer is hoping to get at the time. I find, too, these spontaneous contributions are always narrated with more zest and in a language that is more alive than if he is giving rather stilted answers to carefully directed questions.

On the occasion just mentioned the horseman was giving an outline of his life on the farm: 'I recollect,' he said, 'that were the year I went to Burton. I went up for two seasons, missed a season, then went for another two—and then I got married.' The horseman did not enlarge on the remark at the time and I did not attempt to question him. But I was continually hearing echoes of it from other horsemen; then the remark was further amplified and sensitized by a talk with a Suffolk farmer. We were discussing the growing of barley: 'Many farmers round here tried to grow the best barley so they could get a good price for it by selling it to the Burton brewers. It had to be good though. At that time you'd sometimes hear the comment: "That barley's good enough for Bass", or "He's a-scheming to get Burton barley off that field".'

Eventually it became clear in my own mind that there had been a fairly widespread movement of young farm-workers who followed the barley they had grown in East Anglia to Burton-on-Trent where they worked as maltsters, helping to convert it into malt to be used in the brewing of beer. I decided first to get evidence for the migration from the old workers themselves. As I had found in other fields, the richest evidence came from those men who had been born before about 1885—men who had reached their maturity before the 1914–18 war and the break-up of the old pattern of farming and the social life connected with it. They were able to give me a first-hand report of the agricultural depression which the 1893 Report had described and Rider Haggard, when he toured the country a few years later, found still to be lying heavily on the land. The earliest instance I discovered of a farm-worker going to Burton-on-Trent was Ernest Love of Alburgh, Norfolk. He was born *c.* 1860 and he went to Burton shortly after *Black '79*, the disastrous wet year that began the long farming depression that lasted in East Anglia until the 1914–18 war. Ernest Love, after a few seasons working in the maltings, married and settled down there; and his eldest daughter, Mary, was born there in 1884. Albert Love was born in 1886 after his parents returned to Norfolk but was able to tell me a great deal of what his father had told him about their stay in Burton. The movement continued until 1931 when the level of unemployment in Burton itself had risen so high that the importing of outside labour was unpopular and difficult. William Bolton (born 1900) of Peasenhall was one of the last of the Suffolk maltsters to go to Burton.

The main outlines of the movement emerged very early in the search. Young men who could easily find work in the East Anglian villages during the peak periods of the farming year— haysel and corn harvest—were dismissed by farmers after the harvest, and often spent the whole winter hanging about without work and without any form of subsistence except the *parish* or the charity of their family. These young men jumped at any chance of work during this time. Many went fishing and many went to Burton. For the malting season was complementary to the farming season: as soon as the corn harvest was over the malting began, and it went on right through the winter and early spring right up to the eve of the haysel. One stipulation the Burton firms made before taking these young workers: they wanted big-framed men, strong enough to handle the comb-sacks (sixteen stones each) of barley.

The oral evidence was rich but where were the documents to support it? For many months I tried to get documentary material from the usual sources—record offices, newspapers and libraries (both in East Anglia and Staffordshire), census returns, the British Transport Historical Records[1] and so on—but without finding

[1] The movement between East Anglia and Burton-on-Trent was by rail through Peterborough.

any.[1] Eventually I was referred to Colin Owen, a historian who was researching into the industries of Burton-on-Trent. At this time, too, I had the idea of contacting Bass the brewers whose name figured largely in the memories of the old East Anglian maltsters. The firm's maltings manager, R. A. Dale, kindly wrote that they still had the labour-books of the older firm, Bass, Ratcliff and Gretton and that some of the books dated back to 1900. He sent a digest of the numbers of workers from Norfolk and Suffolk for two malting seasons, 1904/05 and 1926/27 (Appendix Two). Suffolk was the county that was strongly represented: 'In the 1904/5 season 169 men came from Suffolk to this one malting firm out of a total labour force of 315, while in 1926/7 41 men came from Suffolk out of a total of 200. This represents a decrease from 54 per cent to 20 per cent.'

In the meantime I heard from Colin Owen. He had not come across mention of the East Anglian migration during his two years' researches into the history of the brewing industry, and he was doubtful whether the brewers would need maltsters from East Anglia: 'The Burton brewers preferred to malt their own barley and employed permanent maltsters. Large stocks of malt were kept, often from one year to the next.' A little later, however, he wrote: 'Having examined the books to which you referred at Bass and Co. it is obvious that the movement was on a large scale at the end of the nineteenth century and the start of the twentieth, when on the average the firm employed around 200 of these workers from the end of September to early June. The earliest book is dated 1890 but this certainly does not mark the start of the process. My guess would be that it began around 1860 or 1870, by which time the railway (1840) was in being and the Burton breweries were expanding at a great rate. I am hopeful that I may be able to gain further information from Bass or one of the other breweries so that I can trace the movement of workers back to the beginning. It is significant in the books from 1890 to 1910 that, whereas in 1890 most of the Suffolk men returned home at the end of the season, as time went by increasing numbers of them

---

[1] A. Wilson Fox reported copiously on the farm-worker of this period but I have not been able to find any reference to this migration in any of his writings.

came to live in Burton permanently. This suggests that the process had not been long in operation in 1890.'

During the spring of 1968 I went to Burton-on-Trent to talk to some of the older Suffolk maltsters who had settled in Burton and also to some of the Burton maltsters who were of the same generation. I planned to look at the Bass labour-books but found that in the meantime the firm had moved office and the books had been destroyed. Colin Owen, however, generously gave me permission to include a digest of his researches into them; and these are included here (Appendix One). I write the above bare facts of the search for the story of the Burton migration as a prelude to the transcriptions of the memories of East Anglians (chiefly Suffolk men) who went to Burton between 1880 and 1931. But before presenting these it would be as well to outline what exactly was involved in the process of malting. In addition to being worthwhile in itself, it will I think clarify many of the details of the following accounts by the old East Anglian maltsters.

It appears that malting, which is the important process in the making of beer, was known in Mesopotamia from the third millennium B.C., and beer drinking was confined to that area for centuries. The Greeks considered beer a barbarian beverage and rarely drank it. Tacitus also reveals that beer was unknown to him: 'The Germans made a drink from barley or wheat which was fermented in a similar way to the juice of the grape.' The Celts were skilled in the art of brewing from early times as the Elder Pliny recorded,[1] and they also discovered the use of barm or beer-yeast or leaven. But beer did not acquire the taste by which we now recognize it until the Middle Ages: it was not until then that hops were first commonly used for flavour and preservation. The word 'hoppe' is not known in English documents before the fifteenth century. The use of hops in brewing was forbidden by Henry VIII, and the ban remained until the last years of his son's, Edward VI's, reign (1547–53). This seems partly to confirm the old jingle that used to be heard in Suffolk:

> *Hops, Reformation, bacca and beer,*
> *Came into England all in a year.*

[1] *Nat. Hist.*, XIV: 29.

But, as already stated, the malting is the essential process in the brewing of beer. Barley grain contains within it insoluble starch together with certain enzymes which are necessary to make the starch soluble in water. This is effected by the grain's germinating. During germination the enzyme called diastase changes part of the starch into sugar maltose or malt sugar. Malting is, in fact, the natural process under controlled conditions.

The process of malting in an old floor malting house can best be understood by describing what happened in a small three-floor maltings at Bungay, Suffolk. Although the Burton-on-Trent maltings were bigger, containing four or five floors, the malting process was essentially the same. The Bungay maltings were built during the last century by R. W. Mann: they lie alongside the river Waveney and at that time wherries brought the barley from farms in the area right up to the malt-houses. This particular malt-house is now obsolete and lies alongside a complex of more modern buildings owned by Crisp's Maltings.[1] When the barley came in it was dried until it contained the right moisture content; then it was stored. The actual malting process started at one end of the building when the barley was winched up through the loading hole on to the first floor for the initial stage—the steeping of the barley in water. After a short period of steeping the soaked grain was then fed on to the three floors: one below, one above, and one on the same level. The maltsters spread the grain on to the floors to begin germinating. The floors of the malting are constructed of plain *pamments* or square tiles. While on the floor the grain was sprinkled with water which was pumped up by hand-pump from the river. The barley now germinated and sent out small green rootlets and stalks. But at a certain stage the growth was arrested by moving the grain on to the kiln for roasting. The kiln is at the other end of the building, and its pyramid-shaped roof with the tall rectangular-shaped ventilator at the top is a regular feature, easily recognized, of the old maltings. The heat for the kiln floor is provided by a furnace on the ground floor. The kiln floor is placed at a central level at the end of the three floors

[1] I am indebted to Peter Turner of this firm for the information about the Bungay maltings.

so that the grain could be shovelled on to it from any one of the floor levels. The kiln floor is constructed of foot-square malting *pamments* or tiles. Each tile is two inches thick, and its under surface consists of 120 holes three-quarters of an inch in diameter. The purpose of the holes is to allow the hot air rising from the furnace to pass through the tiles to roast the germinated grain which is spread evenly over the kiln floor. But the three-quarter-inch holes do not penetrate to the surface of the tile: if they did most of the grain would then fall through. Each hole penetrates the under side of the tile up to about half an inch from the top: from there a rosette of eight small holes, each about an eighth of an inch across, allows the hot air to pass through to the grain. An old maltings tile which has a rich brown surface with a matt finish is a beautifully-constructed and efficient artefact.

After the grain had been roasted on the kiln, in a gradually increasing temperature, the small rootlets and stalks were screened off from the actual malt-grain and were sold as foodstuff for cattle. The malt-grain was then bagged up by 'an outside gang' and transported to the breweries and factories. The maltsters' work consisted chiefly in handling the barley as it came in: drying it, storing it, then steeping it and shifting it on to the floors where the malting process continued. Once it was on the floor the soaked grain had to be turned regularly to aerate it and to prevent the rootlets and stalks from matting together as they grew. In the larger Burton maltings a foreman or piece-walker was responsible for the germinating of each *piece* or area of barley laid out on the floor. The process of germinating, under the old floor malting system, was naturally affected by the weather, and the piece-walker had to see to it that the temperature was regulated by adjusting the current of fresh air over the malting floor. They did this by opening or closing the windows on each side of the floor. Because temperature is so critical to the malting process the maltsters' hours were irregular. They worked a seven-day week and had to gear their hours to the rate of germination of the grain. They might, for instance, have to return to work at a late hour to *load a green kiln*, that is, move a piece of grain that had reached the final stage of germination, on to the kiln for roasting.

While the grain was sprouting on the floors it demanded skilled and careful attention. For this the maltsters had various tools. The chief was the wooden malting shovel. It used to be a beautifully-made implement, carved from one piece of wood; and it was very much like an old casting shovel which was used for winnowing corn by hand in the barns of East Anglian farms. In some districts it was called a *scuppit*. Today the maltsters use aluminium shovels. Lightness was the first requisite of a malting shovel; but some of the Burton maltsters did not consider theirs were light enough, and they spent a lot of their time surreptitiously whittling them down with pocket-knives to make them even lighter. The malting fork was also made of wood. As far as possible all the tools were wooden to avoid bruising the grain unduly. The Burton maltsters also wore specially designed boots which had wooden pegs in the soles instead of iron rivets; and in some departments of the malt-ings, for example the stores, they had shoes with canvas bottoms. The shoes and the boots supplied by the brewing companies at Burton often figure in the old maltsters' recounting of their seasons there.

The heaviest work while the green malt was on the floor was in the constant turning it demanded. One method called *double-turning* is analagous to the double-digging of a garden. Here is a simplified description of the process:

A piece of grain on the floor was first divided equally, A and B in the diagram. The grain from the rectangular strip at the top of B (b1) would be turned with a malting shovel on to the similar strip of grain at the top of A (a1). Then starting at B the maltster would move the grain forward into the now empty space, b1; and then he moved all the grain in B forward in a methodical manner until there was an empty space at the foot of B (b2). Starting next at the foot of A he moved the grain across to fill strip b2. He then continued moving all the grain in A, including the double quantity in a1, until it was all spread out evenly. This method ensured that all the green malt was thoroughly turned, and the circular flow of the turning meant that it was done with the least expenditure of energy.

An iron malt-rake was sometimes used for raking the green

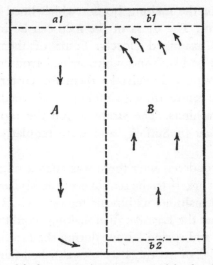

malt; but as the blades were in contact with the floor there was little bruising of the grain. The malt-rake was also drawn lightly in a careful, jerking movement over the grain, leaving ripples or corrugations, thus exposing a greater surface of the grain and aerating it more effectively. On the floors, too, the maltsters used scoops for picking up the grain: eight of these scoops would fill a sack of malt grain. For sweeping the floors they used a special kind of malt-broom. The photograph [Plate 28] shows a group of maltsters from the Barking and Battisford districts of Suffolk: they went to the Bass maltings at Burton-on-Trent near the beginning of this century. It also shows many of the tools they used in the maltings. The man at the back wearing a cap is the kiln fireman, and he is holding a furnace poker. Next to him is a man holding a stick-plough which was used for turning the green malt when the piece was unusually thick: it was pushed in a semicircular direction. The two men sitting on the right are holding floor shovels; the one on the left a kiln shovel. The man on the extreme left is grasping an implement, probably a rake. In the centre a maltster is tilting the beer-can which each man used in turn to draw the group's daily allowance of beer. The baskets were for transporting the grain on the floor and for hoisting it from one floor to another. The stamp on the shovels, *Bass No. 7*, refers to one of the malting houses which lined Station Street, Burton-on-Trent. The dress of the men can be identified if the photograph is examined closely. Some of them are wearing *sponge-bag check* or black-and-white striped trousers which made one Burton young lady mistake them for costermongers. The two men in the centre are wearing light *cords*, made almost white by constant washings. The straps round the top of the calves were called *lijahs* in Suffolk, and were regularly worn by the farm-workers.

It may be wondered why there was such a migration of East Anglian farm-workers to the maltings of the Midlands when there were dozens of maltings within the region itself. The answer undoubtedly is that the East Anglian maltings could not absorb the surplus winter and spring labour during the farming depression. These East Anglian maltings were established fairly early in the nineteenth century; for instance the maltings at Halesworth were operating by 1844. *White's Directory* for that year has: 'Mr. P. Stead has lately obtained a patent for malting by a new process, and has built a large kiln in tower form, fifty feet high, divided into five stories and heated by steam-pipes and a hot air blast.' Newson Garrett, the Aldeburgh merchant, acquired an interest in a London brewery; and shortly afterwards, in 1854, he began malting at Snape. It was he who started the fine complex of buildings, part of which has become the *Maltings Concert Hall*. These mid-nineteenth-century maltings were mainly concentrations of what had previously been a small village craft or industry which a farmer or a miller operated to serve his immediate neighbourhood. During the last few years there has again been a tremendous concentration of the malting industry in large, hyper-mechanized maltings such as the £2 million *Associated British Maltsters* factory, opened at Bury St. Edmunds in 1967. Big factories like these are making the old nineteenth-century maltings obsolete in East Anglia, and also in other barley growing areas such as Yorkshire.

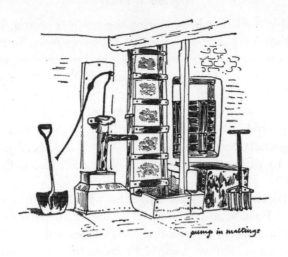

pump in maltings

23 Signing On

Colin Owen discovered that the Burton brewing industry expanded roughly threefold every ten years between 1850 and 1880, and this expansion naturally created a great demand for labour. The brewers solved this problem by bringing in workers from East Anglia. They came from East Anglia for three reasons: the Burton brewers already had connections with the region through the purchase of barley, mainly from the Bury St. Edmunds, Woodbridge and Ipswich areas. Secondly, East Anglian farming was in a state of depression and there was a great number of young men out of work. And lastly—as already suggested—the farming season and the malting season were complementary to one another. 'The migration was a sizeable one. It was in existence by 1880 and had possibly started on a small scale as early as 1860. By 1890 Bass and Company alone were employing over 125 East Anglian workers. By 1896 it had risen to 256 workers. So I would estimate that during the 1890's as many as 400 East Anglian workers were coming to Burton each year. Although Bass and Company were the main people responsible for the migration I think the other breweries did bring workers over as well.

'The malting season had to finish in June because the brewers were unable to malt or brew during the summer season. This was because they were unable to control the temperature in the maltings and brewery at that time of year; and unless they were able to do this they couldn't produce malt or beer of the required quality. The beer had to be of sufficient quality because Burton already had a long tradition of exporting beer. At that time beer was being exported all over the world, particularly to India, but also to Australia, South America, the West Indies and Russia. This beer had to withstand a long sea voyage so it had to be of top quality.'[1]

The majority of the East Anglians who went up to Burton before the First World War were young, unmarried horsemen, young farm-workers who tended their horses and took them out to plough. Some of them described the conditions in Suffolk when they first went up. Albert George Ablett (born 1885) of Sibton Green, Suffolk, first went to Burton in 1903:

[T] 'There were about twenty young chaps without work in one small village like ours. It used to be that when the thrashing tackle came round they'd be going around asking for jobs a month or two before the machine actually got to the farm; and then of course they'd be denied. It was not only in one village; it was everywhere nearly. There weren't nobody a-doing nawthen, hardly. They wouldn't even pay the money to cut the bushes back. The farms were neglected. I mean you'd got big owd fences. Some on 'em would take up half the field—left, you know. They wouldn't pay anyone to do it. The fences all grown up like woods. They used to grow each side of the road till they met, you know.'

John Dennis Kettle (born 1894) of Framsden first went to Burton in 1912. The conditions in the villages were still the same then:

'I was brought up in Earl Soham, and there were about fifty of us young chaps in that area without work after harvest. Farming was in a bad way. You couldn't get work only at haysel and harvest. The farmers didn't want you after the corn-harvest. They'd keep the married men on and the younger workers were laid off.' Sam Friend, also of Framsden, went to Burton about the

---

[1] Personal communication.

same time; and he had a younger brother, Ernie, who went up just before the outbreak of the 1914–18 war:

[T] 'Well, I was lucky. I was a horseman and I niver had to lose time [through bad weather]. But my brother lived along o' me and I seen him come hoom on Saturday nights and give my mother five shillings. That's all he'd 'arned in the week! And he'd look at these five shillings and say: "Well, Mother, I'm a-going to git a red coat. I'm going to 'list." I sometimes used to go down to Cretingham *Bell*, and I say to him, "Come and have a pint, Arnie"; and he'd come down and have to change a two-shilling bit. So I suppose he find two bob somewhere. Poor owd Mother used to give it to him. So he didn't go and 'list. But he went up to Burton—him and his mate; and he came home 'arly in 1915 and joined up and went to Mesopotamia. He got killed in September 1918. And my mother niver had a medal for him. Niver found out anything about it, but of course she got a pension.'

Conditions in the farming areas of East Anglia remained exactly the same—except for the brief intermission during the First World War—until the migration to Burton ceased. Hector Moore, the Brandeston blacksmith, recalled the tail-end of the movement: 'I can remember the Christmas of 1930–31 when things were really bad. We were catching sparrows on the chopping-block with an old *break-back* trap—catching 'em for Christmas dinner! Things were very hard. That's why, I suppose, I can remember it so well. That particular year we moved—we moved back to Kettleburgh— the summer of 1931, and things were still very bad then. But I can remember one man in the village of Kettleburgh coming home from Burton in the summer, bringing his two children with him. He'd walked all the way from Burton. He'd got his daughter in the pram. She was a cripple and he'd pushed her all the way in the pram, and his son was walking beside it.'

At the end of August and the beginning of September the Burton brewers sent agents down to various centres in East Anglia to engage the young farm-workers. Bass and Company sent a circular letter to each malting worker who had been employed during the previous season—if he had proved satisfactory. The letter gave the date when the agent would be in a particular locality. The place was usually a public house—*The Station Hotel*, Ipswich, Framlingham *Crown* and so on.

[T] 'They used to sign us up at the *Crown*. The agent was a man called Johnny Clubs, a good owd bloke, and later a Mr. Whitehart come down. You went into a room and he looked you up and down to see if you could do the work, see if you were well set-up. Then he asked you the name of your last master so he could get a character. Then you signed the paper.' This was the agreement form (opp. page). When Sam Friend went up in 1912 each worker was supposed to be at least twenty-one years of age; but at an earlier period it appears that as long as a worker looked strong enough his age was not questioned. James Knights (born 1880) of Little Glemham, Suffolk, went to Burton when he was nineteen:

[T] 'I went to Burton because I thought there was bigger wages. That's what I went for. I was ploughman at Thistleton Hall, Burgh; and the farmer says: "You've got a pair of good horses, and you're a good man and I'll give you a shilling a week more than I give anyone else," and he says, "I don't see what you want to leave for." Eleven shillings a week was the wage for a horse-man and I was getting twelve. He thought a lot of me and I could do my work all right, of course. But I went up to Burton and the first job I done I went carrying barley—*store-room trot*. That was about a hundred yards carrying a sack of barley. I only had that two days; and then I went into the malt-house and I was making malt for all the rest of the time I was there. Very hard work it was. There was lots of fellows, lots of fellows, young fellows went up there and that killed them. Four or five died during the time I was up there from the hard work. They were all young chaps went up, from seventeen to twenty-five. They wouldn't never have old men.'

It is probable that for this reason the company later insisted that every worker engaged should be at least twenty-one years of age. But this rule did not prevent some of the younger men putting on their age in an effort to escape a winter of unemployment. John Kettle of Framsden recalled: 'The agent was an Irishman, a very pleasant chap. I remember him well: he was very fond of

105

Sept 10th _1925._

In consideration of Wages at the rates herein stated being paid

to me, I, _F. Gilbert_

of _Burton_ County of _Stafford_

do agree to serve to the best of my ability in the Grain Department of

M srs. Bass, Ratcliff & Gretton, Limited, of Burton-on-Trent,

from this _10th_ day of _Sept_ 1925 to 31st May, 1926.

This Contract may be cancelled by either party giving to the other
Twenty-eight days' notice.

WAGES.

All Maltsters when employed in work other than in Malt-making will
be paid the S.R. rate.

Maltsters when employed in Malt-making 66/6 per week.

Sundays - - - - 4/6 extra per day.

Xmas Day, Good Friday, Boxing Day, Easter Monday and
Whit-Monday, double pay.

Hours of Working according to Foreman's Instructions.

Witness my hand this _10th_ day of _Sept_ 1925.

F. Gilbert

We agree to pay the aforesaid Wages,

For Bass, Ratcliff & Gretton, Limited.

Witness _Marson_

In addition to the Wages stated in this Contract Note, Messrs. Bass, Ratcliff
and Gretton, Limited, are prepared to give on the 31st May, 1926 (or on an earlier
date if the Maltster leaves on account of illness or any unavoidable occurrence)
to each Maltster in their Employment on that date, a present of Two Shillings
for every week he has been engaged in Malt-making for them from this date.

his beer. He sat by himself in a room at the *Crown* and we went in one at a time. I recollect I went in one year and he asked me how old I was. "Twenty-one," I say. He looked at me some hard and then at the list he had in front on him and he say: "Outside! You were twenty-one years ago." I'd forgotten I'd put my age on before; I was so keen to get up there. He was sharp, but I got there eventually.'

Once the worker had signed on, the agent gave him a *single* railway ticket from the nearest railway station to Burton-on-Trent, and he went up on the following Monday. But as the villages were often a fair distance from the railway the men had to arrange to get to the station as best they could. Sam Friend recalled an occasion when he went up to Burton:

[T] 'A lot of us from round here went to Framlingham Station. Walter Mays used to keep a shop and he drove us down in his horse and trap. I went up on the 5th September and got on famously. But of course my mate had gone up the Monday afore. He came and met me at the station in Burton. Of course he'd got me lodgings next door to where he was lodging in Station Street. But I was telling you about the journey. There was one of the blokes who come with me from Cretingham in the horse and trap and he couldn't read nor write. So his mother gave him a postcard and say to him: "As soon as you get there do you post this. Then I'll know you're all right." Well, the fust thing he done when he got to Framlingham station was to find a post-box and shove in the postcard to send to his mother. That's how we used to go on at that time o' day. But none of us had never been in a train afore. That was the fust time I went in a train when I went to Burton. And everything—the compartments and so on—were some strange.'

Sam Friend gave me an inkling of the impression this journey made on the young East Anglian workers by recounting two of its noteworthy points: 'When we came back home from Burton I recollect you could allus start an argument in a pub by saying outright: "I've seen 'em a-cutting wheat in March!" Of course, they wouldn't believe that, and there'd be bets and arguments. You could pick up a pint as easy as winking because when you came to prove it you could say that when you went to Burton last September the train passed through the Fens, and alongside the town of March you saw 'em a-cutting wheat. But you couldn't play that trick often.' And more seriously: 'Going up to Burton by train they used to say: "There ain't no Sundays once you've passed Leicester corner." You were going into a seven-day week and you couldn't tell a Sunday from a weekday.'

The same recruiting organization obtained in Norfolk, as Albert Love of Wortwell recalls: 'A number of young men used to go up to Burton at the beginning of the century; though my father had been and lived up there I niver went up myself. They came from all the surrounding villages and they all came together at Homersfield station like soldiers and they went up to Burton together. There were two or three men from each of these villages: Earsham, Denton—I knew many of 'em: a family called Revell went up from there—Bedingham, Woodton, Alburgh. About twenty-five to thirty went up each year from Homersfield Station.'

24 The Work

When I went to Burton-on-Trent I asked a retired maltster about the malting process: 'Go to Will Gosling. He'll be the lordly man to tell you about that.' William Matthew Gosling (born 1899) is a second-generation Suffolk man who has lived in Burton all his life:

[T] 'Father was a Suffolk man. He lived at Belstead near Ipswich, though he was born at Creeting St. Mary. At first he used to come up every winter to malt; and then he'd go back again in the summer months when the Burton men used to clean the maltings down. My father when he settled up here had only sixteen shillings a week. He was a wagoner for Bass's. He was single and got only sixteen shillings: the married men got eighteen. He got married up here and settled down. But he never lost his accent. I can remember to this day when I took my father's dinner to the malthouse: as soon as I pushed the door open the first words I heard was: "Blast, bor, your nearly pulled thet door off!"

'But it was hard work. By gosh, it was hard work, needing good strong healthy men. I found that out myself. I mean there's chaps like myself—about twelve stone ten pounds—you were expected to carry bags of barley at sixteen stone four; and sometimes there wasn't a job for you in the hard days when there was a lot of men out of work. And there was one boss—well, if he couldn't spell your name you'd had it. You'd got to go! I remember one man called Paternoster: that's a good old Suffolk name. Yes, there wasn't a job for you if you couldn't carry the barley. It was all manhandled in those days. About eight men and a foreman had to get 300 quarters of barley off the wagons for a day's work. You had to do, that's your day's money. And the biggest—the biggest godsend that ever came to Bass's in the maltings was the endless belt. It used to carry the barley to where you wanted it instead of you having to carry it on your shoulders. I've come home once or twice with blood coming from my back-collar stud-band and my shoulder bones. You know, the skin rubbed off with carrying the barley. It was awful! I reckon it was the hardest job next to coal-mining. And coal-mining was only worse through the danger of it being underground. I've gone home at nights with clothes drenched with sweat from head to foot and the wife has had to pull my socks off, they've been that wet inside my boots. That was the heat of the kilns.

'When I was at Bass's they used to soak the barley for three days, and then it was turned on to the floors. It was divided between three floors. Then it was spread out on the floors to grow. Bass's method was to try and get as much root out of the corn before the stalk came out at the other end of the grain. Of course it wasn't always possible, but Bass had a method of doing it for which they got a very well-known name for making malt. And they relied on all these old Suffolk chaps that came up to do the work. Then when the barley was put on the kiln it stopped on the kiln for four days, starting from about 130 degrees Fahrenheit the first day, 140–50 the second day, 160–70 the third, and up to the required heat for the fourth day. With the strong ale beer, the very dark, it used to run to 215–18 degrees.'

James Knights of Suffolk described what happened to the malt afterwards. This was at an earlier period—about 1900—when methods were primitive even by the standards of a decade later:

[T] 'The malt came off the floor and it would go into a garner, and then it all had to be screened. They did this on the screens they called *Joe and Charlie*—two big screens. You'd get your good barley and the muck would go behind the screens. You had to throw the malted barley up against the screen. It was done by a fan as well. It was hot: it would nearly kill you. We had to have masks for this. When it had been screened you'd got to be in there and the malted barley would come out of a big hole just big enough to get a comb-sack through; and it used to run into a big heap; and you'd got to be inside there a-throwing on it back so it didn't bung up the hole. When you come out of there you was drunk from the dust of the malt—without having nawthen to drink! No, you didn't want anything to drink. You was drunk. When you come out of this you was absolutely drunk! Then if you'd lie down for a few minutes, have a few minutes' sleep, you were right again.

'For the work we used to do up there we used to have all the beer we could drink. There used to be a chap told off every day to fetch us beer in two nine-quart cans. I often had eight or nine pints before breakfast; and breakfast was at eight o'clock, when we used to get to work at two o'clock in the morning. You never got drunk from that: you were used to it and you always had it. Sweated it out turning the barley and turning the malt. But it was all rush and go: one to beat the other. Of course that was three storey high: a floor here, then the next floor, then the top floor. Three floors in a malt-house. One floor would be up against another.'

This competition between the men working on different floors was confirmed by many of the maltsters. The men on one floor would complain, for instance, that they had a thicker *piece* of barley to turn than the men on the floor above them: 'The top floor is not spreed [spread] as thick as this 'un', and so on. It was harder, therefore, to turn, and since they were on piece-work they were afraid it would affect their wage.

Will Gosling added a note about the allowance of beer the men got:

[T] 'In all steel-works and in every job like that where men lose a lot of sweat it has to be replaced with five pints of something— whether it's water, tea, milk or beer. They used to supply us with allowance beer. Five pints in my time; we used to have a pint at six o'clock, a pint at ten, another pint at midday and another two pints during the afternoon. Then if you had to come back after tea to turn the kiln you had another pint for that. In between times you was given two pints of beer called *lack*. They called it *lack* because it was lacking a lot of things. It was a very mild beer, but it was wet: it was moisture. And of course you had different pints of beer for doing little odd jobs, just picking kiln dust up and getting ashes out, bagging up the rubbish and all that. They thought in those old days that a pint would cover you for all your expenses. But things have altered now.'

Albert Ablett of Sibton spoke of an earlier period when he referred to the allowance beer:

[T] '*Lacksie* was the beer you had while you were doing this [screening], a mild beer. But if you got their best beer you'd only want a pint and you wouldn't work. Thet would be too strong for you to drink—with the heat and so on. You could have as much lacksie as you liked. A man who was working with me drunk twenty-one pints of beer before breakfast. That was the time when we got up at two o'clock in the morning. (You had to get up at all times of the night when the foreman said it [the piece of barley] was ready to start.) Twenty-one pints afore he had his breakfast! That's a good day's drink, ain't it? He was a great big strong fellow. He came from Debenham. His name was Pearl.'

In the close season after the malting finished, the buildings were cleaned down thoroughly. One of the essential jobs was to clean the perforated kiln-bricks or tiles. I first heard about this job from Mrs. Gwendoline Hancock of Ipswich. She used to go kiln-pricking in the maltings at Manningtree, Essex. For this she used a bent knitting needle with a cork to protect her hand. Tom Wood (born 1910) of Burton described the process: 'During the school holidays we used to go *kill-pricking*. We used to prick out the holes in the malting tiles. They'd get fouled up with barley and dust during the malting season. Through these holes the hot air rose from the *kill* underneath and roasted the barley, so they had to be clear. When we were kill-pricking we used to put a sack down on the floor and lie on our bellies using a bodkin to clear the holes. We used to work down a row of bricks or tiles. We got a penny for each brick, and it was a wonderful thing for us to earn some money during the school holidays. We also used to catch greenfinches that came on to the barley. We caught them with a net and we used to sell them as cage-birds.'

Visitors to the *Maltings Concert Hall* at Snape will notice that the walk below the restaurant on the east side of the building is paved with old malting tiles taken from the floor of the original maltings.

25 Living in Burton

William Denny (1882–1968) was one of the oldest surviving Suffolk men who went to the Burton maltings at the end of last century and the beginning of this. Just before he died, he gave me an account of his four seasons in Burton. Will Denny was typical of the early wave of men who went up from East Anglia. When I first met him he was an old man of eighty-five, but one could still see the remnant of his former strength and stature, of the time when he was a young man over six feet tall, weighing sixteen stones and fearing no man or job he had to tackle. He was courteous and had a simple directness that made listening to him a pleasure:

'I first went to Burton when I was nineteen. I worked on the farm before I went up there. I was fit and strong and I wouldn't be messed about by anyone. The hours on the farm were six-thirty to five-thirty in the summer; seven o'clock till five o'clock in the winter. But you'd do a haysel and a harvest and perhaps they didn't want you after that. So I signed on for Burton at the Ipswich *Railway Hotel*. I signed on a Thursday and my ticket was waiting for me at Ipswich Station ready to go up on the Monday. My first job was in the store, a-bushelling barley, putting the barley into sacks, doing the carrying jobs and so on. Store-room work they called it. They paid you twenty-one shillings a week for a six-day week. The store chaps didn't work on Sundays but they stood by in case one of the regular maltsters was away from work. Then I went into the maltings. For this I got four shillings a day, five for Sunday. If you came any morning an hour or so early—you had to do sometimes—you got a shilling extra. If you got through your malting season you got fourpence a day as well as your wage. Some called it holiday money. This was added to your last pay before you came home. I recollect in my first year I got £2 4s 2d: the extra tuppence was for a half-day I stood in for a mate of mine.

'In the maltings the grain was taken up from the bottom floor by the scuttles—through the loading holes. I recollect that thirty years after I left Burton I went back on a visit with my son—we were returning from north Wales—and we saw a foreman called Smith who was there in my time. This man told my son: "No one could handle the scuttles better than your father." I aren't a boasting man but it was the truth, and it was good to hear it.

'After coming home from work and having some tea we'd go round the town, having a pint at one pub and then at another. There was the *Wheatsheaf, Punch Bowl, Golden Ball* and many more. We were a crowd together and we used to enjoy ourselves. We used to sing, and one thing we used to do up there was to step-dance on top of a barrel. In all the pubs up there you could get a free clay-pipe at that time—with the pub's name on it. After my first season in Burton I recollect I brought ninety clay-pipes home with me. We were in lodgings, most of us, paying twelve shillings a week. Some got on well, but we didn't. I once lodged in Canal Street, and a sixteen-year-old girl looked after the meals for me and another chap named Stover. I had a fancy for something tasty, and one night I gave her a pig's fry and asked her to cook it for us for next day. When we came home it was hardly warmed let alone cooked. The girl wasn't there when we ate it, and didn't we swear! I was courting one of the Burton girls. Her name was Good or Wood—I forget now. She was a nice girl and I bought her a pair of shoes. But her mother noticed her new shoes and asked her where they come from; and when the girl couldn't give a good account of the shoes her mother chopped the heels off! Talking about girls, there was a man up there in the maltings, a piece-walker called Runnacles. This one was strict and made us work. But one day he say to me he knew Ashbocking where I come from.

He was a-courting a girl there. But I was right surprised when he told me the name o' the girl because I knew her: she had a face like a bullace pudding gone wrong!

'Bass used to give us a piece of beef at Christmas at that time— 1901 it was when I first went up. They used to give six pounds for the single chaps and ten pounds for the married ones. It was good beef, too. Some of the chaps used to sell it; some of 'em used to send it home to Suffolk. I gave a bit of it to my Burton landlady. But you needed suthen like beef. You didn't go up to Burton for a holiday!'

The tremendous and sustained physical effort involved in the old process of malting demanded good food with a high protein content. The brewers recognized this, and it was the purpose of the Christmas beef allowance. Albert Love of Wortwell remembers his father telling him that when he and his wife set up house in Burton they took in lodgers, three or four young Norfolk men from the Homersfield area. While they were there he often used to call at the butcher's and take home a stone or a stone-and-a-half of beef to feed the men who were in the house. George Alesbrook, a Burton maltster, recalled one Suffolk man who made sure he was going to be well fed:

[T] 'I just forgot where he come from. But when he come back he used to bring a load of sausages back with him. Their own make; and it was good stuff and all.' Sam Friend told me that they could cook themselves breakfast in the maltings:

[T] 'They packed up a lunch for you to take. But you had a frying-pan or an oven in the cabin and you bought bacon and eggs and anything you fancied and you could fry it up and have a good hot breakfast. We used to light a fire. One of us would do it one morning, then someone else on another morning. I always used to light the fire on a Friday.' But as half the day's work was done before breakfast most of the men had a 'sustainer' before they started work. The daughter of one of the East Anglian workers who settled in Burton remembered that her father used to get up at two o'clock in the morning to be in work by three. Before he went out he drank two raw eggs beaten up in his mug of tea. The need for a full diet for maltsters was emphasized by Mrs. Lester Brett of Framsden in Suffolk. Before she was married she lived in Stonham

Aspal and was one of a large family. Her mother used five stones of flour in a week and baked forty loaves for a family of five men and four younger children. Her brother who worked at the nearby maltings at Stonham used to take sixteen rounds of bread with butter, cheese and pork for his meal while he was at work.

Will Denny went on: 'The job was slavery. One year I remember I was taken bad, and I couldn't go on and I went to see the doctor. He was an Irishman, and as soon as I went into his sargery he say to me: "You don't want to tell me what's the matter with you. Bass's pick up you young chaps and bring you up here from the country and they work you to *dead!*" Some of the work was a bugger, a job we called *Joe and Charlie* particularly. This was screening the malt. As the malt comes off the kiln after roasting there is the roots or the *combs* loose with the grains. We then threw the malt with wooden shovels through this sieve and the combs would pass through. Well, when we were a-doing this you couldn't see across the room for the steam and the dust.

'We used to finish at the maltings towards the end of May. But before you went home you had to have a new suit. You dussn't come home from Burton wearing the suit you went up in. I used to buy my suit at a Burton shop called Tarver's. I believe it's still in the town. The suit had what we used to call a *donkey-dealer's* jacket. It was cut long, half-way down your thigh, and it buttoned up tight almost up to your neck. It had a long centre-vent at the back and a shaped waist with a couple o' buttons. You could get a good suit with a good style of cloth for £2 10s. One regular thing, too, before you came back home was to buy a teapot. I recollect I bought one to take home to a family I was lodging with in Suffolk. My Burton landlady say to me: "Aren't you going to give me the teapot?" but I told her I was a-taking it hoom to Suffolk. It was a rare teapot; it held about six pints and they made them at Woodville just outside Burton. When I got it hoom the old lady I was a-staying with was as pleased as a cat with nine cocks. We usually travelled down on Whitsun Saturday; we all went down to Suffolk in the same train. That was a load I can tell you. What weren't sober were drunk. We had a two hours' wait at Peterborough on the way down, and the chaps used to go out into the town. One year I recollect they went out and started lifting fruit—oranges, bananas, anything they could put their hands on. The police followed 'em back to the station, and I were right worried because I wanted to get back hoom like most of 'em. But as luck would have it, the train came in and we were away and nawthen came of it.

'There was a visit from the King one year we were up there, and they made a special brew of beer, extra strong *Royal Ale*. He did nothing, of course, just turned the tap on. It cost a lot o' money, about a shilling a pint as far as I can recollect. Some of the boys brought a gallon of Royal Ale hoom with them. My mate did. And when we got to Ipswich I was the last out of the carriage and a saw a jar of ale left there in the rack. So I took it thinking it were my mate's. But when I caught him up at the *Railway Hotel* just across the road I saw that he'd got his jar of ale. So he say to me: "Don't go a-searching for its owner now. Keep it. If you call out, everybody will own it."

'After I came back following my last season up in Burton I worked for Arthur Pratt, the Suffolk horse-breeder at Morston Hall, Trimley. They were a right good family, Mr. Pratt's. He say to me after harvest: "You're not thinking about going back to Burton, are you, Billy?" and I say: "I reckon I am, Mr. Pratt. You can be under cover up there during the bad weather." But he say: "You can be under cover here," he say. So I stayed and worked with him for a few years until I went into the pub business, and I went to Ashbocking *Nelson* where I stayed for nigh on fifty year.'

Mrs. Mary Wightman, born 1881 near Burton, married a maltster from the Framlingham district of Suffolk. They set up house in Burton and Mrs. Wightman took many of the young men from that district as lodgers:

[T] 'Yes, I had as many as four at a time. They were very good, very nice young men they were. I will say that about them. They came from good homes so why shouldn't they be nice? They were like a lot of townspeople: there's good and bad, I suppose. Twelve shillings a week, that's what the board was. I was country-born and I got on very well with them. I was born on a farm so I knew ... well, most of them were farm-workers who came up here; and of course I understood their work a little better. But they used to look forward to the end of the season. Some of them used to say: "Oh, roll on the thirty-first of May!" But I mean it was just to get home. That used to be their Framlingham Gala what they used to look for. As long as they got home for that they didn't mind.'

Many of the young Suffolk workers lodged in company houses, boarding houses owned by Bass or one of the other brewers. Albert Ablett recalled:

[T] 'I lodged in a company house. Very often of a night the buggers used to come home drunk. Some on 'em weren't satisfied with what beer they had in the maltings, they'd go round the pubs, a lot on 'em. The food was good, done well. I went out at night sometimes and you had the papers and books to read. I got on all right with the Burton chaps. Some on 'em were rough, we know—got to fightin'. But they were all nationalities and they used to knock one another about.'

The East Anglians were called *Norkies*, *Suffolk Punches* or *Suffolk Jims* and appear, on the whole, to have got on well with the Burtonians though there was the inevitable fracas occasionally. James Knights told me that he and his mate were once in a fight with two Burton men, and his mate—a Halesworth man—died in his lodgings two days later. The trouble usually started in a pub and Sam Friend recalled how the East Anglians would recognize some of the signs. If a Burton man turned his empty beer-pot upside down on the table they knew there was going to be trouble. So they could either stay or disengage, as it suited them. The East Anglians stood out from the local people, both by reason of their speech and their dress. Mrs. Wightman remembered:

[T] 'When I first saw them I thought they were costermongers with their black and white trousers. They used to be made at Mr. King's in Station Street. He used to make the black and whites and the black coats with a silk stripe; and I quite thought they were costermongers until I went to help a friend of mine—she kept a public house—and I met quite a lot of them there. So I found out who they were and what they were. They were very nice men. But we could hardly understand them sometimes in their Suffolk talk, you know. They talked peculiar.'

Mrs. Violet Topley (born 1900) of Burton worked for forty-eight years as a cashier in Messrs. Tarver, clothiers and tailors of Burton:

[T] 'These men used to come down from East Anglia in quite big numbers. In fact they came down for years and years, but I remember them when they were taken on in the 'twenties. They used to come in to Tarver's shop at the end of the season and spend their money—their well-earned money—and buy a suit. They could get a good suit, made to measure, for three to four guineas —which was a lot of money in those days. They'd got to work hard for that.

'Incidentally, the materials we used for these suits came from Suffolk, from Gurteen's of Haverhill chiefly. This material was very strong, dark greys. But then, in the 'twenties, the ordinary suit was coming in—the suit with the shorter coat, you see. But in the old days they wore them very much the same style as the gamekeeper. They had a tail to the coat, two buttons at the back, and I think it was one on the sleeve, and white stripes and a waistcoat. And they always had an extra piece of material at the bottom of the waistcoat, a kind of sateen lined thing that covered the back, for warmth as we used to say in those days. And the trousers were like the modern youth is wearing today. They were narrow and no turn-ups. They looked very smart, very smart indeed. And they always used to have one of those suits to take home with them. The trousers were the drop kind—*whole-falls*—like the sailor's. For work they had corduroy trousers, and they used to have to wear them when they worked at the malt. They were almost the same colour as the malt, with tapes round the knees to save the dust going right up their legs, because it was very dusty. And they always had a scarf or neckerchief as they were called in those days.'

John Kettle told me about the suits he got in Burton: 'All the young chaps would have new suits coming back from Burton, and Ipswich station on Whitsun Saturday night was a sight, with the girls on the platform meeting them. They made fine suits in Burton. They took some wearing out, I can tell you. They were made from Melton cloth. You couldn't punch a hole through it. It wouldn't wear up. I bought a coat in 1913 or '14, and when I joined the army

I let my brother have it. He wore it for five years and when I came out of the army it were not wore up then. I had to finish it. I bought a suit in the early 'twenties and it cost £9 10s. It would cost more like forty guineas today and the cloth would be nawthen like the quality. The suits were very well made: horse-shoe buttons, double stitching, and narrow trousers. You could wear a suit for twenty years and it would still be respectable.

'A number of men who went up from Suffolk stayed up there and got married to Burton girls. They often went as horsemen, driving the horses in the beer-drays. This company, too, kept a hundred horses just for shunting alone—moving the wagons about in the railway sidings. My wife's brother married a Burton girl and stayed up there. He became a fireman in the maltings, a responsible job: he had to make sure the grain was processed at the right temperature. He was a big man; he made twenty-one stone. There was a lot o' big people up at Burton. Burton was a master place for big people. They say it was the smell of the beer that made them all so big; but a-supping on it helped a bit, you may depend.

'My last season at the maltings in Burton was in 1922. The malting season finished towards the end of May, and this year instead of coming straight home I went to Epsom for the Derby. I remember I had a pound on the race but I didn't back the winner. After it was over I was walking around and I met a fellow who asked me whether I was a-looking for a job. I thought he were pulling my leg. I didn't think he were worth tuppence, let alone hiring someone to do a job. He was wearing old cord trousers, and he was smoking a clay pipe. But he seemed to be in 'arnest and he said: "If you want a job you can start now—just over the fields there." It turned out he farmed over a thousand acres—him and his son. He had a big herd o' Red Polls, and he grew a little corn as well. I signed up with him on the London rate of fifty-two shillings a week, with harvest paid by the extra hours you worked. I lived cheap, too: I slept in the barn and ate in the farmhouse. That was in 1922. If I'd been working in Suffolk at that time I'd have been 'arning twenty-seven shillings a week, with £7 harvest bonus; that was about half as much as I was 'arning at Chessingham—that was the name of the place.'

26 Interludes During Work

When the young East Anglian maltsters were not working they *played* hard, often violently. This was an understandable reaction to the gruelling nature of the work. There was also a certain amount of natural fun and horseplay in the maltings themselves when the foreman or piece-walker was out of sight. There were also the tales and small activities to recount when break-times for meals gave them a short relief. Will Gosling knows a great deal of the folklore of the East Anglian maltsters because he was so closely connected with them through his father:

[T] 'I've never been down to the place in Suffolk where my father was born. But I took him down to Yarmouth for a holiday one year, and he went from there down into Suffolk. He came back with four rabbits. And it appears from what he told his mates when he came back up to Burton-on-Trent that the gun hadn't been down from over the fireplace since he left over twenty years before. They all reckoned that the rabbits must have been killed by the rust from the barrel.

'There's a lot of East Anglians I remember. There's Bill Burgess —he's just retired—and his son, John; Barney Beckett, my own workmate—but he just died last year. And there's Bert Wightman, still about. And I remember Fred Chambers from Fressingfield. He comes up every now and again to see me. His brother Bill, he's still working in Burton-on-Trent. Bert Atkins, the little fellow and his long pal, Tiny Crane—he's gone now. I've not heard from Tiny Crane for years. There was Roley Last, one of the old stalwarts that first came up when I was a lad. I remember the tricks he used to play at work and at home. There was one tale about him coming home for his dinner, and his wife was down the garden gossiping. So he took the pudding out of the saucepan and replaced it with a brick. I don't know what end that came to. I remember one day at work when Roley came into the cabin to look for a bottle of beer he'd put by for a rainy day. He found it and he had a little pull of it and said: "Blast, bo', thet look like soft water." He took the cork out and had another sip, and then he said: "Blast! it is soft water." Someone had taken his beer.

'We used to have fun with the Norfolk lads. I told you that the company used to supply all the boots. (Sometimes the floor was so hot it used to burn your boots and you'd have to come off and stand in the *foot-low* if you couldn't put up with the heat. These boots used to be hand-made at Bass's. There were no steel nails in them: there were wooden pegs like matches in the square holes they used to bore in the soles of the shoes. And for the barley-room men, in the store, they used to make a special boot—with a leather bottom and a canvas top so the corn can't sink down and get in the boots. Of course one corn would cripple you, whereas a shoe full is not too bad.) But I was telling you about these Norfolk chaps—one of them was called Tiny Crane. He was a Lifeguards-man, and when he came up to Bass's we hadn't got a shoe to fit him. First of all they took the largest size they'd got—I think it was elevens—and they slipped a toe-cap on to the uppers. But after that, when he started to come regular, year after year, they made his boots special for him; and Bass's have still got the last pair that wasn't issued to him. And that's a size fourteen! There used always to be jokes about Tiny Crane's feet. They'd say: "We haven't got a pair of fourteen for Tiny. Better give him two pair o' sevens!" He was one of the nicest chaps you'd ever meet; and he took it in good heart and laughed with us. He used to say that when he got back home he'd sit on one side of the table and two of his children would sit opposite on each big toe. There used to be some

games on the floor between Tiny and Bert Atkins, the little fellow.
Bert would always be trying to wheel a barrow over Tiny's feet, and
Tiny used to chase him about the floor, with the little 'un ducking
under the blows—you could hear the air *whishing* as he missed him!
I believe Tiny was from the Pulham Market area: I don't know if
he's alive today. I don't think he is.'

Albert Ablett recalled the occasion over sixty years ago when a
girl very rashly walked on to the malting floor when the piece-
walker was not about:

[T] 'We got a young lady in there once. She'd come there, I
don't know how. But she was a funny one I expect. I mean she got
into this barley with us; and there was some playing about. Two
or three of us, we pulled her down into the barley and pulled her
drawers down and filled 'em with barley. Of course we didn't
interfere with her, just pulled down her drawers, you know, and
put the barley in and let her go.'

The buying of a teapot was part of the Burton ritual that helped
to give variety to the East Anglian's stay in the Midlands. These
large, rather crudely decorated, earthenware teapots were made
at Coalville and Swadlincote, and many of the East Anglians who
went up before the 1914–18 war brought 'Burton teapots' back
with them because it was part of the experience of going to
Burton, like buying a new suit. Many of the teapots—which are
identical with the old bargee's teapot—have since become family
heirlooms in East Anglia; Sam Friend still has the one he brought
back with him in 1912:

[T] 'Well, they used always, well most of them would bring
their mother a teapot; just to say, "That come from Burton"; and
some would bring a set of jugs. Just before we come home I
wanted to go to Swadlincote for a teapot, and I asked the floor-
man, and he say, "Yes", but kept a-putting on it off. So I say to
my mate, Rowley: "If you go to get my teapot I'll pay your fare,
and I'll give you a couple of bob to spend. And I'll go back at
night and turn your kiln for you and you can take the money."
He went all the way and got the teapot. He lived in Station Street,
Burton; and when I come out of work I went down there and I
said: "I hear you've got my teapot, Rowley." But he said: "No,

they ain't got no more!" Then he laugh. He'd got the teapot indoors. I brought it home, and there it is now. It cost two shillings and tuppence. I've been offered a lot of money for it, scores of times but I won't part with it now.'

Another article the young men brought home with them was a belt. Most of them were young horsemen on the East Anglian farms and a braided belt was almost part of the dress. Most of these belts came from a nearby village of Winshill. Albert Love remembers that the young workers who went to Burton used to bring back braided leather belts from Burton for their friends. They cost half a crown each before the First World War. 'All the young Norfolk horseman used to wear them. It was the practice to walk out of a Sunday with the braided leather belt showing just below your waistcoat. A mate brought me one down from Burton well over sixty year ago—and here you see I still got it. It was in 1902, it was; a man named Plumb got it for me. You see the fastening on the belt are all made like the horse-gear: the buckles are stirrups, and the clasp a snaffle-bit with a horse-shoe in the centre. But I found out the way to braid leather myself. I once went to a saddler in Bungay who sold these belts ready made up. I offered to braid them for him; and he paid me five shillings for half a dozen I did for him.'

During the 'twenties when Will Bolton of Peasenhall used to go to Burton, the old *Statute Fair* used to be an attraction soon after they arrived. [T] 'The Fair was in the street and while it was on no traffic was allowed. There were hurdy-gurdies, horses, a boxing-booth—everything. But they told me it used to be an old hiring fair when the farmers used to come in and hire workmen for the following year. We used to do a lot of singing and *stepping* in the Burton pubs. Outside the Burton *Wheatsheaf* they sometimes had a lorry, and two of the lads got up on this lorry to step-dance, to see who could do it the best. Young Freeman, a mate of mine could do it well, you know. He could rattle his feet. The *Barley Mow* was one of the songs we used to sing up there.'

The high spirits of the young maltsters come out in this story James Knights told me of his landlady and his two friends from Halesworth. It happened over seventy years ago: and the story also

shows the narrative skill of some of the people of the old culture
which was almost entirely an oral one:

[T] 'Well, when I first went to Burton I lodged with a woman
called Mrs. Oakby; and I didn't get on much there because she'd
got only one son and he went to college. So I didn't get on much
with him. Two or three doors away there was a couple of other
boys come from Halesworth. And I said to them:

"What sort of grub are you getting?"

'They said: "Ours is all right."

"Well," I said, "Have you got room for another lodger?"

'He said, "I should think so."

"I'll come around and see the old woman," I said.

'So I went and see the old woman[1] and she said: "Yes, I could
do with another one. There'll be three of you." She lived alone.
The old woman lived alone. So I went there to live; and it went
on, well on, I should think nearly into June; and I said:

"I should like to play a trick with this old woman."

'These ones say: "Well, what would you like to do?"

"Well," I say, "I'll tell you what I should like to do: I should
like to get her to go to bed one night," I say, "and I'll get underneath her bed and lift her out of bed."

'So the other two, they say: "Well, I don't know how you are
going to work that."

'I say: "I know how to do that well. Tonight I shall get some
soot out of the chimney after she's gone to bed," I said, "and
put it in paper and I'll take it upstairs with me tonight; and I'll
go to bed tomorrow night—early."

'Which I did. I went to bed and I went upstairs and blacked
my face all over, and before she come up I got under her bed.

'Well, when she come to bed I could hear she was just going
to sleep because she was a tidy old gel for her drink—she'd soon
drink a couple or three pints of beer. She always had beer in the
house of course. And when she got sort of dozing off, I heaved
up, you see; and she began to roll about the bed; and I gave her
another heave and she come out on the floor.

[1] See photograph [Plate 29] with the landlady and her three lodgers. James
Knights, who is wearing a braided belt, is on the left.

'The other two boys was downstairs, so I said to myself, "What am I going to do now?" She flew at the window and got half-way out of the window: she was going to jump out of the window; and I pulled her back and I jumped out of the window myself.

'The other two boys come upstairs to want to know what was up with her. She laid on the floor and Bert Freeman, he say: "Well," he say, "we shall have to give some brandy." She was queer. I went out and come down and washed myself and everything; and the old woman say:

"Well," she say, "I don't know who it was but it ain't Jimmy because he's in bed."

'So we carried on with it and she was laid there till one o'clock in the morning, the old gel laying there and they was putting brandy into her. Well, there was some laughing! And the next morning she goes down to the police and she said that there was a black-man had broken into her house and had gone underneath her bed and turned her out of bed.

'That morning the police come out to me at the malthouse and wanted to know if I'd suspicioned anybody. I said: "No, I never knew anybody, but she said it was a black man." Of course that was me all the time. The police went to the other two boys in the malthouse to find out what they could about it, but they never did find nothing out about it. We had some sport over that and the old woman never knew it was me.'

Other times, other manners: but if it seems today that this was a much overestimated form of amusement, the historian of polite society could remind us that bed bouncing was a favourite pursuit among the ladies of Queen Victoria's court and a frequent diversion at country-house parties.

Conclusion

In most of the examples given in the previous pages I have tried to show the use of the oral tradition at the present time. I have taken these examples chiefly from the last generation of country people who grew up under the prior culture, and I have gone to farming and its related crafts for most of this illustrative material because farming was the base of this culture in East Anglia and shows an outstanding continuity over a long past. But the old country community is not unique in this respect: the town can afford many examples of the usefulness of the oral tradition. Living men and women can illuminate its social and industrial history during the great changes of the last seventy-five years (the chapters concerning Burton-on-Trent are an example), and occasionally they can supplement evidence that is of wider general interest than the particular town itself.

An example comes from Ipswich. In the first two decades of this century there were outbreaks of an infectious disease with an alarmingly high death-rate (75–80 per cent). Fortunately, the outbreaks were contained; but it was not until 1910 that the disease was identified. The last cases occurred in 1918. It was the bubonic plague, *The Plague* that had swept through England in the fourteenth century, and had recurred at intervals during later centuries.

As soon as the cause of the Ipswich outbreaks was known, their source was traced to the black rats which came up the estuary of the Orwell with the ships that were bringing in grain. The port of Ipswich at that time could take ships of only a shallow draught; therefore the grain ships were anchored in the estuary at a point called Butterman's Bay, and the grain was *lightered*—that is, transferred to barges or lighters and brought to the quayside. The black rats, carrying the plague-infected fleas that transmitted the disease to human beings, escaped from the ships at Butterman's Bay and got ashore, later fanning out over the surrounding countryside. One of the health authorities' main tasks was to trace and exterminate the rats and attempt to contain the outbreak in this way. With the aid of the village policemen they traced the rats over an area, which in one direction was about ten miles from the presumed point of landing, and the disease-spread was halted.

An Ipswich consultant physician, Dr. D. van Zwanenberg, is writing an account of the outbreaks which are sufficiently documented. But in addition to studying all the available written sources, Dr. van Zwanenberg has gone to the survivors of the outbreaks; and from their memories he has been able to gain useful information to fill in the material he has gained from documents. The survivors were able to answer his questions about living conditions; for instance, the number in family of those who suffered, whether or not they lived in the old *two-up, two-down* type of dwelling, and where they got their water from. Some of them also had memories of the quarantine ship with its yellow flag and its place of anchor down the river. In addition to the physical details they were able to give the human, as opposed to the clinical and statistical, side of the outbreaks.

But the conditions for this kind of occurrence, and for the recording of much of the material previously given, have passed away and are not likely to be repeated. Therefore it would appear at first sight that when the last members of the prior culture in this part of Britain have gone, the main function of the oral tradition will die with them; because with all the present-day techniques of documentation, document-preserving, and recording, oral transmission of what is happening today is not likely to be of equal value to the historian or sociologist of the future. Without doubt, there will always be room and use for the *I saw it; I was there* or *I knew him* type of evidence, as the recent accounts of the 1914–18 war, against the perspective of half a century, have so well shown. But there is another reason why the reservoir of men's memories will have continuing value in the future: this is the great speed of change during the present generation, the lifetime of people who were born during or immediately after the last war. A quotation will illustrate from the technological point of view how quickly the succeeding generations during this century acquire the fossil-imprints of obsolescent modes and techniques. But they cherish them as well, and this is reflected in the widespread looking back to the immediate past and the setting up of various organizations dedicated to preserving old engines, photographs, motor-cars, tools—almost any old object—and in the wide interest in antiques: all the expression of a natural, compensatory attitude that inevitably accompanies a period of rapid change. The 1830's were another similar period when social unrest, parliamentary reform, and increasing technical and social change saw the deepening of an interest in the past and the founding of many local antiquarian societies. But here is the quotation:

'Man has changed the terms of his existence more in the past twenty-five years than in the previous ten-thousand years. In the space of one generation—in the lifetime of the children born since 1945—we have telescoped eras each as significant as the Bronze Age, the Iron Age, the Renaissance, and the Industrial Revolution. We have mushroomed into the Atomic Age, been programmed into the Computer Age and been rocketed into the Space Age. We have discovered and released as a bomb, the Secret of Matter. We have broken the gravitational fences of our planet. We are, in the studies of DNA and molecular biology, in predictable possession of the Secret of Life. But man neither evolves nor adapts as fast as the conversion of his own discoveries. His institutions do not change. His habits may, but reluctantly. His institutions—educational, political and religious

—cannot ignore, but only slowly accept, the revolutionary forces.'[1]

For many years to come, therefore, men and women will be able to give vivid accounts of social conditions and old industrial techniques which will illuminate the massive documentation that is accumulating. But more important still, they will be able through their memories to guide the student and the ordinary enquirer to the relevant sector of the documentary maze that is yearly becoming larger and more complicated. Ten years ago, Lord Evershed, then Master of the Rolls, said that the *Public Records Office* was acquiring documents at the rate of one and a half miles of shelves a year: the rate is probably greater now. This is only one of the central depositories; there are others not only in documents, books and newspapers, but in photographs, film, and recorded sound. In addition to these there are the industrial and local records that will at least double the total amount of records centrally stored. But the future student is not likely to be troubled so much by the question, *Where to look?* (a computerized central information bureau should be able to deal with that with comparative ease) as the problem, *What to look for?* Amid such a vast coverage of a past age where is he to begin? The memories that men still have of that age will be reliable first-indicators of where he should search, because it is in the minds of men themselves, through a process of instinctive selection, that the topics, the areas of interest, that are vital to man as an evolving being, will most probably remain.

At the more immediately practical level the oral tradition is likely to be of future use in its natural context—the family. Information passed from grandparent to grandson was of vital importance in older societies for obvious reasons. The elders of the tribe or the community were the sole carriers of and the instructors in the tradition. In modern society the older generation has largely lost this function (perhaps owing to the speed of change they are 'outdated' so quickly): instead, interest in the

---

[1] *Radio Unesco:* A series of ten programmes concerned with the future of mankind. Edited and introduced by Lord Ritchie-Calder. Programme 10: 'Who are the Custodians?'.

past as a stabilizer during a period of rapid change has been focused in things—old machines and objects, as we have seen. Yet the older generation's memories are of great value in the family itself, helping to knit it together as a continuing social group under pressure from many of the disruptive forces that are incidental to accelerated social change.

Family memories could also be of value to the teacher of history in schools. Many teachers find that they have some difficulty in engaging a proportion of their students' interest in formal history. These cannot identify with people or things remote from their own limited experiences: they cannot *latch on* to the idea of history; and having no interest in it they do not acquire the percepts out of which the concept of history is formed. But in the small circle of which the family is the centre the experiences of children and young adults are rich: they are deeply interested in their family and identify themselves with it. If a potentially larger experience can be related to the family this natural interest could well carry over, or at least will have a good chance of doing so. This area of untapped family history is not, as already suggested, confined to the country; almost equally great changes have taken place in the town within living memory. The fairly recent study, industrial archaeology, has in a short time revealed the tremendous historical potential in a town's old buildings, factories, canals, and warehouses. A town-child's parents and grandparents can supply valuable footnotes which would help quicken his interest. This approach would be particularly valuable in those families where there has been a craft tradition over many generations (in printing, milling, farm-machinery, shoe-making, transport, mining—to name only a few). And where a craft tradition is strong, a child or young adult may well be able to bring important historical evidence to his group. But more to the point, he himself will have both feet in the domain of history almost without knowing it. It is not claimed there is anything new in the above suggestion. Proceeding from the known to the unknown, tracing history backwards are two of the clichés of history teaching. What is perhaps new about the idea is its suggested loosening of the rigid, academic concept of history. History, at

T

this present fertile time with a rich historical foreground waiting to be gleaned, should in my view be allied with a concept such as folk-life where a living community is still able to help in drawing the lineaments of a recently displaced culture which from any standpoint is already impeccably historic.

In relation to the continuing role of oral testimony another point is worth considering. It has been suggested that we are developing towards an entirely different kind of culture, moving out of the culture of print, the *Gutenberg Era* as Marshall McLuhan calls it, to a more oral culture conditioned by the telephone, the radio, television, the film, and the tape-recorder. The oral tradition will, on this assumption, regain some of its status within a society not committed so strongly to an almost total reliance on what is printed. Some of the signs of this are already visible: the changing role of the newspaper within our society, the increasing desire to hear poetry rather than see and read it on the page, and the setting up of such organizations as *The National Institute of Recorded Sound* which will be in the future as important an archive as any that deal with the written or printed word. Many will consider that all this shows an evolving society where the spoken word will have increasing worth and a new acclaim. It is certain that the oral tradition will have a continuing use in the humanities, both in supplementing the information and the insights that have been obtained elsewhere, and—perhaps most important of all— in correcting the present over-emphasis on things and lifeless data and in bringing the disciplines back to their central and committed concern: man himself.

Appendix One

❧✿❧

Hiring of East Anglian farm-workers by Bass, Ratcliff & Gretton Ltd.,
for work in Malthouses in Burton-on-Trent, 1890–1891 Season

Name of worker	Home Village	Nearest railway station
ADDISON, George	Melton	Woodbridge
ASHEN, Henry	Flempton	Bury St. Edmunds
ASHEN, William	Flempton	Bury St. Edmunds
BALDWIN, William	Alburgh	Harleston
BARBER, Walter	Martlesham	Woodbridge
BEAUMONT, Peter	Baylham	Ipswich
BETTS, Arthur	St. Cross	Harleston
BACKHOUSE, Jesse	Sutton	Woodbridge
BLOOMFIELD, Richard	St. Lawrence	Harleston
BRAGG, John	Bardwell	Bury St. Edmunds
BRETT, Charles	Martlesham	Woodbridge
BROOKS, Alfred	Pakenham	Bury St. Edmunds
CALVER, Frederick	Alburgh	Harleston
CLEVELAND, James	Rumburgh	Halesworth
CARVER, William	Kirton	Ipswich
CARVER, George	Kirton	Ipswich
COLE, Arthur	Westhall	Halesworth
CALLINGFORD, Sam.	Butley	Woodbridge
CALLINGFORD, Geo.	Butley	Woodbridge
COX, Edward	Somersham	Ipswich
CLEMENTS, David	Ufford	Woodbridge
CARR, George	Ipswich	Ipswich
CALEY, Samuel	Butley	Woodbridge
CARR, Jonathan	Gt. Bealings	Woodbridge
COBB, Edward	Somersham	Ipswich
COPPING, George	Grundisburgh	Woodbridge
CRANE, Jonathan	Burgh	Woodbridge
COX, Jonathan	Gt. Dunham	Swaffham
DAWSON, William	Saxlingham	Norwich
DAWES, Jonathan	Chillesford	Woodbridge
DAVEY, David	Burgh	Woodbridge
DRUMETT, Robert	Badingham	Framlingham
DYSON, Harry	Barrow	Bury St. Edmunds
DURRANT, Albert	Saxlingham	Norwich
EMMERSON, Samuel	Mendham	Harleston

283

Name of worker	Home Village	Nearest railway station
EMMERSON, Charles	Mendham	Harleston
FENN, George	Linstead	Halesworth
FLATT, Charles	Linstead	Halesworth
FOSTER, Edward	Charsfield	Woodbridge
FOSTER, William	Cookley	Halesworth
FRESTON, Ernest	Witnesham	Ipswich
FRIEND, William	Burgh	Woodbridge
GARNHAM, James	Bucklesham	Ipswich
GILES, Arthur	Barham	Ipswich
GOODALL, Walter	Bucklesham	Ipswich
HOOK, William	Saxlingham	Norwich
HUNT, Joseph	Hargreave	Higham
HOGG, Robert	Bardwell	Bury St. Edmunds
HART, George	Pettistree	Woodbridge
HISKEY, Alfred	Elmsett	Ipswich
HOCKLEY, Robert	Trimley	Ipswich
HART, William	Witnesham	Ipswich
HALLS, Alfred	Thurston	Bury St. Edmunds
HEAD, George	Swaffham	Swaffham
JAMES, Arthur	Baylham	Ipswich
JACOBS, William	Sutton	Woodbridge
JOHNSON, William	Hepworth	Bury St. Edmunds
KNIGHTS, Samuel	Ramsholt	Woodbridge
KEELEY, Clement	Topcroft	Bungay
KEABLE, Jonathan	Denton	Harleston
KING, Alfred	Mildenhall	Mildenhall
LING, William	Beccles	Beccles
LORE, William	Alburgh	Harleston
LAMBERT, William	Barking	Ipswich
LEWIS, James	Boyton	Woodbridge
LAWES, Matthew	Market Weston	Thetford
LAMBERT, Henry	Bardwell	Bury St. Edmunds
LAST, Robert	Burgh	Woodbridge
MANBY, Charles	Needham Market	Ipswich
MOORE, Frederick	Saxlingham	Norwich
MOORE, Andrew	Saxlingham	Norwich
MANN, George	Shottisham	Woodbridge
MILLS, Thomas	Iken	Wickham Market
MORTLOCK, Obediah	Barrow	Higham
MANN, Arthur	Earl Soham	Framlingham
MEADOWS, Philip	Leiston	Saxmundham
MEADE, Philip	Beauchamp Otten	Ipswich
MOYES, Arthur	Wolverstone	Ipswich
NOLLER, William	Hasketon	Woodbridge
NEEVE, Isaac	Dennington	Framlingham
NORMAN, Alfred	Flowton	Ipswich
NASH, William	Hempnall	Norwich
POINTS, George	Saxlingham	Norwich
PRENTICE, David	Diss Heywood	Diss
PETTITT, George	Chediston	Halesworth

Appendix One

Name of worker	Home Village	Nearest railway station
Pratt, Arthur	Butley	Woodbridge
Panment, Arthur	Mildenhall	Bury St. Edmunds
Pearce, E. J.	Newton Flotman	Harleston
Pearce, Frederick	Metfield	Harleston
Rushbrook, William	Trimley	Ipswich
Rivett, Jonathan	Kirton	Ipswich
Richardson, Edward	Bredfield	Woodbridge
Raine, William	Witnesham	Ipswich
Riches, George	Woodton	Bungay
Sharman, Jonathan	Framsden	Woodbridge
Sharman, Arthur	Framsden	Woodbridge
Self, Henry	Marlesford	Wickham Market
Self, Albert	Marlesford	Wickham Market
Steward, George	Spexhall	Halesworth
Smith, Charles	Melton	Ipswich
Stannard, William	Bardwell	Bury St. Edmunds
Stiff, Harry	Thurston	Bury St. Edmunds
Spall, Edgar	Witnesham	Ipswich
Spall, William	Kirton	Ipswich
Scopes, George	Sutton	Woodbridge
Sharpe, Jonathan	Westley	Bury St. Edmunds
Taylor, Frederick	Akenham	Ipswich
Tubby, James	Fritton	Norwich
Titshall, William	Burgh	Woodbridge
Turner, Ernest	Henley	Ipswich
Trary, E. R.	Newton Flotman	Harleston
Tyrrell, Walter	Saxlingham	Harleston
Turner, Frederick	Ashbocking	Ipswich
Turner, Joseph	Ashbocking	Ipswich
Vincent, Robert	Mendham	Harleston
Wame, Reuben	Blaxhall	Wickham Market
Woods, George	Higham	Higham
Wright, Harry	Hedenham	Bungay
Woollard, Samuel	Clay Hall	Bury St. Edmunds
Williams, William	Bredfield	Woodbridge
Whitting, William	Stockton	Beccles
Wells, Edward	Creeting Bottom	Ipswich
Ward, George	Cookley Grange	Halesworth
Woods, Elijah	Barham	Ipswich
Youngman, Wm.	Saxlingham	Norwich

(Source: Bass & Co.—'Eastern Counties Journals for the engagement of men')

Appendix Two

❧❦❧

Suffolk men hired by Bass, Ratcliff & Gretton Ltd.
during two seasons

1926/1927:

Ashkettle
Bolton
Barns
Brigg
Bedingfield
Barker
Baxter
Barham
Burgess
Baldry
Button
Cattermole
Chambers
Debbage
Davey
Freeman
Fisk
Gordon
Goodhilde
Goult
Good
Hollingshead
Kemp
Mayhew
Mealing
Mortlock
Mayhew
Norris
Pratt
Paternoster
Roper
Roper
Reynolds
Sheldrake
Snell
Sharpe
Townshend

1904/1905:

Archer
Aldous
Aldous
Abbott
Andrews
Bloss
Bloomfield
Bloomfield
Browne
Brewster
Battle
Branche
Burgess
Brister
Bragg
Burgess
Brundle
Baker
Burch
Clarke
Cox
Chaplin
Cotton
Colthorpe
Crackwell
Cobbold
Clarke
Creasey
Capon
Clarke
Capon
Chapman
Clorer
Cook
Carter
Coppings
Chennery

Everett
Earl
Emery
Dickerson
Emmeus
Flack
Flatt
Franks
Forsdyke
Flatt
Frerid
Frerid
Ford
Fryatt
Fiske
Fryatt
Forsdick
Friend
Goodchild
Gooch
Goodwin
Goodchild
Halls
Hammond
Howlett
Hatcher
Hood
Harris
Juby
Kaye
King
Kerridge
Kemp
Kersey
Leech
Larknis
Lambert

Pratt
Pipe
Poacher
Peck
Payne
Page
Peck
Plant
Pearl
Reeve
Rivers
Revell
Rush
Rogers
Rudderham
Rose
Rose
Read
Robinson
Steels
Steed
Spall
Salter
Sutton
Stammers
Saxby
Saxby
Stokes
Smith
Smith
Scace
Sheppard
Smith
Smith
Stockridge
Salisbury
Tacon

Appendix Two

Versey	Cant	Leonard	Thorpe
Woods	Clark	Last	Titshall
Wink	Cook	Leek	Talbot
Worledge	Dyson	Last	Thorpe
	Diver	Leech	Threadkell
41 men from	Davidson	Laughlin	Taylor
Suffolk represent-	Durrant	Leek	Taylor
ing 20 per cent of	Dunnett	Mason	Upson
total labour force	Denny	Marsh	Welham
during 1926/27	Denny	Mayhew	Wightman
		Matthews	Watling
		Marsh	Watling
		Marjoram	Welkham
		Martin	Warren
		Mayhew	Ward
		Meadows	Woolterton
		Moulton	Warne
		Mann	Welham
		Norris	Wood
		Newson	Webb
		Neeve	
		Newson	
		Nunn	
		Osborne	
		Pilbrough	169 men from Suffolk,
		Pinner	representing 54 per cent
		Peck	of total labour force
		Pipe	during 1904/5

Selected Written Sources

꧁꧂

Arnold, J., *The Shell Book of County Crafts*, London, 1968.
Ashby, E. K., *Joseph Ashby of Tysoe*, Cambridge, 1961.
Bell, Adrian, *Corduroy*, London, 1951.
  Silver Ley, London, 1951.
  Cherry Tree, London, 1951.
Charbonnier, G., *Conversations with Levi-Strauss*, London, 1969.
Ekwall, E., *Concise Oxford Dictionary of English Place Names*, London, 1960.
Ernle, Lord, *English Farming Past and Present*, London, 1961.
Evans-Pritchard, E. E., *Social Anthropology and Other Essays*, New York, 1964.
Fussell, G. E., *From Tolpuddle to T.U.C.*, Slough, 1948.
Graves, Robert, *The White Goddess*, London, 1961.
Grigson, Geoffrey, *The Shell Country Alphabet*, London, 1966.
Gruffydd, W. J., *Yeoman's English. Gwerin*, II, 2, (Ed. Dr. I. C. Peate), Oxford, 1958.
Hartley, Marie, and Ingilby, Joan, *Life and Tradition in the Yorkshire Dales*, London, 1968.
Hill, Christopher, *Intellectual Origins of the English Revolution*, Oxford, 1965.
Hillyer, Richard, *Country Boy*, London, 1966.
Hudson, Kenneth, *Industrial Archaeology*, London, 1967.
Hymes, Dell (Ed.), *Language, Culture and Society*, New York, 1966.
Jenkins, David, *Arfer Ffarm a Ffurf Cymdeithas* (Farm Custom and Social Structure), Journal of Welsh Agricultural Society, Vol. xxviii, 1959.
Jenkins, John Geraint, *Traditional Country Craftsmen*, London, 1965.
  Studies in Folk Life, (Ed.), London, 1969.

Lawson, John Cuthbert, *Modern Greek Folklore and Greek Religion*, Cambridge, 1910.

Levi-Strauss, Claude, *Structural Anthropology*, New York, 1967.
The Scope of Anthropology, London, 1967.
The Savage Mind, London, 1966.

Levy, G. Rachel, *The Gate of Horn*, London, 1963.

McLuhan, Marshall, *Understanding Media*, London, 1964.

Mayhew, Henry (Ed. Peter Quennell), *Mayhew's London*.
Mayhew's Characters.
London's Underworld.

Mays, Spike, *Reuben's Corner*, London, 1969.

O'Donovan, J., *The Economic History of Livestock in Ireland*, Cork, 1940.

Vansina, J., *The Oral Tradition*, Chicago, 1965.

Van Zwanenberg, D., *The Last Epidemic of Plague in England? Suffolk 1906–1918. Medical History*, Vol. XIV, No. 1.

Wright, Joseph, *The English Dialect Dictionary*.

Index